S0-ATK-237

ABOUT THE AUTHOR

John Sweeney is a reporter for BBC Panorama who became a YouTube sensation in 2007 when he lost his temper with a senior member of the Church of Scientology. Before joining the BBC in 2001, Sweeney worked for twelve years at *The Observer*, where he covered wars and revolutions and unrest in more than sixty countries including Algeria, Bosnia, Chechnya and Zimbabwe. He has helped free seven people falsely convicted of killing their babies, starting with Sally Clark and Angela Cannings. Over the course of his career John has won one Emmy, two Royal Television Society prizes, one Sony Gold award, the What The Papers Say Journalist of The Year Prize, an Amnesty International prize and the Paul Foot Award. His hobby is falling off his bike on the way back from the pub.

ALSO BY JOHN SWEENEY

FICTION

Elephant Moon

NON-FICTION

Big Daddy – Lukashenka, The Tyrant of Belarus
Wayne Rooney: Boots of Gold
Purple Homicide
Trading With The Enemy: Britain's Arming of Iraq
The Life and Evil Times of Nicolae Ceausescu
North Korea Undercover: Inside the World's Most Secret State

THE CHURCH OF FEAR

JOHN SWEENEY

SILVERTAIL BOOKS • *London*

First published in 2013 by Silvertail Books
www.silvertailbooks.com
Copyright © John Sweeney 2013

The right of John Sweeney to be identified as the author of this work has been asswerted by
him in accordance with the Copyright, Design and Patents Act 1988

A catalogue record of this book is available
from the British Library

ISBN 978-1-909269-03-3

All rights reserved. No part of this publication may be reproduced, transmitted, or stored in a
retrieval system in any form or by any means, without permission in writing from Silvertail Books
Typeset in Ehrhardt Monotype

To my father, Leonard Sweeney.

'Your next endless trillions of years and the whole agonized future of every man, woman and child on this planet depend on what you do here and now, with and in Scientology.'

                                                      - L Ron Hubbard.

'Some people, well, if they don't like Scientology, well, then, fuck you. Really. Fuck you. Period.'

                                                          - Tom Cruise.

'Ours is often called an age of scepticism. Let us see whether this is not, on the contrary, an age of fatuous credulity.'

                                                          - CH Rolph.

CONTENTS

INTRODUCTION

Welcome to the Church of Fear. Tom Cruise and John Travolta and a host of Hollywood's finest will tell you that the Church of Scientology is a force for good, that it helps you communicate better, understand yourself more, become a more superior kind of being.

But beware: the Church is not what it seems. Go, for example, to the organisation's recruiting centre on London's Tottenham Court Road and you will see L Ron Hubbard's Dianetics in the window, illustrated by a volcano erupting red-hot rocks. That's a subtle hint, some say, to the Church's secret cosmology, its belief that man's inhumanity to man is caused by a space alien Satan massacring space aliens in volcanoes 75 million years ago. The Church denies that, and much else.

Instantly, reader, you should be aware what the Church says of me: that I am a bigot and a liar, that I am psychotic. A member of the Church of Scientology has said on his blog: 'John Sweeney is genuinely evil.'

I used to be a war reporter. From Algeria, Bosnia and Chechnya to Zimbabwe I have been shelled, shot at, bombed, arrested, threatened and a Serb devotee of Slobodan Milosevic once stuck two sticks of dynamite up my nose. But never, ever, in all my times in all those wars have I felt under such harrowing psychological pressure as I did inside the brainwashing section of the Church of Scientology's exhibition, 'Psychiatry: The Industry of Death' on Sunset Boulevard in LA in the spring of 2007.

I am not a timid man but I was afraid then and am afraid now, afraid of them and afraid of it. I fear that by even attempting to write this book I risk ruin. I am afraid of enormous legal bills breaking me and my family; afraid of not telling the whole truth, and letting down the ordinary, extraordinary people who have had the courage to get out and who have suffered so much because of the Church; afraid of letting down general readers because the book may be too faint-hearted, the story too legally constricted to understand. But if I write too bluntly, I fear the Church will strike me down. I have wrestled with those fears for five years.

Back in 2007 in the brainwashing section of their exhibition, I was afraid they were brainwashing me. I was afraid that I was about to lose my grip on reality and I lost my temper with a volcanic passion that still frightens me, that makes me wonder where it came from. I roared at Tommy Davis, a leading acolyte of the Church, close friend and, in a bad light, lookalike of its number one Hollywood apostle, Tom Cruise.

John Sweeney: No Tommy you stop there …
Tommy Davis: Brain washing! Brainwashing is a crime!
John Sweeney: You listen to me!
Tommy Davis: Brainwashing is a crime!

*John Sweeney: YOU WERE NOT THERE AT THE BEGIN-
NING OF THE INTERVIEW. YOU WERE NOT THERE.'*

The YouTube video of me losing it, released by the Church
a few days before our BBC Panorama on the Church, went
viral. If you add up the figures from the main sites I got seven
million hits. And then a kicking from the global media.

In the United States, news shows fronted by Styrofoam-
bouffant-haired presenters with names like Cindy and Scott
raised eyebrows at my outburst. In Britain, the headline in
Rupert Murdoch's News of the World ran: 'TV MAN IN A
FURY: A Panorama reporter has shamed the BBC with a hysterical rant during an investigation into Scientology. Balding
TV veteran John Sweeney flipped while interviewing Tommy
Davis, son of actress Anne Archer. He screamed, sprayed
spittle into Davis's face and jabbed his index finger in a row
over brainwashing.' Charles Moore wrote in the Spectator:
'If you want to see how BBC people can behave when they
are feeling righteous, do watch John Sweeney of Panorama
screaming dementedly at some members of the Church of
Scientology (available on YouTube) when they objected to his
interview techniques. He looks and sounds like a secret police
interrogator.'

I apologised then and I apologise now. I was wrong. Civilised discourse is the engine oil of democracy and by losing
it and doing an impression of an exploding tomato I let down
the values I cherish. It was a propaganda gift from heaven to
the Church.

But that was not the moment when I felt most crushed by
the power and reach of this thing I fear. The worst moment

was not being followed by creepy private eyes on the streets of Los Angeles; not being shouted at; not being called a bigot relentlessly by Tommy Davis, the son of the actress whose bunny got boiled in Fatal Attraction; not returning to our hotel in Florida to find the Church's agents waiting for us at midnight; not the creepy strangers harassing us in the States; not the creepy stranger knocking on the door of my neighbour back in London; not the mystery person who appeared in the shrubbery at our wedding in a fort in Cornwall. No, it was none of those.

The worst moment came a couple of weeks after I had lost it in LA but before our documentary made air. I was walking out of White City tube station in west London, towards the grim Grey Lubyanka, the concrete cardboard box that then housed the office of the BBC Current Affairs department. My colleague Patrick Barrie got a call on his mobile. He listened, said a few words and then killed the call and gave me the strange news.

We'd just been to film a woman who counted herself a victim of the Church. The mother, let's call her Betty, made us comfortable in the front room of her spotlessly clean house. She was elegant, house-proud, funny, sweet but her story was unbearably sad. Betty was a hard-working single mum, with two grown-up children, let's call them Phil and Samantha. Phil had died a few years previously in an accident on Friday, the 13th. Every anniversary of that grim date Betty and Sam would meet up for a chat and a cry. If one or the other was away, they would get on the phone and mourn their loss.

Then Sam joined the Church of Scientology. Betty told me that her daughter – a beautiful, loving, kind, considerate woman – turned, she said, into a stranger, someone cold, unfeeling, hard. Her mum became worried beyond words, not just because Sam was spending so much time and money on the Church, but because it felt like she had mutated into an entirely different being. Sam 'disconnected' – it is a term of art in Scientology - from her mother: no contact, no phone-calls, no birthday cards, no Christmas cards, no Mother's Day cards, but worst of all, no contact on the anniversary of Phil's death. No Friday the 13th, no mourning of a dead son and brother.

Betty dared to visit the restaurant where Samantha worked because she missed her so. Sam didn't ignore her mother. That was too weak a word. It was as if Betty did not exist. It was, Betty told me, horrible: 'it kills me. Through the mirror I could see her turn round quickly and she said, "have I got thick written across my head?" I said, "no", and she said, "you are not doing any favours coming in here with your innocent face" and I said, "I just like coming", and she said, "I don't want you in here."

Betty walked away from her adored child. 'I cried and thought, "this is my daughter... What am I going to do? How long is this going to go on?" Her mind, said Betty, 'seems totally twisted and taken over and I can't get through to her. They say it's a religion. I don't class it as a religion. In my opinion it's a cult.

'There is nothing religious about Scientology. How can this organisation who say or think they are religious, how can they hold their heads up when they do nothing but split fami-lies up, they break them up into pieces until there is nothing left? What can be religious or God-giving that turns a daughter away from her mother?'

Betty got hold of Sam's new mobile number and rang her on her birthday. 'She said, "hello" and I just said, "Hi, sweetheart, this is Mum just phoning to say Happy Birthday" and she put the phone down. How can you disconnect from your mum?'

Tom Cruise, the most famous Scientologist, says it has helped him. What did Betty make of that?

'It doesn't help. I remember the questionnaire Samantha had to fill in and the results were that she was lacking in confidence, that they could help with her personality. There was absolutely nothing wrong with Samantha. People would tell you she is the most bubbly, bouncy brilliant person. They just put the problem there, and say, "yes we can sort it out for you" but it's not free. It's all money.'

What did Betty think had happened to her daughter?

'She has been hypnotised and brainwashed. It's like a staring, a glare almost icy, fixed, hardly a blink and the eyes look larger than normal. It is a trance. That is the only way I can describe it. Samantha is a victim and she has been recruited into Scientology and she has been brainwashed. It is like Samantha is deep down inside and this cocoon is being made around her, and this totally different person is there now.'

Tom Cruise in a leaked video said: 'I think it's a privilege to call yourself a Scientologist, and it's something that you have to earn… Being a Scientologist, you look at someone and know absolutely that you can help them… When you drive past an accident… you know you have to do something about it because you know you're the only one that can really help… So it's our responsibility to educate, create the new reality.'

And then he chuckles.

What did Betty feel about the Church's celebrities, Tom Cruise and John Travolta?

'I almost feel sorry for them in a way because they are almost victims of it. They have been recruited in the same way.'

Betty said she still loved her daughter and hoped one day that she would get her back. 'I want to give her a hug and I want to love her, I love her anyway, but love her properly, and I can't because there is me, there is Samantha and there is Scientology in the middle. And I can't seem to get her back. Her mind has been absolutely taken over and that is really, really frightening.'

Betty's advice to anyone contemplating entering a Church of Scientology was clear: 'For God's sake, don't walk through the door.'

In three decades and more as a reporter, this was one of the most unutterably moving interviews I have ever carried out.

On the train back to London, a woman sat opposite Patrick and I and engaged with us. I was suspicious. She said her iPod had run out of juice, and could she borrow my laptop, on which I was pounding away, to charge it. I politely said sorry, I could not. Paranoid, I suspected that she was an agent, working for the Church. Of course, I could have been entirely wrong.

We got the tube back to White City and were walking towards the office when Patrick's phone rang. It was Betty, in tears. After almost two years of no contact, her daughter had walked through the door shortly after we had left. She'd told her mum: 'Let's be friends.'

The next day Betty phoned Patrick again. Her daughter had asked her to pull the interview with Panorama.

How on earth had they found out that we had interviewed Betty? One could make the deduction that they were spying on us – a charge the Church denies.

We pulled the interview and I have changed names and details. But the essential truth of the story remains. A broken-hearted mother, weeping about her lost daughter on camera to the BBC, and the same lost daughter walks through the door before we got back to the office. Of all the things that have happened to me personally while I have investigated the Church of Scientology, Betty's story, and their success in stopping us from telling it, is the one that troubles me the most.

This book tells the story of Scientology from the perspective of people like Betty, from the other side of the gloss and the celebrities. It is the story of people who used to serve Cruise and Travolta but who now describe themselves as slaves and say the Church of Scientology is a force for evil. And it is the story of the battle between the two sides, the multi-billion dollar Church, its multi-millionaire stars on one side; the heretics on the other. It presents not the eagle's eye view, not that seen by the celebrities, but the worm's eye view, the story of ex-Scientologists who spent decades inside the belly of the Church, of critics demonized by it, at least one of whom ended up committing suicide, and my personal experience of the Church's attempts to break me during five weeks of madness in the spring of 2007 up to the present day.

It is a Church, or more accurately, a thing of great wealth

and power and if you anger it, it will try to destroy you, as I
found out.

CHAPTER ONE
first contact

I magine two groups of people, one lot on the outside, one on the inside. The insiders believe they are defending their religion to the utmost from bigots; the outsiders believe the 'religion', if religion it be, is bad science fiction. The insiders believe the outsiders are brainwashed into thinking they are free when in fact they are slaves to a space alien Satan. The outsiders see a confidence trick inside a space alien cult masquerading as a religion; they believe the insiders live inside an invisible box, walled with mirrors, marked: religion. The outsiders believe the insiders are brainwashed, full stop.

That is the best short-hand description of the Church of Scientology I can come up with in one hundred and one words exactly. The alternative is to go see it for yourself. I did, but I would not recommend it.

Drive through the gates of Saint Hill Manor, a country estate a few miles from East Grinstead in Sussex, and you notice that something is immediately and obviously wrong. The English ruling class has a certain style for country houses. It's not good form to show obscene wealth. So they let things slide a little, a gate off its hinges there, wild flowers running amok here, chipped and peeling paint, stray dogs, strayer children, the whole artifice generating a sense of artfully constructed neglect.

Saint Hill looks like a Hollywood set designer's idea of an English country house. Fifty acres, hedged with rhododendron bushes, boasting a fake turret and a real lake, it's so perfect in every detail it's plastically unreal. In the heart of the English countryside it is that worst of things, un-English. Over-gardened, eerie, empty of people, Saint Hill exudes the atmosphere of a high-end psychiatric clinic, the kind of place where billionaires dump their mad aunts. Saint Hill is the British base of the Church of Scientology. Nothing here comes cheap. The Saint Hill Special Briefing Course will set you back £20,300.

No-one laughed. It was creepy.

They believe that humanity is trapped inside a prison of the mind and only the Church of Scientology can get us out, can end the insanity all around us. 'We are the saviours of humankind.' John Travolta, the older of the Church's two great Hollywood apostles, once said: 'There's no doubt about it that the people that didn't make it in Hollywood - and I mean survived - if they'd had Scientology or Dianetics they'd have been here today, whether it's Elvis or Marilyn.'

In other words, Scientology can save your life.

Tom Cruise is the younger but the greater apostle, the living embodiment of Scientology. His divorce from Katie Holmes in the summer of 2012 notwithstanding, Cruise is no ordinary human being. He is, they say, the second most powerful Scientologist in the world and an Operating Thetan and that means, they say, Tom Cruise has special powers, of knowing and willing cause over life, thought, matter, energy, space and time. He can levitate too.

If you just take those two stars together, Travolta and Cruise, hundreds of millions of people have seen them in films like *'Saturday Night Fever'*, *'Pulp Fiction'*, *'Top Gun'* and the *'Mission Impossible'* series. Some of those millions may have reflected that if Scientology has led Cruise and Travolta to fame and success, then it could be wonderful for them, too.

But the evidence that the Church has abused its servants is strong and compelling. The evidence that the Church abuses the trust of its star parishioners is also strong. There is no evidence to suggest that the Church of Scientology gives you powers over life, thought, matter, energy, space and time. Nor is there evidence that the story of the space alien Satan is anything more than inter-galactic mumbo-jumbo. Rather, the evidence points to the Church of Scientology being a brainwashing cult.

The Church of Scientology denies that it is a cult; it denies abuse; it denies spying; it denies betraying the secrets of the confessional; it denies brainwashing.

It was founded by the late Lafayette Ron Hubbard, known as 'Mr Hubbard' or LRH or L Ron, in 1954. There are people I know who still believe in Scientology, who still revere Mr Hubbard but no longer trust the Church as an institution, and they are good people and have a right to believe in whatever they want to believe in, and, uncomfortable as it is for me, I defend that right. But that right is not telescopic.

Scientologists inside and outside the Church hold that Mr Hubbard is the saviour of humanity. Others question that. Paul Thomas Anderson's brave and good film, *The Master*, is

loosely based on Hubbard. The film's tortured main character, a true disciple, is warned: 'You know he's making it up as
he goes along.'

The Master shows a fictional character like Mr Hubbard as
a man of immense charismatic power. That portrayal helped
me understand something: that, in the beginning, there was
big magic that sucked people in. To others, L Ron was a ginger-haired pulp fiction writer who knocked off a story about a
space alien Satan and re-baptized it as a religion. He launched
his theory of Dianetics in *'Astounding Science Fiction'* magazine in 1950. The name of the magazine is a clue.

Dianetics soon became a philosophy and a therapy programme, and that quickly morphed into Scientology, which
shape-shifted into a 'Church'. The movement appealed to
something missing from people's lives in 1950s America. But
grave anxieties started to be raised. For example, the effect of
Scientology's mind exercises was to create a trance-like state,
suitable for hypnosis. Could that lead to a kind of brainwashing?

Scientologists were in thrall to L Ron's 'tech' which ena-
bled Scientologists to improve their communication skills. L
Ron developed or borrowed a kind of 1950s 'lie/truth detector' technology he dubbed 'auditing' in which adherents
would confess to an auditor, but with the added dimension of
an 'Electro-psychometer' or 'E-meter' to test that they were
telling the truth. The E-meter is a machine with leads running to two 'tin cans' which you grip with your hands. The
sweat from your hands increases when you are anxious, and
that anxiety shows up on a needle-and-dial dashboard which
the auditor studies. Having a steady or gently floating needle

is cool. If your needle jerks, then you've got issues and you may be lying - an 'overt' - or withholding the truth - a 'with-hold'. Confessions are recorded. In the early days the auditor took detailed notes; in the twenty-first century by state of the art pin-hole cameras. But could the recorded secrets of that confession, once given, be used against you – a kind of black-mail? No, says the Church. Yes, say ex-Scientologists.

What kind of man was Mr Hubbard? Charismatic, cer-tainly. According to the Church he created, L Ron had an amazing life story: he'd been an acclaimed explorer, a nuclear physicist, a war hero and he'd been to deep space: 'I was in the Van Allen Belt. This is factual. You'd be surprised how warm space is.'

'It is all lies. None of that is true,' Russell Miller, his very unauthorised biographer, told me. 'The whole religion is based on the word of a congenital liar and a brilliant confi-dence trickster.' In his biography, Miller reports an ex-Scien-tologist, Gerry Armstrong, painting an unflattering picture of L Ron: 'a mixture of Adolf Hitler, Charlie Chaplin and Baron Munchausen. In short, he was a con man.'

Hubbard was a friend of Aleister Crowley, the Occultist and Silly Twit who the papers called 'The Wickedest Man in the World'. Hubbard said of Crowley: 'my very good friend... signs himself "the Beast", mark of the Beast 666...'

Some point to the distinctive sign of the Church – the cross and the star – and note its similarity to Crowley's Tarot card design, with a cross in the foreground and a star shape behind.

In the early 1950s sceptical reporters in America started writing negative stories. They called it the Church of the

Rondroids. Hubbard hit back, calling the ordinary, non-Scientologist world, inhabited by people like you and me, 'wog', defining the word as 'common, everyday garden-variety humanoid ... He "is" a body, doesn't know he's there, etc. He isn't there as a spirit at all. He is not operating as a Thetan.'

By the late 1950s Mr Hubbard was suffering a blowback as ex-members were admitted to mental hospitals. Psychiatrists, on behalf of patients who were disaffected Scientologists, started investigating, then castigating Scientology. Scientology investigated, then castigated, psychiatry. Others condemned Hubbard as an unusually inventive confidence trickster. Worse, the law enforcement authorities in America were beginning to give L Ron a rather beady eye. So he decided to up sticks and move to England. Mr Hubbard, by now a multi-millionaire, snapped up Saint Hill in 1959. The estate once belonged to the Maharajah of Jaipur, an aristocrat whose princely statelet back in India was gobbled up by democracy and whose princely fortune was left untended while he enjoyed his chukkas on the polo field. The Maharajah died, as he had lived, falling off a polo horse.

Hubbard once boasted that he 'sort of won' Saint Hill in a poker game. By the time he was interested in Saint Hill, the Maharajah was dead and it seems unlikely that his estate's solicitors would have used it as a stake in poker.

In 1959 L Ron moved in, announcing to a reporter from the *East Grinstead Courier* that he was an expert on plant life. 'The production of plant mutations,' *the Courier* gushed, 'is one of his most important projects at the moment. By battering seeds with X-rays, Dr Hubbard can either reduce a plant through its stages of evolution or advance it.' A black and white photograph was taken of L Ron attaching electrodes to a tomato – the vegetable (botanically a fruit) that I replicated in the Industry of Death exhibition. This is one of my favourite photographs in the whole wide world.

The Church grew from a tiny base to number tens of thousands of adepts, but some of those people left and what they had to say was not good. It suffered international notoriety. In Australia, Mr Justice Anderson concluded in 1965: 'Scientology is evil; its techniques are evil; its practice is a serious threat to the community, medically, morally, and socially; and its adherents are sadly deluded and often mentally ill... [Scientology is] the world's largest organization of unqualified persons engaged in the practice of dangerous techniques which masquerade as mental therapy.' Anderson's report is the first to touch on the theme of the Church subjecting its adherents to 'mental enslavement', but not the last.

In the late sixties, the British health minister, Kenneth Robinson – a former Lieutenant-Commander in the Royal Navy – blocked foreign Scientologists from coming to Britain: 'The government is satisfied that Scientology is socially harmful. It alienates members of families from each other and attributes squalid and disgraceful motives to all who oppose it; its authoritarian principles and practice are a potential menace to the personality and well being of those so deluded as to become followers; above all, its methods can be a serious danger to the health of those who submit to them... There is no power under existing law to prohibit the practice of Scientology; but the government has concluded that it is so objectionable that it would be right to take all steps within its power to curb its growth.'

The Church did not turn the other cheek. In 1967 it took on the local community around Saint Hill, suing East Grinstead Urban District Council, a teacher at a local convent school, the Chairman of the Urban District Council's Health and Housing Committee, a farmer whose land adjoined Saint Hill Manor, and who had spoken disapprovingly of his neighbours, and thirty-eight people who had written critical things about Scientology in the papers. Most of the law suits were subsequently dropped but the Church sued the local Tory MP, Geoffrey Johnson-Smith. The libel trial lasted six weeks in 1970. The Church lost.

To counter-attack, Hubbard created a policy called 'Fair Game' where enemies of the Church could be 'injured, tricked, sued, lied to or destroyed'. Russell Miller says he faced a terrifying campaign of harassment by the Church for his heretical biography.

What did Miller think of the Church's claim that it is a religion? 'It exhibits all the symptoms of a classic cult. It draws people in when they are vulnerable; it causes them to disconnect from their friends and family; it makes them believe that the truth is within the cult and the world is a dangerous place.'

L Ron's Church suffered scandal after scandal in the sixties and seventies. On the run from the authorities, it went, like the owl and the pussycat, to sea. Miller tells the story hilariously in his book on Hubbard. After one stormy crossing too many the Church and its Founder ended up back in the United States. Perhaps the darkest days for the Church were in 1977 when the FBI discovered that the Church had been running two operations, one to frame the journalist

Paulette Cooper by sending bomb threats to itself as if from her and the other to penetrate the US Government. The FBI arrested Mr Hubbard's wife, Mary Sue and other senior Scientologists, and LRH himself went on the run, vanishing off the face of the earth.

In 1984 the Church was accused of blackmailing its adherents to stay in, lest their intimate secrets be leaked out. Blackmail is a heavy word. But it was used by Judge Breckenridge sitting in the Los Angeles Superior Court, in his ruling against the Church and in favour of a group of ex-Scientologists, led by Gerry Armstrong, the chap who'd previously compared Mr Hubbard to Chaplin and Hitler. The Church had asked Armstrong, a dedicated Scientologist, to prepare documents for a planned biography of the Founder. Armstrong duly dug around the attic at Gilman Hot Springs, an old gamblers' den on the edge of the Californian desert, handpicked by the Church as its secret base, now known as Gold or Int. In the attic Armstrong found a treasure trove of paperwork on Mr Hubbard but they proved to Armstrong's satisfaction that Hubbard was a liar and a fantasist. He ran for it, taking the documents with him. The Church sued Armstrong and his fellows, and lost.

Judge Breckenridge wrote in his judgment: 'The picture painted by these former dedicated Scientologists, all of whom were intimately involved with LRH, or Mary Jane Hubbard, or of the Scientology Organization, is on the one hand pathetic, and on the other, outrageous. Each of these persons literally gave years of his or her respective life in support of a man, LRH, and his ideas. Each has manifested a waste and loss or frustration which is incapable of description.'

Judge Breckenridge found: 'Each [ex-Scientologist] has broken with the movement for a variety of reasons, but at the same time, each is still bound by the knowledge that the Church has in its possession his or her most inner thoughts and confessions, all recorded in "Pre-Clear (P.C.) folders" or other security files of the organization, and that the Church or its minions is fully capable of intimidation or other physical or psychological abuse if it suits their ends. The record is replete with evidence of such abuse.'

Judge Breckenridge continued: 'The practice of culling supposedly confidential "P.C. folders or files" to obtain information for purposes of intimidation and or harassment is repugnant and outrageous.'

The judge cited a 1970 French police investigation into the Church, which concluded that 'under the pretext of "freeing humans" (it) is nothing in reality but a vast enterprise to extract the maximum amount of money from its adepts by pseudo-scientific theories... pushed to extremes (a machine to detect lies, its own particular phraseology) to estrange adepts from their families and to exercise a kind of blackmail against persons who do not wish to continue.'

Nothing much had changed, said Judge Breckenridge: 'From the evidence presented to this court in 1984, at the very least, similar conclusions can be drawn. In addition to violating and abusing its own members civil rights, the organization over the years with its "Fair Game" doctrine has harassed and abused those persons not in the Church whom it perceives as enemies. The organization clearly is schizophrenic and paranoid, and this bizarre combination seems to be a reflection of its founder LRH. The evidence portrays a man who has been virtually a pathological liar when it comes to his history, background, and achievements. The writings and documents in evidence additionally reflect his egoism, greed, avarice, lust for power, and vindictiveness and aggressiveness against persons perceived by him to be disloyal or hostile. At the same time it appears that he is charismatic and highly capable of motivating, organizing, controlling, manipulating, and inspiring his adherents. He has been referred to during the trial as a "genius," a "revered person," a man who was "viewed by his followers in awe." Obviously, he is and has been a very complex person, and that complexity is further reflected in his alter ego, the Church of Scientology.'

Hubbard died in 1986, a weird recluse. His autopsy said he was full of VISTARIL® or hydroxyzine hydrochloride, prescribed for disturbed or hysterical patients, and, of course, the very kind of psychiatric drugs the Church condemns.

But that was all a very long time ago. In the 21st century the Church is engaged in a pretty much successful global march to win respect and the right to call itself a religion. The church boasts of having 11 million square feet of property around the world, a somewhat idiosyncratic index of holiness.

In October 2006 the Church was set to open its spanking new £25 million centre in the City of London. Our Great British Weather, sadly, rained on their parade. Drizzle, drizzle, relentless drizzle. I came along to do a spot of filming from the street. As soon as we started, an official of the Church, Janet Laveau, asked us to stop filming. I told her we worked for BBC Panorama and the law allowed us to film in a London street. She said that they had blocked the street, it was a private function and she had a problem with Panorama. Janet was referring to the BBC Panorama documentary, '*The Road to Total Freedom?*' filmed in 1987, 23 years before I joined the BBC. I repeated that that the BBC is allowed to film in London streets. We could not film inside the Church (or Org, in *SciSpeak*) but we could film on the street. I pointed out to her that had I been a car, she would have had a point because cars were not allowed on the road today. But I was not a car.

We filmed a top City of London copper, Chief Superintendant Kevin Hurley, splendidly reassuring in his uniform, walk up to the podium. The police chief praised the Church as a 'force for good' in London, 'raising the spiritual wealth of society'.

It was time for the pope of Scientology to wow the faithful. David Miscavige bounded onto the stage to the rapture of the crowd, not perhaps as big as the organizers had planned. The Church of Scientology claims to have more than 10 million devotees worldwide, with 123,000 in the UK but the crowd did not look much bigger than a thousand people, if that. Quite a few seemed to be European, not British, as if they had been shipped in to bulk the numbers. But they all loved Miscavige. In the flesh, he has the manner of a high-end estate agent, smooth, polished, markedly short. The drizzle never stopped. The umbrellas twirled prettily.

'Thank you very much,' said Miscavige. 'It's a pleasure to join you on a day that genuinely qualifies as momentous…'

Miscavige is an Angel to some, a devil to others. A former Catholic high school drop-out, born in Philadelphia and raised in a suburb of that great city just across the state line in New Jersey, Miscavige suffered from asthma and allergies until his father, a trumpet player, took him along to a Scientologist and he was cured. The family embraced Scientology and moved to Saint Hill in England, where Miscavige, a precocious achiever, became an auditor at the age of 12. He joined the Sea Org – the Church's priesthood – and became a favourite cameraman and messenger of Mr Hubbard. When the old prophet died in 1986, Miscavige rose to the top, proclaiming to grieving Scientologists that LRH had 'discarded the body he had used in this lifetime.'

Intense, clever, Miscavige is known in the Church's peculiar corporate-speak as Chairman of the Board or COB. He is given to grand claims: 'If you've heard we're the fastest growing religion on earth - it's true.'

To the Church's apostles, like Cruise and Travolta, Miscavige is a great servant of mankind. Some outsiders might consider that he has proved to be a deft and formidable operator, especially good at exploiting the weaknesses of those who criticise the Church. Ex-members of the Church, some of whom remain Scientologists and some of who no longer have anything to do with Scientology, say their experience of Miscavige was somewhat different, to put it mildly.

Whatever the truth about its leader, it is a fact that under Miscavige the Church of Scientology has been gaining acquiescence around the world.

In Germany, forever fearful of repeating the terrible mistakes of history, the Church of Scientology has faced serious, government-backed scrutiny for decades because of fears that it is a totalitarian organisation. The Church has fought back. In 1996 a number of famous Americans wrote an open letter to the then Chancellor, Helmut Kohl. Signatories included Bertram Fields (who just so happens to be Tom Cruise's lawyer), Goldie Hawn, Dustin Hoffman, Larry King, Mario Puzo, Tina Sinatra, Oliver Stone and the late Gore Vidal. They wrote: 'In the Germany of the 1930s, Hitler made religious intolerance official government policy. In the 1930s, it was the Jews. Today it is the Scientologists... We implore you to bring an end to this shameful pattern of organized persecution. It is a disgrace to the German nation.'

In 2008, Tom Cruise starred as the great anti-Nazi German hero, Claus Von Stauffenberg in the film '*Valkyrie*'. That raised the question whether Scientology's number one parishioner, Cruise, had made a brave film about a German hero. Or whether he had pulled off a great PR coup by taking on the role of a great enemy of totalitarian power, while being a member of what some say is a totalitarian cult – and in so doing subtly undermining one of the Church's strongest critics.

In the United States, it is a similar story of official hostility to the Church weakening under attack, then morphing, first into acquiescence with the Church's assertion that it should be classed as a religion, then actively promulgating that claim to other countries. The Church of Scientology had long been considered a business, not a religion, in the United States. In 1993 that changed when during the Clinton Presidency the Inland Revenue Service reversed its previous position and declared the Church a religion, saving it millions in taxes and giving it a shield against those who would dare criticize it. A week after the great breakthrough, 10,000 Scientologists went to an arena in LA. Chairman of the Board Miscavige took to the stage in black tie and spoke for two-and-a-half hours flanked by two flaming torches. He denounced the Church's enemies, swayed by a hive-mind of psychiatrists, 'pea-brained psych-indoctrinated mental midgets' bent on creating a 'slave society', damned the IRS civil servants as 'vampires' and warned the Church's foes: 'We know who they are and we'll get to them last.' Miscavige's trademark manner of address seems to include common themes of vilification and revenge.

Miscavige announced the headline news: 'There will be no billion dollar tax bill which we can't pay. There will be no more discrimination. There will be no more 2,500 cases against parishioners across the US. The pipeline of IRS false reports won't keep flowing across the planet. There will be no more nothing – because on October first, 1993, at 8:37 p.m. Eastern Standard Time, the IRS issued letters recognizing Scientology and every one of its organizations as fully tax exempt! The war is over!'

Everyone clapped.

On this side of the Atlantic, many councils give the Church local tax breaks but as far as the Charity Commissioners are concerned, for the purposes of English charity law: 'Scientology is not a religion.'

In Britain, Scientology's war, as it were, is not over.

L Ron Hubbard was, whatever else you think of him, a shrewd man who knew that harnessing the power of celebrity to his cause was a smart thing to do. He jumped on the celebrity bandwagon faster than most. Miscavige has followed in his master's footsteps. Ex-Scientologists say that the Church under Miscavige deliberately groomed and cocooned its celebrities, making life sweet for them in its own Celebrity Centres. In return, the Church's celebrities have banged the drum for Scientology. Its film and TV star apostles include Cruise, Travolta,

Kirstie Alley from *'Cheers'*, Anne Archer, Nancy Cartwright, the actress who voices Bart in TV's *'The Simpsons'*, Elisabeth Moss, who played Peggy Olson in *Mad Men*, and, before they left the Church, Jason Beghe, star of *GI Jane* and TV dramas like *CSI* and *Californication* and Larry Anderson of *Star Trek: Insurrection* and *Aliens Go Home*. *'The Fresh Prince of Bel-Air'*, Will Smith, has never publicly committed to Scientology, but Smith has said: 'I just think a lot of the ideas in Scientology are brilliant and revolutionary and non-religious.' In 2010 Smith gave $1.2 million to a school in California he founded which uses L Ron's 'Study Technology'.

In Britain, again the picture is not so rosy. The Church can point to just one MP who has told the House of Commons it is not a cult and a single man of the cloth, the Bishop of Norwich, who has questioned the 'unexamined assumption' that it is a cult. There are no celebrities who have embraced the Church of Scientology hook, line and sinker. The nearest the Church got to landing a British celeb was Peaches Geldof, who appeared to have a brief fling with the Church in 2009. She is now out.

TV stars like Top Gear's Jeremy Clarkson and Jonathan Ross entertain Tom Cruise on their shows and do not seem to question him much or at all about Scientology. Perhaps this is not remarkable but in his autobiography Ross gives the Church the benefit of the doubt. Ross writes in his book, *'Why Do I Say These Things'*: 'I don't think Scientologists get a fair deal. I don't know enough about the religion itself... But I do know that the handful of people I've met who've happened to be Scientologists have been some of the nicest and most courteous of any it has been my pleasure to spend time with.' Ross cites John Travolta – 'very happy and stable and together', Will Smith – 'if he is one' – and Tom Cruise: 'incredibly down to earth for a star of his stature. When he walks into a room, he pays attention to everyone, no matter what job they're doing on a shoot – getting the coffee, doing the make-up, lugging the camera or sound equipment around – he doesn't differentiate... when he leaves the room, everybody loves him'.

And yet ex-Scientologists say Cruise is a recruiting sergeant for a brainwashing cult. What is so strange about the world of the Church of Scientology is that evidence for Cruise being both a charming and thoughtful man and a cult's recruiting sergeant co-exists. Throughout this book, you will come across examples of black-white conflicts, again and again. The Church and the middle ground do not flourish.

Wikileaks shows that American diplomats regularly took foreign governments to task for failing to respect the religious entitlement of the Church. Tom Cruise led Scientology meetings with the then French President, Nicolas Sarkozy, in Paris and reportedly at Downing Street, pushing home the message that Scientology was a religion like any other.

To that end, Miscavige embarked on a multi-million pound building spree, opening new Orgs or churches across the world. The new London org was yet another example. He was still at it, still speechifying: 'A day when the moment we pull down that ribbon it goes down in history... In this city L Ron Hubbard... ... defined the human spirit ...an immortal being... technology... the root of our religion...'

He cut the ribbon and everyone cheered. The London

drizzle drizzled on.

What is the secret of the Church of Scientology's success? One answer is, critics say, brainwashing. It may have been a coincidence but when I lost my temper with the Church's Tommy Davis, we had been arguing about brainwashing inside the brainwashing section of an exhibition that says that psychiatrists are brainwashing humanity. As I holler, Tommy says, over and over again: 'Brainwashing is a crime.'

The Church of Scientology denies brainwashing.

What is 'brainwashing?' is the title of the opening chapter of Robert Jay Lifton's classic study of mind control, *Thought Reform and the Psychology of Totalism: A Study of "Brainwashing" in China*. I was introduced to Lifton's work by Bruce Hines, at one time an auditor – Scientology's word for confessor – who used to minister to Nicole Kidman, Kirstie Alley and Tom Cruise. Bruce is now out, neither a member of the Church, nor a Scientologist.

Lifton, an American military psychiatrist, interviewed Allied ex-prisoners who had been captured during the Korean War and held in North Korea and then Chinese and European victims of Chairman's Mao totalitarian state. He explains that the term 'brainwashing' was first used by the American journalist, Edward Hunter, as a translation of the colloquialism *hsi nao,* (literally, 'wash brain') which he quoted from Chinese informants who described its use after the Communist takeover. In his book, which everyone seriously interested in understanding the Church of Scientology should read, Lifton quotes the Indian philosopher Radhakrishnan: 'When religion becomes organised, man ceases to be free. It is not

27

God that is worshipped but the group or authority that claims to speak in His name. Sin becomes disobedience to authority and not violation of integrity.'

Later, Lifton set out three defining characteristics of a cult: firstly, 'all cults have a charismatic leader, who himself or herself increasingly becomes the object of worship, and in many cases, the dispenser of immortality. Spiritual ideas of a general kind give way to this deification of the leader.' Secondly, in cults there is some kind of 'thought reform', popularly known as brainwashing. Thirdly, 'there is a pattern of manipulation and exploitation from above, by leaders and ruling coteries, and idealism from below, on the part of supplicants and recruits.' To sum up Lifton's definers for a cult: one, the Leader is God; two, brainwashing; three, harm.

In his book Lifton sets out eight tests for brainwashing. The third test is 'The Demand for Purity': the 'world is sharply divided into the pure and the impure, into the absolutely good and the absolutely evil... All "taints" and "poisons" which contribute to the existing state of impurity must be searched out and eliminated.' A follower of a thought control cult can off-load his inner guilt by hitting out at the outside world: 'one of his best ways to relieve himself of some of his burden of guilt is to denounce, continuously and hostilely, these same outside influences.'

Let's apply Lifton's test number three to the Church of Scientology. Does it by any chance denounce the impure? Are there any subtle signs of that? The Church's Freedom Magazine produced an attack video which described ex-Scientologists I had interviewed and me as follows:

'Disgraced. Liar. Perjurer. Callous. Insulting. Bullying.

Notorious. Shameful. Laughing stock. Poor work ethic. Can't hold a job. Failure. Known drunk. Disaffected. Angry. Vengeful. Malcontents. Disgraced. Incompetent. Serial sexual misconduct. Sells soul. Abhorrent. Deranged Abuser of women. Wrecks of men. Posse of vindictive liars.'

Thank you. One of the Church's official spokesman, Mike Rinder, called me 'an utter lunatic' and 'an asshole' in 2007. Five years on, he still stands by both judgments, although there is a twist to that tale, more of which later. Tommy Davis, the other, more senior spokesman, called me 'psychotic', a 'tabloid bottom-feeder' and repeatedly, a 'bigot'.

One Scientology blog calls for my permanent end: 'Growing up on a diet of things like Star Wars and Indiana Jones, one gets a chance to see a fair number of good guys & bad guys. In the movies, the bad guys are commonly depicted as being so low, so loathsome, that by the end of the movie even the most sweet and innocent housewife is picturing in her mind the most violent, grisly and **permanent** way for the bad guy to meet his end, because there's no question at all that the bad guy is just plain **bad** for everyone, and has just *got to go*. But in real life, you seldom come across such a bad guy that can be as utterly loathsome, so low, so cowardly and yet so holistically evil that they can be agreed upon as a total villain. Well, I think our wait is over. Enter BBC Panorama's John Sweeney.'

The title of the blog? 'John Sweeney is genuinely evil.'

Brainwashing is a heavy word. It's also a serious charge to make against a multi-billion dollar entity like the Church. In 1984 British High Court judge Mr Justice Latey said: 'Scientology is both immoral and socially obnoxious ...It is corrupt, sinister and dangerous. It is corrupt because it is based on lies and deceit and has its real objective money and power for Mr. Hubbard... It is sinister because it indulges in infamous practices both to its adherents who do not toe the line unquestionably and to those who criticize it or oppose it. It is dangerous because it is out to capture people and to indoctrinate and brainwash them so they become the unquestioning captives and tools of the cult, withdrawn from ordinary thought, living, and relationships with others.'

Language, grammar orders the mind. Subvert language and you subvert sanity. George Orwell, that great enemy of totalitarianism, knew and feared the power of that subversion when he witnessed it done by Stalin's men in Catalonia during the Spanish Civil War. That's the substance of his invented language, *NewSpeak*, in *1984*. The charge against the Church is that it confounds meaning and minds while presenting an artificial front to the world, a charge it denies.

The Chinese Communist torturers, and before them, Stalin's men, and before them, the Spanish Inquisition had brutal force to fall on if the wretches in their hands did not mentally submit. What is so strange is that we are considering people in fundamentally free societies who, it is said, have submitted to mental enslavement. They could just walk away. This is a conundrum raised in the TV series 'Homeland', just as it was in Richard Condon's 1959 novel, *The Manchurian Candidate* – how can the brainwashing be so strong that it keeps its spell even when you are free to leave?

One month after the opening of the London Org, November 2006, Tom Cruise married his third wife, Katie Holmes, in one of the most beautiful castles in the whole of Italy. The happy couple were conjoined according to the Scientology wedding rite scripted by L Ron, calling on all those present to note, 'girls need clothes and food and tender happiness and frills, a pan, a comb, perhaps a cat.' The Book of Common Prayer it is not.

Miscavige, the Leader of the Church, was Tom Cruise's best man. The word is that he came along on the honeymoon too, a story the Church denies.

In the spring of 2007 we engaged with the Church. So that's how I ended up in Saint Hill. Mole and I approached the front door. Mole is the BBC producer some believe best able to keep me on the professional straight and narrow. Mole (first name: Sarah) is so quietly spoken you can barely hear a word she says and she looks completely harmless. Don't be fooled: she combines the attributes of Mother Theresa and J.V. Stalin.

Hundreds, perhaps even a few thousand Scientologists, live in the East Grinstead area. This patch of Sussex, some of the most lazily beautiful countryside in England, is served by two Conservative MPs, Nicholas Soames (grandson of Winston Churchill) and Charles Hendry – the political heir to Geoffrey Johnson-Smith, who was unsuccessfully sued by the Church in 1970. Soames once threatened to sue the Church after it used images of his grandfather in their publicity material.

Hendry, a government minister from 2010 until the summer of 2012, is a different kettle of fish. In 2004 Hendry went to the premiere of Cruise's film Collateral. Tom Cruise chatted to the MP and his wife and phoned up Hendry's step-daughter to wish her happy birthday. The MP told the East Grinstead Courier: "'Clare thought it was the coolest thing ever." Mr Hendry said he and Mr Cruise spoke about Saint Hill, an L Ron Hubbard detox centre the actor set up in New York for victims of the September 11 terrorist attack and a bit about the film. "It was a very special evening and a real treat to be invited. I thought Tom was absolutely amazing for spending so much time speaking to people who had waited for him for hours and the film was full of suspense." Graeme Wilson, public affairs director at the Church of Scientology, said: "The premiere of Collateral was quite an experience and it was a real pleasure to be able to invite many of our friends from the East Grinstead area. It is a really excellent movie.'"

In 2005 the House of Commons debated an amendment to a controversial bill protecting religions from hate speech which some, including the comedian Rowan Atkinson, feared threatened free speech. The amendment proposed that the following groups should not be covered by the law: Satanists, Nazis, cannibals, believers in female circumcision and Scientologists. Up popped Charles Hendry: 'I hope my honourable Friend will understand that although Scientology may be very controversial, people who are Scientologists find it profoundly offensive to be included in that list. As he may be aware, Scientologists in this country are based in East Grinstead, which is just outside my constituency, and many hundreds of my constituents are Scientologists. They will be mystified by their inclusion in such a list, particularly as many other groups, such as those who practise voodoo, are not included. This debate has already caused Scientologists offence. On Second Reading, my right honourable Friend the

Member for Suffolk, Coastal (Mr. Gummer) said that "it is...a dangerous organisation that preys on people with mental illness". That is a characterisation that many people in my constituency would find peculiar and to which they would not relate. I am not familiar with the details of Scientology as a religion or as a set of beliefs, and having heard the Minister's comments earlier, it would be hard to decide on which side of that boundary it would fall. Those who practise Scientology would say that it is a religion, but many others would contest that. Undoubtedly, as human beings they do a great deal of good.' Hendry praised the Church's drug treatment programme. He went on to say: 'Certainly, as an organisation, Scientology has gone through serious hoops in terms of ensuring that it has the right to broadcast on television by satisfying the Independent Television Commission [ITC] that it is not a cult. It is a not-for-profit organisation, and that is well recognised.'

The bill became law but the clause Atkinson objected to was dropped.

In 2012 I raised Hendry's 'not a cult' stance in the *Independent* newspaper and Hendry wrote a letter to protest: 'Mr Sweeney quotes me as saying of Scientology that, "It is not a cult". The actual words I used in Parliament were that Scientology has been able to broadcast on television by "satisfying the Independent Television Commission that it is not a cult". To say he was quoting selectively was an understatement.'

The ITC no longer exists but a spokesman for the British agency that regulates advertising, the Advertising Standards Authority, told me: 'To be clear there are no rules in the Broadcast Advertising Code relating to cults. So neither the

ITC nor the ASA today would have a role in judging whether an organisation was – or was not – a cult.'

Hendry was the only MP to stand up for Scientology and his enthusiasm for the Church contrasts strikingly with Soames and his late predecessor, Johnson-Smith. Hendry's constituents who fear the Church may perhaps be assured that it is a not-for-profit organisation.

Mole and I got to Saint Hill's grand door and were met by a lawyer and three Scientologists – an interesting ratio I had not come across before in a House of God. They all wore suits and gave off a whiff of corporate power, as if they were from a multinational commodity broker or a mining company. The lawyer was Bill Walsh, a near-silent American who said that he was not a Scientologist but a Human Rights Counsel – that's fancy talk for a lawyer. The Englishman was an ex-London fireman called Bob Keenan. He, too, didn't say that much. Bob and Bill were flower-pot men, nodding their heads but contributing little theatre.

The two others were to be our 'handlers', we later realised: an Australian-American called Mike Rinder, a spooky, sallow-faced and hollow-cheeked man, and Tommy Davis, son of film actress Anne Archer. Tommy was younger than Mike but by some unspoken corporate osmosis more senior. Teeth gleamed, dark hair flopped, the nose aquiline, the smile cherubic. Nattily attired in what looked to me to be a $2,000 suit, crisp white shirt and dark tie, Tommy not only physically resembled Tom Cruise, he acted like him, intense, passionate, smiley, weird. In the idiom of American TV cops shows like *Starsky and Hutch* or *Hawaii Five-0* that used to wallpaper my childhood, Tommy was the smart, rich guy who almost

34

certainly was the baddie; Mike had all the hallmarks of the bloke who gets gruesomely murdered in the first five minutes.

The pecking order was established from that very first day: Tommy Davis was the boss, Mike a corpse-in-the-making. You could tell from their suits. Tommy looked magnificent; Mike looked Zombie-esque, as though he'd just come out of prison. That did not turn out so far from the truth.

Tommy is a prince of Scientology, his mother an Academy Award nominee, his father a real-estate tycoonette: family fame and money made him a member of its Hollywood Brahmin caste. He is a close friend of Tom Cruise. Three years before we met, Tommy had been on hand to improve Tom's chances with Iranian beauty Naz Boniadi, whom he dated before dropping her and going out with Katie Holmes, according to *Vanity Fair*. The magazine alleges that Tom Cruise used the Church, with Miscavige's blessing, to scout for and groom a suitable mate for him, an allegation that the Church and Cruise hotly deny.

Vanity Fair's version is that Tommy and his then wife, Nadine van Hootegen, and his now current wife, Jessica Feshbach, all went ice-skating and had sushi with Cruise and Naz on their first date. Perhaps co-incidentally, Naz had been previously asked what was her dream date? Ice-skating and sushi. Everything went well between Cruise and Naz until she met David Miscavige and his wife, Shelley, the magazine alleged. Naz, born in Iran but raised in London, couldn't properly understand the fast-spoken Philadelphia rasp of the Chairman of the Board, Miscavige, says *Vanity Fair*. This is a common failing. Ex-member of the Church Steve Hall, a scriptwriter and a man with a laconic wit, said that disentangling Miscavige's mixed messages and super-fast delivery was a nightmare. Pity Naz. The magazine said that after Naz was perceived to have failed to respect Miscavige, Cruise had her dumped. All of this the Church, Miscavige and Cruise deny.

Tommy and Jessica Feshbach had both gone to the great wedding in Italy when Cruise got hitched with Katie Holmes. Jessica was widely described as Scientology's minder for Katie, introduced as Katie's 'best friend' when the media interviewed Katie about *Batman Begins*, in which Katie starred as an assistant DA in Gotham City and a childhood friend of Batman. Jessica's father, Joe, was a multi-millionaire investor and a major donor to the Church. Back in 1993, the Feshbach family business took over a chocolate company in California, introduced Scientology's technology and a number of staff left, complaining that they were being force-fed not chocolate but Dianetics.

Plugged into the very top of Scientology although Tommy Davis may have been, the power relationship between Posh Tommy and Zombie Mike seemed, on reflection, to be the wrong way round. That's because Mike, whose family joined the Church when he was six years old, was a professional PR man for Scientology who had been defending the Church to the media for years, and whose preferred technique was to block, not to engage. Tommy was new to this game, and happy to fight, and that makes good telly but bad PR.

Very early on at Saint Hill, the mind-games started. Tommy told us it was a shame that we hadn't told them about the BBC team filming me driving in through the gate, because they would have helped us. That was generous and kind and slightly creepy because we had done a few driving set-up shots on the road outside of the estate. How did they know we had been filming? This was the first time with the Church that I felt as though I was treading on a step that wasn't there. It would not be the last. Bob chatted to Mole about her being based in Northern Ireland. They knew quite a lot about us. Funny that. We didn't know it but they were filming us on their CCTV, footage that would be subsequently shown in their splendid film on us, called *'Panorama Exposed'*. Watch it. I am the baddie.

Inside, Saint Hill was like a show mansion. Or a film set. Everything looked right. Nothing felt right. Plush, carpeted, scrupulously clean, eerily quiet, empty, creepy-creepy-crawlie. They showed off the novelty feature of the house, a ghastly mural in garish colours by John Spencer Churchill, nephew of Sir Winston Churchill, of a load of monkeys, 145 in all, featuring a score of species. A capuchin monkey painting under a tree portrays his Uncle Winston. I cracked a joke about Stan and Hilda Ogden's 'muriel' in ITV's *Coronation Street*, a cross-cultural reference they were never going to get in a billion years. Mole looked at me witheringly so I shut up.

Out came the snaps. Tommy and Mike showed us lots of family album-style snaps of empty Scientology churches or Orgs. In Scientology, there is no mass worship. It consists of one-to-one therapy sessions, which is one reason why some question its claim to be classed as a religion. Once you've seen one shot of an empty Org in Nebraska, you've seen too many. Mole is naturally polite; I am not. Under the cosh from her to play nicely I said little and was on my best behaviour. Albums over, a film, again, high-value sequences of empty Scientology Orgs, then its Narconon programme.

Narconon is a programme for drugs addicts, devised by Mr Hubbard, based on the notion that if you spend long enough in the sauna and take lots of Vitamin B tablets the harmful drugs will ooze out of your pores with your sweat. This is rubbish. There is no independent scientific validation for Narconon, though some, including the former minister Charles Hendry MP, praise the Church's programme.

The Narconon base in Arrowhead, near New Bucket, Arkansas – or somewhere like that – was illustrated on video with lots of swooshing camera dives of knitting pattern magazine mannequin-style extras playing drug addicts walking crossways across the main field of view. They look good and they have big hair, so the film seems like a bad 80s American detective series, but one with not enough or, in fact, no dead bodies. My notebook gives a flavour of it: 'psychiatry: bringing down the hammer on a criminal agenda... largest disaster relief organisation on earth... the tech...'

The notes in my notebook continue: 'this is welcome to reshaping the destiny of earth... Bingo... psychiatry... taking them down... Psych... 6616 Sunset Boulevard...'

The video showed Mike Rinder introduce Chairman Miscavige. On the tape, Rinder seemed to be a cardinal of the Church, not the zombie underling in front of us. The leader bounced onto a vast stage, applauded to the echo by an audience of Hollywoodesque luvvies, all booted and suited in black tie, as if were some kind of eschatological Oscars.

The film continued: 'psychiatry an industry of death... the horror of psychiatry... 100 million aware of psych horrors...368 psychs doing time... 2006: Phase One: Global Demolition... Global Obliteration... hand grenade.'

Hand grenade?

It made little sense but I got it that they didn't like psychiatry. After an hour of it, I wanted to run away. I said I needed a loo break. Tommy said that the film lasted another two hours. What? It was a surreal exercise in non-communication. We said goodbye and arranged to meet them the next day in London in Fitzroy Street where L Ron first stayed in London. Mole recalls that very sweetly they gave us as a goodwill gesture a picnic of cheese and pickle sandwiches.

At Fitzroy Street they showed us L Ron's room, a wacky shrine of a kind, complete with a peaked white naval hat to remind us of his service in the US Navy, in which heretic Russell Miller says he shelled Mexico by mistake. We were given a lunch of sandwiches wrapped in cellophane, served by a distractingly beautiful woman who vanished in seconds. It was clearly some kind of trick and it worked on me brilliantly. On Mole, it did not.

The five of us sat down over a fantastic platter – spring rolls, cheese things, smoked salmon enrobed in delicious what-nottery – Tommy, Mike, Fireman Bob, Mole and I. Tommy did most of the talking. I noticed that Mike's Australian accent was watered down or conflicted by a smattering of English idioms and an icing of Americana. He was, in short, one crazy mixed up Aussie.

I asked Tommy: 'Can there be such a thing as a good psychiatrist?'

Tommy: 'No.'

Mole tried to play diplomat. She recalls saying that we wanted to find out more about Scientology for the documentary, and maybe they could show me some Scientology techniques or go through the process of what it would be like to become a Scientologist. 'Until this point,' Mole says, 'Tommy had been charming. But he suddenly switched and accused me of being disingenuous. He said he knew that I'd been filming with anti-Scientology protesters a few months ago opposite the Church's Tottenham Court Road assessment centre and so I clearly had a negative agenda. I was very surprised because, yes, I had filmed the protestors the previous autumn but I hadn't identified myself to the Church. I realised that they must have taken pictures of me and either matched me up to the person who was sitting in front of them or they had done some kind of other investigative work to find out my name and that I worked for the BBC.'

The anti-Scientology protesters back in 2006 were small in number but big in volume. They would encamp immediately opposite the Church's long-time Tottenham Court Road recruiting centre and their leader, a classic English eccentric in a rather splendid straw trilby, would intone through a microphone in a fine sing-song baritone: 'Don't give money to Scientology. It's a scam, it's a con, it's a cult.'

Mole tried to negotiate access with Tommy, Mike and co. I wrote down their terms in my notebook: '1) Not a cult.' In our proposed film we were not to mention the word 'cult'. '2) No crazies. 3) No anonymous – unnamed – sources.'

Again and again they pressed the point that the Church of Scientology was a religion like other religions, and that it should be respected. This line of argument had clearly been played out before, successfully to the United States IRS back in the 1990s, to President Sarkozy in France, reportedly to Tony Blair in Number Ten. It's a powerful argument but not one that is beyond scrutiny.

There is a cultural dimension to the question of what is and what is not a religion. The United States of America was founded by Puritans fleeing religious persecution at the hands of the King of England and the established Church of England in the seventeenth century. For the founding fathers, religious freedom was a right which they hard-wired into the American constitution. It is as if there is in the United States an eleventh commandment: 'Thou shalt not criticise another man's religion.' The danger is that in America they are so afraid of religious un-freedom that they fear to discriminate between a religion and a confidence trick.

Henri IV of France, born a Protestant who converted to Catholicism because, as he put it, 'Paris is worth a Mass', summed up my take on God: 'Those who follow their conscience are of my religion, and I am of the religion of those who are brave and good.' Later, Henri was assassinated by a bigot.

In the twenty first century, everyone has a right to believe in nothing or whatever they want to believe in and that includes the right to believe in Scientology. It may be useful to make a distinction between faith and religion. A faith is a universal belief system which individuals can respect; a religion is a universal belief system which society, by and large, respects. If people believe in Mr Hubbard's teachings, good luck to them. Some people I know do, and, uncomfortable as it is, I defend their right to believe in him. But not everything that claims it is a religion has an automatic right to be treated as a religion by society. It could be a multi-billion corporation like Coca Cola or a racket like the mafia or a brainwashing cult. The Church of Scientology is, some say, all three.

The Church's conditions – no use of the word cult, no anonymous interviews, no interviews with people the Church defines as 'haters' – were a line in the sand. We could not make a film about the Church of Scientology without addressing that core issue, that it is not a fact that it is a religion but a claim – and a claim that is open to scrutiny. Others dispute it. It is a fact that many of its ex-members call it a cult. We could not possibly make a film on the Church without examining whether or not it is a cult.

The Church through those awfully nice legal people at Carter-Ruck denied setting the conditions. Mole and I are clear: they set three conditions. She's smart; I was sober.

We politely declined their terms and left. We did not tell them but we were going to carry on. We were determined to make our film, come what may. The question is would the Church let us get on with it? Or would they try and intervene, to try and exercise control?

L Ron's unauthorised biographer, Russell Miller, warned me: 'First, you are going to be followed. Unquestionably you will be followed wherever you go. They will dig into your background, they will try and dig up some dirt about you and find out any scandals about you and they will certainly make them public and they will keep as close as possible tabs on you as they are able to do so.'

Mole had a cunning plan. She and cameraman Bill Browne flew to Florida a day ahead of me.

My father, Leonard Sweeney, had died the week before, a loss I strove to keep from the Church of Scientology. He was a good man, a poor working class boy from Birkenhead – on the increasingly fashionable west bank of the Mersey, across from Liverpool – who left school at the age of fourteen, joined Cammell Laird's shipyard as an apprentice and at the age of 19 became a ship's engineer during the Battle of the Atlantic. After the war he left the sea to raise our family, support Tranmere Rovers from a distance and tell stories. Modest about his war, after a pint and a half he could be persuaded to talk about what it felt like being hunted by Nazi U-boats. He did an impression of the sound of a Royal Navy anti-U boat depth charge going off when you're stuck far below sea level in the engine room: BOOOOM! In the pub, it was a show-stopper.

He was a lovely chap but old age was catching up with him. Sitting in 'the captain's chair' at home with mum, he had a massive heart attack and died in hospital. Far better to go out like that with a BOOOOM! than a long lingering death covered in tubes. In death, as in life, he was a gentleman.

I drove down to Hampshire for the funeral. Lots of people turned up, many from Lymington Bowling Club, where he'd been some kind of Supreme Being. I gave the address, reading out the score of a football game that will never happen: 'Manchester United nil, Tranmere Rovers seven.' We gave him a good send-off. I felt guilty that I did not cry.

The next day I flew to the United States and battle commenced.

CHAPTER TWO
'What do my socks have to do with spiritual freedom?'

There is something unearthly about the quality of the light in Clearwater, halfway down Florida's thigh facing the Gulf of Mexico. Perhaps it is the light which lured L Ron to appoint Clearwater as Scientology's Mecca in the 1970s, when he tired of wandering the oceans of the world. It is to this small, sleepy coastal resort that Scientologists the world over come to study. Here, there are more members of the Church per head of population than anywhere else on the planet.

A word about the weather. Throughout our time in the United States in the spring of 2007 the weather was unremittingly glorious: clear, bright sunny days, not too hot. It never rained. This lack of drizzle weakens moral fibre.

It was the late Mr Hubbard's birthday party, and Miscavige was speaking at a major event in a hall which seats 2,200 people. We went along and tried to get in, but were rebuffed, and left, but not before their CCTV cameras filmed us not getting in and then leaving. For the record – and perhaps I am being overly defensive because of what happened later in California – I was polite and correct throughout.

At Clearwater the next day we met our first two defectors from the Church who were willing to go on camera and talk openly about their experiences inside, Donna Shannon and Mike Henderson. Mole arranged that we film the couple in a country park, populated by raccoons, who took a mild interest in our conversation. By and large, the ex-members of the Church I've met are nice people: bright, funny, self-deprecating, keen to help. They are not dumb. What is extraordinary is what they endured in the name of something they believed in.

Mike is a gentle giant, six foot nine inches tall, a pilot and a sweet man. When we met, he still believed in some of Scientology's teachings but had fallen out with the Church as an institution. Donna was an 'out-out', a vet and also a pilot with her own small plane and someone with real oomph about her: a feisty lady. She had been an ordinary or as they call it 'public' Scientologist but was so enamoured with the Church she was persuaded to sell her vet's practice and moved with husband Mike to Clearwater. There, they entered the Church's Holy Order, the Sea Org – Scientology's version of monks and nuns, who give up worldly pleasures to better serve the organisation. Donna and Mike were based at FLAG, the name of the Church's massive HQ in Clearwater, endeavouring to make the world 'clear'. As a parishioner or 'public' Scientologist, Donna had worked in the outside world, coming in to the Church to study and pay her way up the varying levels to clear and beyond. As a member of staff at FLAG, she became, she said, their slave.

'In the Sea Org, on staff,' said Donna, 'you are controlled by derision, ridicule, being screamed at the top of someone's lungs right in your face. They train people how to scream at somebody and how to intimidate somebody and how to make them feel like dirt. It is called ripping your face off. You get right up in somebody's face, nose to nose, and spittle flying out of your mouth, scream in their face.'

Can you scream back, I asked, foolishly? Remember this conversation took place a whole week before I did exactly that. The answer was no.

Mike Henderson gave me an illustration of life in the Sea Org: 'One of the first weekends we were there, room inspection. And the Sea Org ethics officer comes in and inspects. And if you drawers aren't in order, if your socks and your underwear aren't stacked neatly, it is a flunk. And the first time this happened Donna just said right to the guy's face "you have got to be fucking kidding me". And I couldn't believe she said that to him, but that's Donna.'

He said that with awe.

Donna chipped in with a theological point of some force: 'What do my socks have to do with spiritual freedom?'

At Saint Hill and Fitzroy Street, everything we had seen was immaculate and subtly expensive. Living conditions for the Sea Org, behind the scenes, were, they said, somewhat different.

'Termites, roaches, stinky old carpets,' listed Donna. 'Bare light bulbs, holes in the wall. Mike put in tiles, fixed the holes in the wall, put in a new toilet that worked. He got the old leaky dishwasher taken out, all that stuff. We did $2,000 worth of work on that room so it would be liveable.'

At Saint Hill and Fitzroy Street in London, the food was exquisite, I droned on, beautiful women giving us tea and coffee. Everything top notch.

'For the staff, if you are a single person you will live in a room with four, five, six other people of the same sex, all stacked up.'

If you transgress, you are punished, she said. 'They made an example of someone. He had to run up all the stairs of the Fort Harrison Hotel, ten floors. So here you have a person in their fifties who is not really in great shape and they are running them up and down ten flights of stairs. It is a wonder somebody doesn't drop dead.'

Mike chipped in: 'One night Tom Cruise spoke for five minutes at a graduation. He was there on a break from OT7' – Operating Thetan Level 7. 'He gave his wins' – *SciSpeak* for self-enhancement – 'and that was it. Donna was in the audience. But I never saw it because we were busy running tables and chairs up the freight elevator till one o'clock in the morning. When you are on staff you see the other side of the Scientology.' His disillusion was deep.

Donna ended up on the Estates Project Force, a kind of paramilitary boot camp. And that is where she met Tommy Davis, she said. Suddenly, one day, the ethics officers and some of the higher ups came storming out of that room with Tommy. 'They had him by the ear or by the hair and they dragged him out and held him up in front of the class. They started screaming about what a liar and terrible person he was. They were just trying to ridicule and shame him in front of everybody else. Then they slammed him back in the room. And we were left thinking: what was that about?'

Tommy Davis and the Church deny these allegations, vehemently. The Church makes the counter-accusation that Donna sought to extort money from it by making up absurd

47

claims of abuse, and that her attempts at extortion failed. Donna and Mike deny these claims.

Back in England, I had asked the three Church spokesmen, Tommy Davis, Mike Rinder and Bob 'Fireman Bob' Keenan, about what some say is the Church's secret belief, that they are engaged in a trillion year war against a space alien Satan who has brainwashed humanity into believing he does not exist. His name is Lord Xenu. Is Xenu real, I asked. They all guffawed, incredulous at my incredulity. Clearly, Xenu was nonsense. Or was it?

What did the defectors think about Xenu? Mike was uneasy, and said that he had signed a bond agreeing not to talk about it. I found his reluctance to discuss Xenu both proper, for him, and strangely disturbing. It suggested to me that there was something in it that he did not want to talk about. Donna had signed the same bond but she now believes that she did so in some strange hypnotic state: 'It is just a game to get money. I don't think there is any more truth in it than if I declare a raccoon god. And I don't feel that anything I signed there can bind me to anything, because I was lied to, I was conned. I think Scientology creates a form of insanity. You are hypnotised, you are brainwashed.'

On Xenu, Donna came out, guns blazing: 'It's all made up, utter space garbage.'

Stop there. Three members of the Church's Holy Order, Tommy Davis, Mike Rinder and Bob Keenan had all denied the existence of Xenu; Mike had declined to discuss Xenu; Donna said, effectively, that it was bad science fiction. Who to believe?

The 1987 Panorama *'The Road to Total Freedom?'* (available on YouTube) says followers of the Church of Scientology go through a series of levels to become an Operating Thetan. When you get to Operating Thetan Level III – OT3 – you cross through 'The Wall of Fire' and learn the great mystery at the heart of Scientology, that it is secretly engaged in an endless war against a space alien Satan. The 1987 *Panorama* depicted an animated cartoon treatment of Scientology's core cosmology. Hubbard, the BBC reported, wrote that seventy five million years ago Lord Xenu, the head of the Galactic Confederacy, brought life-forms called Thetans to planet Earth and blew them up in volcanoes with hydrogen bombs. Humanity's wretchedness is due to our being infected with the souls of the dead Thetans.

Ex-Scientologists maintain that Xenu *is* part of Scientology's Holy Writ. They say the exploding volcano that illustrates L Ron's great work, *Dianetics*, is a cunning reference to this great secret. They say that if you ask a Scientologist about Xenu, they can't tell you because the truth could kill you. Sceptics who think the Church is a con trick are, in fact, brainwashed by Xenu. They are Suppressive Persons, to be feared and attacked. The Xenu thing is, to some, an extraordinarily powerful narrative that has consumed the lives of thousands and thousands of people. To others, it's bad science fiction.

Panorama in 1987 depicted Xenu as a bald cove, boasting a sinister goatee, heavy black eyebrows and a silvery jacket with shoulder pads so sharp they could poke your eye out. Xenu looks like a cross between Emperor Ming The Merciless in *Flash Gordon* and The Hood in *Thunderbirds*. It looks like, er, bad science fiction.

The Xenu story, critics say, is only secret because it is a clever way of squeezing money out of people. They only learn the great secret after spending years studying and paying for Scientology's lessons, which do not come cheap. The critics say this makes Scientology less like a religion and more like a lobster pot – in that you are tempted by theological bait but that it is not fully revealed to you until you have entered so deep you are well and truly trapped in the pot. Ex-Scientologists insist that that the believing Scientologists were lying to me, out of their own peculiar sense of necessity.

Perhaps Tommy, Mike Rinder and Fireman Bob had no choice. If you believe in Scientology and confirm Xenu to the uninitiated, you place them in grave danger.

Enter a Church – Catholic, Protestant, Orthodox or Coptic – and they will tell you that they believe that 'Christ has died, Christ is risen, and Christ will come again.' Enter a mosque and they will tell you: 'Follow the teachings of the Prophet.' Enter a synagogue: 'Marry a nice Jewish girl/boy and don't eat bacon sandwiches.' Enter a Church of Scientology Org and no-one will tell you about the space alien Satan they're fighting. Xenu is a logic bomb inside the Church of Scientology's claim to be treated just like any other religion. A 'religion' that hides its core belief from the world is not a religion because a true religion must be open about itself to all. That is the essence of the British test set by the Charity Commissioners in London, and one the Church of Scientology fails.

Mike Henderson refused to discuss Xenu, whereas Donna was happy to spill the beans. Mike's position was, in some ways, the more telling: he still felt under an unbreakable mental bond to a thing he no longer belonged to; and that bond over-rode his natural courtesy to explain Scientology to us. The split over Xenu between Donna and Mike seemed natural and honest and indicated at least the possibility that if a believing Scientologist denied Xenu to us they were doing so in the service of humanity's higher good, and that trumps any obligation to tell anyone from the ordinary world the truth.

Truth to tell, my mind at that moment was stumbling towards the distant glimmer of this observation. The most striking thing back then was the chasm between the two camps: Xenu was nonsense, said the Church officials; Xenu was real but garbage, said Donna the heretic and, the Church says, extortionist. None of this is easy to get your head round.

Let's think about it in a slightly different way. Remember this: 'They peel them with their metal knives, boil them for twenty of their minutes, then they smash them all to bits'. The words of the spindly-bodied, big-headed, metallic-voiced cackling Smash Martians from the 1974 advert for instant mash potato in the UK. Imagine creating a religion out of the Smash Martians. As they are to earthlings, so adepts of the Church of Scientology are to simple, earthbound humanity. 'They are clearly a most primitive people,' as the Leader of the Smash Martians puts it. But imagine this: the Smash Martians are real, and the rest of us have been brainwashed into thinking they're just a silly joke in an ad campaign. But really they are just a silly joke in an ad campaign and the people who believe in the Smash Martians are crazy. Try and hold both propositions in your head.

We moved on from the Church's somewhat tricky cosmology to how people are treated inside the Sea Org. Donna set out the gap between the high theology of the 'religion' and the human reality. Sea Org members are encouraged to travel on buses from the accommodation to FLAG. The buses are 'grossly overcrowded, just horrible, there is no room to sit. Now these are Sea Org members, Operating Thetans, these higher beings. When the bus comes, it suddenly turns into a madhouse, like a bunch of stray dogs they just go crazy clawing to get on the bus.' If you don't fight, you will miss the bus and get into trouble for being late, she said.

Mike said, 'You have the smiley face experts who handle the celebrities. Tommy Davis is part of that crew, to make sure that Tom Cruise, Kirstie Alley, get the best treatment. They hold elevators for them, they never have to wait for anything. They get the top level of smiley face Scientology treatment. And the only time I ever saw that as a public Scientologist, was the more money I had available, or the higher the credit limit was on my credit cards, the more smiley face I got. And then I figured it out that the smiley face is dependent on your status as a celebrity, or how much money you are worth.'

Mike spent 34 years inside the Church. Why stay so long? 'It becomes like a carrot attached to a donkey by a stick, out in front. You just keep chasing the carrot. And every time you take another two or three steps it costs you another hundred thousand dollars.'

They both felt that it was a pay-as-you-go religion. Donna spent a decade inside the Church, spending $1million. Mike spent $500,000.

But worse, far worse, than the money is the effect on family life.

Mike said: 'I have 35 family members in Scientology:

my mother, my brother, my four sisters, my 22 nieces and nephews, and my son. And the only ones that are outside the church are myself, my daughter, and my father. And everyone is estranged that is not in the Church. My father's kids won't speak to him with me being the exception. And I didn't speak to him for four years. And after I left the Church I re-established ties with him and it is difficult to describe how a man of 76 years whose proudest accomplishment in life is his six children, and they won't speak to him.'

Mike, a great haystack of a man, was crying his eyes out. It was unbearably moving.

I told Donna and Mike that the Church's spokesmen had offered us access on condition that we did not use the word cult.

Donna said: 'If you actually understand what a cult is, look it up in the dictionary, all of the things fit. It is funny to me that when you first get into Scientology you are trained on how to handle people that tell you it is a cult. They say they have nothing hidden. Everything is hidden. The Xenu story is hidden. The staff conditions are hidden, the real agenda of Scientology is hidden. They are not there clearing the planet, they are out there getting money. It is a con game. They are a cult.'

After the main interviews, Bill Browne, our cameraman, took some set-up shots of Donna and Mike. I powered up my phone and BBC Radio Five came on, asking me for a reaction to the news that Sally Clark had died. Sally was the English mother of two baby boys who suffered cot deaths. Cruelly, she was charged, tried and convicted of murdering them, in part on the evidence of Professor Sir Roy Meadow who told the jury that the chances of this happening naturally were '73 million to one'.

One of my first radio documentaries for BBC Radio Five in 2001 was called '73 million to one' in which that number, and much of the rest of Sir Roy's expertise, was demolished, and we set out the evidence that Sally had been the victim of a monstrous miscarriage of justice. Two years later she was freed by the Court of Appeal, but the trauma of false accusation and prison had broken Sally's heart. I gave Radio Five an interview, switched off the phone, and in the middle of a country park in Florida I burst into tears, grieving for a good woman destroyed by bigotry. And then it was back to the day job.

Mike and Donna took us on a tour of Scientology Town, past the Power building, a half-built monstrosity, still being completed after years and years of refurbishment, past the Fort Harrison hotel where the Operating Thetans do their courses. We got out of the car and filmed them walking around Clearwater pointing out all the sites. We expected to be filmed or challenged. But downtown Clearwater was eerily quiet, as if the whole Scientology population had been ordered to keep off the streets lest Bill film them off-guard.

We took Donna and Mike to dinner to thank them for their time. I knocked back a bit of wine while Mole scowled at me. Surely, I was allowed some time off? It was late when we said our goodbyes to Donna and Mike. We got back to our hotel in Clearwater at midnight, to find the Church of Scientology waiting for us in the lobby.

CHAPTER THREE
Ill-met at midnight

Tommy Davis and Mike Rinder were sitting in the hotel's comfy chairs along with a Scientology cameraman, clad in black. Damn the wine. I should have drunk lemonade.

'Hi Mike, Hi Tommy,' I said, as if it was perfectly natural to bump into two Scientologists in your hotel lobby at midnight, and proffered my hand.

'I'm not going to shake your hand,' said Tommy, rising from his chair. He was wearing a suit, dark tie and white shirt. 'I find it considerably obnoxious what you've done. The time that I took – spent two days with you straight. Offer you cooperation and who do you spend your time with?'

His tone was that of an outraged Victorian husband furious that his young wife had dallied at the regimental ball of the 19th Foot and returned at midnight with a tendril of hair uncoiled and her bonnet askew.

The Scientology cameraman was fully kitted out with camera top light and microphone on a lead, so he could catch every word of Tommy berating me for my atrocious conduct. It was the perfect video ambush – or it would have been had not Mole brought along a small video camera to dinner, just in case. They were video-ambushing us. We were video-ambushing them back. The Scientology cameraman switched on his light. I engaged with him: 'Hi I'm John Sweeney from the BBC.' He said nothing but we later found out his name was Jesse Radstrom.

'And you spend the day with Mike Henderson and Donna Shannon? What are these people?' said Tommy, full of wounded pride. 'The people who you spent the day with?' I stepped away from Tommy. He stepped towards me. Mike Rinder edged closer to me, the cameraman boxing me in.

'Ok, from my perspective?' Suddenly, I was sober as Mr Justice Latey. 'Are you sure you're getting good sound? Shall I hold that?' I grasped the microphone wielded by the black-clad cameraman and opened fire. 'You' – Tommy - 'and you' – Mike - 'and the Church of Scientology have been spying on the BBC. You have been spying on our hotel. We didn't tell you where we were staying so you've been spying on us. And I find that, if I may say so, a little bit creepy. Here's your microphone' – and I handed it back, not to the cameraman, but to Tommy.

'Thanks,' said Tommy, perhaps – I might be wrong – a little forlornly.

I hadn't finished. 'And secondly, what's wrong with talking to people who are critical in an open society, who are critical of an institution?'

'Nothing,' said Tommy.

'Have they no right to speak?'

'There is nothing wrong with that. But that's not what I'm taking about.'

The hotel receptionist was not used to this kind of theatre

of absurd in her lobby at midnight. She said: 'Excuse me, you two need to go outside or I will call the police.'

'OK,' I said, 'but you can do that anyway.'

I walked out into the fresh air, and Tommy, Mike and the Man in Black followed me out. I still hadn't finished: 'So the question is: have you been spying on us?'

'No,' said Tommy. 'The locals in town were talking,' said Tommy. 'A camera crew – an English guy.'

The population of Clearwater is 100,000. It being a BBC Current Affairs budget, we were staying in an adequate hotel with fine views of a freeway on stilts, a good few miles out of town.

'Oh and they said they're staying at this hotel?'

'Yeah. Absolutely. But that's immaterial,' said Tommy.

'It's not immaterial. Because it means that you're invading our space. We're not going to come round to where you sleep and say hello. And come in the middle of the night. Don't you think that's a bit weird? A little bit strange?'

'You know what? I'm not even going to talk about it. We spent two days with you. We offered you so much and what happened in return?'

If you work in television, two days not filming is two days wasted. I batted back his offer of 'so much', calling it nothing.

'What are you talking about?' asked Tommy, incredulous at my stony lack of gratitude. He was back to doing his outraged Victorian husband routine. I had lost my bonnet for good. This palaver went on for what seemed like a very long time. I put it to Tommy that Donna had told me she had seen people grab him by the hair. He denied it. He accused Donna of demanding money from the Church, of being an extortionist. Then it was back to attacking me: 'What is baffling to us is that we tell you we're open and willing to communicate...'

And then the Clearwater Police Department cruiser turned up. The police officer got out of the car and sized the situation up: two men in suits and a cameraman in black filming one man and a woman and a cameraman filming them. Or the other way around. The police officer asked: 'The hotel wanted to know what you are filming?'

'We're filming each other...' I replied, unhelpfully.

'So who's staying here? I guess for the rest if you want to get a room... otherwise you might want to get going.'

Tommy and Mike started backing off into the night: 'That's fine we don't want to cause any trouble...'

Tommy shook the police officer's hand, and they were gone.

The next morning we discovered that the Church was opening a new Org in Plant City, an hour's drive east of Clearwater. We thought we would pop along and see the opening for ourselves. Scientology's favourite colour is uranium yellow – and there was a sea of yellow bunting and tents and a lot of people milling around, none of whom would talk to us and one, two, three Scientology camera people who filmed us. After a knife-slash of time, a PR lady called Pat Harney found us. I wanted to go into the new Org and look around. Would that be possible?

'No,' Pat said firmly but sweetly, 'but you can come over here with me.'

Why no?

'From all the reports I've heard, you haven't exactly been

very friendly.'

I told her I was a pussycat. Nothing doing. After a fair while Mole's face split into two halves, horizontally. I couldn't work out why she was so happy, but she motioned behind my back. I turned around to see Tommy, looking extremely natty in dark sunglasses. He'd changed his tie, swapping the dark one he'd worn the previous night for a striped black and white number.

'Hello Tommy!' I squeaked. 'How are you? I was just wondering where you were, and there you are, fantastic. How did you know we were here?'

'I actually didn't, we have the opening here so I was going to that.'

'Very good,' I replied. (By the way, if you shoot me in the foot, I would say: 'Very good.' It's a phrase I use when I mean the exact opposite.)

Yackety-yack, we went, yackety-yack. Tommy said that of course the Church would have offered us access to Plant City had we asked the previous night. I replied, words to the effect that it might have slipped my mind after he turned up at the hotel at midnight, and 'that was rather...'

...Clickerty-clack, clackerty-click. An enormously long goods train thundered by. What was odd was that both Tommy and I knew there was no point in saying anything to each other because the sound would be too poor quality for our respective audiences: for me, the BBC's viewers, for Tommy, who knew? Clackerty-click... I've always wanted to stow away on an American goods train and see where I'd end up – Hoboken? Somewhere in Alaska? – but now wasn't the time. Still, I cannot see a good trains in America without marvelling at the country's immensity. Clickerty-clack, clickerty-clack, click-erty-clack, into the distance...

'...creepy,' I finished.

'Not nearly as creepy,' answered Tommy, as showing up at LRH's birthday event and asking to interview the Leader.'

Who is the creepiest? That is the question. We tossed that around for a bit. I mentioned their conditions for access, including no mention of the word 'cult'. He called me: 'disingenuous', 'shocking' and 'utterly unprofessional'. He talked about them being open; I challenged his attack on the meaning of words.

'I have a real problem with your use of the English language,' I said. 'You say you are open and everywhere we go the doors are closed: "you are not coming in." But what does happen is, we have another silent gentleman here filming us.'

I pointed to a Scientology cameraman, doing exactly that. Tommy replied: 'We are absolutely filming it because you don't know how to conduct yourself. We are actually documenting your bias and all the things that you are doing. You are in violation of OfCom' – the British agency that controls broadcasting standards – 'and your broadcasting guidelines because of how you are conducting yourselves and the unprofessionalism and how rude it is. And we have a world wide religious movement, millions of members...'

On and on we went, on and on. Donna and Mike, space aliens, the cult-word – I fired at him. Notoriety seekers, ignorance, bigotry – he fired back. The only worry was would we run out of tape? Would Bill's battery run flat? We carried on clobbering each other like the Black Knight and his adversary in *Monty Python And the Holy Grail*. And then Tommy said something rather troubling.

'Well, I give the little badge of honour for you. I know where you live.'

'What do you mean you know where I live?'

'Like I know where you reside as a person. Your... your basis of... I don't know where your house is, no, I don't know where your house is. I have no interest in knowing where your house is.'

He seemed to be doubling back on what he had just said, as if he had said it to taunt me, then realised that it was a foolish own-goal.

Did the Church of Scientology know where I lived? A few weeks later, after we had returned to London, one of my neighbours in Wimbledon, Anne Layther, told me that her 11-year-old son answered the door to a stranger. She described him to me as blond, very well-spoken Englishman, 5'7", thin. He was carrying a rucksack and wearing a cap and struck Anne as 'odd'. He said that he was looking for John Sweeney. Anne said she gestured vaguely that I lived in that direction. He said something like: 'I've just come from there. Do you know if he's away?' He went away and returned ten minutes later, saying: 'I've got a package for him.'

'Who are you?' Anne asked.

A courier, he said, but he struck Anne as being not right, too posh, for that kind of job. He said the package was for 'John Sweeney of the BBC.' Anne offered to take the package for him but he said he needed to check with his boss. Anne went out to her back garden and called out to me. I came out into our back garden. I had been home the whole time, but the mystery courier with his package looking for me had never thought to knock on my door. How very odd.

Back at Plant City, Tommy moved away from where I lived to what he called my partially unveiled attack on his religion, my disingenuousness and my twisting of what he was telling me.

'It is wholly absurd,' I replied. 'The question is: is your organisation an honest and open organization? Can the word of the Church of Scientology be trusted? And the answer is well they are very strange. They are actually a little bit creepy because they come along to my hotel...'

'I am creepy?' asked Tommy, incredulous.

'As I said...'

'I am strange and creepy?' Tommy's incredulity thickened like gravy after stirring.

'You came to my hotel at midnight, that's creepy.'

'People who sit down with you and talk to you about my religious belief is something like...'

Ding-Ding, Round Nine.

'But some people say,' I said, 'it is a sinister cult. Now L Ron Hubbard? Some people say he is a fantasist and a liar.'

This got to Tommy. 'I would just like...I would just like to, and I hope somebody is shooting this, OK, good...'

We were heading for a video shoot-out in the OK Corral. I counted five cameras: Bill with his big camera, Mole with a second smaller one, just in case, and three separate Scientology cameras. I set out to list them: 'To be fair, there is one camera from the BBC, one camera from your...'

'Now you listen to me for a second,' snapped Tommy, his anger rising by the second, his face etched with aggression, my face reflected in his dark glasses.

'You have no right whatsoever to say what and what isn't

a religion. The constitution of the United States of America guarantees one's right to practice and believe freely in this country. And the definition of religion is very clear, and it is not defined by John Sweeney. And for you to repeatedly refer to my faith in those terms is so derogatory, so offensive and so bigoted – and the reason you keep repeating it is because you wanted to get a reaction like you are getting right now. Well buddy, you got it, right here, right now. I am angry. Real angry.'

We were nose to nose. Had I puckered my lips I could have kissed him. He announced that we were done.

'We are not done,' I said. From the age of five to ten I lived in Manchester. While riled, my vowel sounds flatten. 'We are not done,' I repeated, as if an extra on *Coronation Street*, up for a fight with Tony Gordon.

'If you use that term one more time about my religion…'

'We are not done because…'

'I can't be responsible for my actions…'

'Now my friend it is your turn to listen to me. I am a British subject, not an American citizen and in my country we have freedom of speech. We have a freedom to speak and we have exercised that freedom for centuries. And, if people say to me that they think your…what you claim to be a religion is in fact a cult, I have a right to report that. I have got a right to report that Tommy…'

He trotted away, past a road works thingy, and jogged across the main road. I lumbered after him, a rhinoceros picking up speed. He called me a bigot, four, five times. That bounced off the rhino's hide. I was holding up, so far.

CHAPTER FOUR
One man against the crowd

That afternoon we headed back to Scientology town – Clearwater – to meet one man who stood apart from L Ron's crowd. He was a fruitcake, a loner, a weirdo and a brave man, all rolled into one. His name was Shawn Lonsdale. Originally from New England, Shawn had been in the US Navy and while still a youngish man he had settled in Clearwater. Years before, he'd been caught by the police having consenting sex with men. Later, at a local council meeting, he had clashed with a Scientologist and suddenly they were on his case.

People who don't like Scientology leave Clearwater. For example, in the late nineties Patricia Greenway, the Vice President of the Totally Fun Company, an amusement park design firm, aired her reasons for the company quitting town: 'The downtown area has taken on the look and feel of a military base. The presence of thousands of uniformed Scientologists and their "security police" swarming the downtown area is oppressive.'

Shawn was different. He stayed, and took them on, single-handed, and that is, by itself, strange. He got himself a video camera and spent weeks filming Scientologists for a slot on the local cable TV network.

'*Cult Watch*' – Shawn's show – is cult cult viewing, beyond surreal. What you see is fuzzy, muddy video. The production values are, in contrast to those of the Church, dire. The shots are wobbly, the focus soggy, the sound quality poor. But the content is weirdly gripping. You watch him filming them filming him, close-ups of his feet, then their camera, a big lens, a finger or two of the Scientology camera person, no sound apart from the whirr and odd click from the two cameras staring at each other, recording, recording, recording. This goes on for minute after minute after minute and every second that passes the tension notches up. There is no doubting Shawn's dogged persistence, and the essential strangeness of what he was capturing. He got to film what we didn't see when we went out filming with Donna and Mike: a robotic procession of white-shirted, dark tied young men and women marching from one Scientology base in downtown Clearwater to another, getting on and off buses. You see dozens and dozens of them. If they are studying to become Operating Thetans, they appear to be a very strange species of students. Everyone conforms. It is like watching not a student body but a hive. Creepy with a capital C.

We tracked Shawn down to a rented apartment in a fly-blown part of town, decorated, if that is the right word, with a collection of green space alien dolls featuring their signature over-large, ovaloid eyeballs. He was a fit, lean, wiry man, slow speaking. He had a twinkle in his voice. We drove him downtown some blocks looking for a good place to film the interview and found a great spot on the top of a municipal car park. Behind us we had a view of the Fort Harrison hotel, one of their major complexes. That meant they had a view of us, but we didn't care.

When filming them, Shawn would stick up a cardboard sign on his white 1991 Oldsmobile: 'OT I-VIII for free at xenu.net.' That website tells the story of the space alien Satan for free. The Church might say that what Shawn did was blasphemous. Cynics might add that his sign could have cost the Church, if not millions, then several hundred thousand dollars, in lost fees, by short-circuiting the lengthy, step-by-step ascent to the state of grace where you can find out about the Emperor Ming The Merciless lookalike, Xenu. It should come as no surprise to realise that the Church did not like Shawn one little bit. Back in 2006, Ben Shaw, one of their spokesman, said: 'He is crazy, utterly crazy. He has no redeeming value to anyone anywhere.'

One simple rule of TV journalism: be scrupulously fair to people who make life difficult for you; and with the people who are happy to help you, knock them over the head with a cricket bat, or, probably better, the verbal equivalent thereof. So my opening question to Shawn did not beat about the bush.

'You are a social outcast, a menace, a fruitcake, a nutter. Why would Scientology make those kinds of suggestions about you?'

Pay attention to this question. It pops up later, a kind of a sonic boom boomerang.

'The only thing I can fathom,' replied Shawn, 'is that it is their only hope of trying to embarrass me into stopping doing what I am doing. They try to paint you as crazy, as some sort of social outcast, if you will, so that nobody will listen to you, nobody will take you seriously. It is a common trend to do that.'

Shawn explained his methodology: 'I wanted to get their take on us. And the only way to do that, since nobody would talk to me or nobody would respond to any of my requests for interviews, was to just go up and start filming them. Their events, where they were coming and going, halls or classes down town which is the only time the public sees them. And they took serious offence.'

How do they register that offence?

'It is almost like they have a mind break. If there is something that they can't handle effectively, something happens.'

Shawn explained that he had been filming on the street for three weeks solid when a member of the Church approached him. Shawn said he started yelling obscenities, yelling that he was Nazi, asking him why he didn't go to the Baptist church and call them all a bunch of 'n' words or the Jewish Temple and call them all a bunch of xxxx. He pushed Shawn, who shoved him back, and they ended up scuffling. That was the extreme, said Shawn. 'Usually, it is just pushing or trying to get to the camera to stop you from filming or cursing at you and verbally assaulting you.'

I asked him about the sign on his Oldsmobile.

'Xenu.net is one of the websites which reveals a lot of their upper level doctrine, OT I-VIII [Operating Thetan, level 1 – 8] for free, which is their higher levels, which costs the majority of the money that you will find they charge within Scientology. And all those are on the internet for free. And those were on my car downtown. The various levels [that is, OTs of Scientology] would walk around across the campus down here and see that on the car and I was hoping that they would wonder why they were paying so much money for it when it is free on the internet.'

They say these are confidential scriptures.

'If it is out, deal with it. We had to deal with the bible being out. Others had to deal with the Koran, the Torah, everything is out. I don't know why you would not want somebody to read a religious scripture of yours especially if it had anything good to say in it.'

What had Scientology done to Shawn?

'It is more or less what they haven't done. I was followed continuously for two months, followed by private investigators, followed by several vehicles which I was later able to track back to Scientology owned vehicles. I was yelled at down town numerous times, threatened with death. Cursed at by children in the presence of their parents. I would have never thought that I could stumble upon a scene that was so dramatically absent of peace and goodwill. But then again that seems to be the modus operandi when it comes to doing something that the Church doesn't like. They all band together and act that way towards you.'

What about work?

Shawn got a job in a real estate company but that did not last for long. 'My boss was called down to Fort Harrison' – the Church's main complex in Clearwater – 'by Pat Harney' – the PR lady who had blocked me that very morning from going into the Plant City Org – 'in an effort to try to get me to reveal my motives or stop what I was doing, piecing together footage for the television programme. And almost immediately after that our business went south. I was asked to leave, it was a financial impossibility for me to be there. After that I went to unemployment. There were several calls made saying that I was making money off the books when I wasn't. It was anonymous phone call after anonymous phone call, to every place where I turned in an application, there was always somebody calling with a threat.' He gave what he said was an example: '"I saw this gentleman in your business filling out an application, I know him to be a religious bigot. I will not shop there, my friends will not shop there if I find out that you have hired this individual..." I am a pervert or I am a criminal, something of that nature.'

Shawn said that when the anonymous caller was challenged, 'there was never an answer, there was always a hang-up. And I don't know too many business owners that want to deal with that type of thing. And when you haven't been hired yet it is very easy to pass your application to the garbage bin. So...'

Because you are trouble?

'Evidently.'

'What happened to accommodation...'

I stopped stone dead.

An SUV had suddenly shot up onto the top level of the car park. The door opened and a man got out, in a natty suit, dark glasses, white shirt, black and white striped tie, followed by a cameraman, and started walking towards us. The eerily bright Clearwater light half-blinded me. It was like a scene from the film, *The Matrix*, when the Agents in their corporate suits close in on Neo. Not quite believing the evidence of my own eyes, I squinted...

'...if I am right,' I said, 'that is Tommy Davis.' The figure, followed by the cameraman, approached us. He was carrying a manila envelope.

'Good afternoon,' said Tommy, for it was he. 'You must be Shawn.'

'Mr Davis, I presume,' said Shawn, 'nice to meet you.'

'Good to meet you. I just wanted to make sure that we are on record as far as this gentleman here' – Tommy was speaking to me, but nodded to Shawn – 'who you are with. I don't know how frankly he has been with you, just be pretty public about it.'

Tommy opened his file and began reading: 'In 1990 he was arrested for trespassing, exposure of sexual organs. Unnatural and lascivious act, possession of cannabis, possession of drug paraphernalia. The police report this is from, the undercover officer who he solicited stated: "The defendant exposed his penis to undercover officer, began to masturbate in view of the public. This occurred in a posted no trespassing area. Search of the defendant's vehicle revealed a marijuana pipe and marijuana". And then on 7th June 2000 he was also arrested for lewd and lascivious behaviour. He was caught by a Pinellas County sheriff performing sex on another male in a public area.'

Throughout my battles with Tommy he spoke like an American lawyer addressing a grand jury, or, to be less kind, like Hollywood's idea of a lawyer addressing a grand jury. This was Tommy's moment in pseudo-court, the moment he nailed a credulous BBC reporter being taken in by a sexual monster. Game, set and match to the Church of Scientology? Not quite.

'Now would Scientology,' asked Shawn, 'be able to help

me with any of these problems that I supposedly have?' There was something rather cool about Shawn's sardonic tone with Tommy.

'Now what he does,' Tommy continued, as if Shawn had not spoken, almost as if he was of no significance, 'he does speak about this openly and of course...'

'By the way he is not an animal,' I said. Enough already. 'Answer that question, can't you?'

'I just want to make sure that we document this and I would be happy to speak to him,' said Tommy, matter-of-factly.

'Hold on a second... actually Tommy.... No...' I stumbled to get my words out. I am an old-fashioned reporter and I've seen a lot of stuff in my time, but even so I was knocked off kilter by Tommy crashing our interview. I couldn't quite believe it was happening.

'I am making no comment...' said Tommy.

'Wait a second Tommy, I am interviewing the man.' I turned to Shawn. I had read the article about him in the St Petersburg Times – the local paper that covers Clearwater – in which it mentioned Scientology's demonizing him over his sexual past, that he had been caught by police officers having consensual sex with adult males in a public place several years ago. 'Let me ask that question, excuse me is that true?'

'Actually some of it wasn't,' said Shawn, 'I can go back over it.'

'I have the police reports here...' offered Tommy, helpfully. Or, perhaps, mock-helpfully.

'What page are you reading from?'

At that moment our tape ran out. I was momentarily a bit

71

cross with Bill, for being so unprofessional, blah blah, then I remembered that we had been running for hours, and that the tapes of even the very best BBC cameramen in the whole world occasionally run out.

When the fresh tape was in the camera, Shawn was questioning Scientology's file on him. They'd doctored the file, it seemed. 'Marijuana pipe and marijuana?' Shawn was querying Tommy's 'police report'.

'But I don't see that on a charge sheet any more. That is not a charge.'

'But this is the police report...' replied Tommy, defensively.

'So you have created a summary from a police report of your own,' said Shawn. 'You haven't used the summary that...'

'This is a report the Tampa police department...' Tommy started.

Shawn interrupted: '...You've compiled this first charge sheet and a sheet from the county. Let's say...'

'Yes, from the...'

'So you have taken it upon yourself...'

'See this, this is a Tampa police report.'

'So you have taken it upon yourself to...'

'Yeah to summarise within the police report,' said Tommy.

'Why wouldn't you use the police report summary?' asked Shawn.

'Last time I checked a marijuana pipe was there...'

'Why wouldn't you use the police report summary?'

'OK fine, whatever,' said Tommy, conceding the point of fact to Shawn. I smiled, inwardly.

Is it possible, I asked, that the reason why the Church raises this stuff is because he is a critic?

'We want to make sure that it is on record that you know who it is that you are speaking about,' said Tommy.

Yes I know, I was aware of that, I said.

'He has never been a Scientologist. He has never done services,' said Tommy.

He is a critic, I said.

'He admitted in the St Petersburg Times that he conducted sexual acts on other people when he was low on money,' said Tommy.

'So I admitted that on national news,' said Shawn, 'and in one of our local papers.'

'But I am asking are you aware of that?' asked Tommy.

I said I was. 'But Tommy,' I pointed out, 'just because you have come here and tracked us down again does not give you the right to dictate the conversation... You have invaded our interview.'

'Actually,' said Tommy with logic as round as a billiard ball, 'you turned the cameras on me and started attacking me. I actually didn't say anything.'

This was madness. You can't physically invade a television interview, read out a factually incorrect version of someone's criminal record for minor sex crimes from years ago and then proclaim with wounded innocence: 'I actually didn't say anything.'

Tommy and Shawn battled on while I wrestled with the surreal nature of what was happening. Eventually, I think I sorted it out inside my head and then the words came tumbling out. I have never in my life come across such a distortion of meaning, such a twisting of the English language.

'Tommy, hold on a second. I can talk to whoever I so choose to in a free society.

That is why you invade, that's why the creepy car comes. As far as the Church of Scientology is concerned, I can talk to anybody about you so long as they are not critical of Scientology. But the moment they are, then it seems as though it is very important for you to tell me that they are either an extortionist [Donna] or a sexual pervert [Shawn].'

'No,' said Tommy, 'it is very important that you have the truth. And it is actually in the BBC broadcast guidelines, the codes of conduct, OfCom, in terms of first hand reports, in terms of balanced reporting, it is covered in your own guidelines. And there is actually something...'

'I read them every night before I go to bed,' I said.

Tommy repeated the gist of what he had just said. I asked him for a copy of their file on Shawn. He would not give it to me. Now it felt like my turn to make things a little more surreal.

Where are we going tomorrow? I asked.

'I don't know where are you going tomorrow.'

Well, you will find us I am sure, I said.

'Yeah, we probably will.' He made his point again that the BBC's guidelines required fairness.

'Last time I read the BBC guidelines there was nothing in it that said that every single interviewee had to be vetted by the Church of Scientology before we could speak to them.'

'I actually don't believe that I ever used the word vetted or what I describe as vetted,' said Tommy. 'I said you tell me who it is and I will send you the information on the person, and what you do with it is your decision. '

'No, no, no,' I said. 'Within hours of any time we talk to a critic of Scientology you, within hours, come up and say that is an extortionist, that is a sexual pervert. It is as if you are terrified of anyone criticising your organisation. It is as if you have something that you have got to hide.'

As in Plant City that very morning, Tommy closed in on me, inches from my face. 'I am not terrified of anything. And you know what I have absolutely nothing to hide whatsoever. Zero. You can dig and dig and dig.'

'OK, well, give us some access. Come, let's have some access. Let's go to these places.'

'To a hostile reporter who has no intention of giving a balanced report? You give more weight and importance and now more hours of time to people critical of the Church than you did anyone else.'

'I spent ten hours with you,' I told Tommy. 'I have spent barely a quarter of an hour with Shawn before you pop up from nowhere. But we want access, we want to film with you, but you stipulated: "no mention of the word cult." Shawn, do you think the Church of Scientology is a cult?'

'It is absolutely a cult,' said Shawn. Tommy was off, walking back to his SUV. 'It has all the definitions of a cult. The fact that one of their own spokespersons can't face that question is why they are called a cult.'

Tommy had gone but the silent Scientology cameraman had stayed behind, to film everything Shawn and I said. It was irritating but the United States of America is a free country.

Scientologists staged a poster campaign in Clearwater, denouncing Shawn: 'They put up a lot of posters saying that

I was a pervert, convicted of lewd and lascivious conduct and I needed to be watched. It was just trying to keep me out of downtown. Just trying to embarrass me enough not to show my face down there. But the funny thing about it is they put it on the windows of all the shops that they are associated with behind the scenes, which shows on a grand scale exactly how big their force is in our downtown core. And of course every public Scientologist when asked to do something by the Church doesn't say no. So you can tell who owns what down town.'

My final question to Shawn was pretty similar to my first. 'Why did you pick on them? Aren't you a little bit crazy to do this?'

'It was the 500 pound gorilla in the room. Here in Clearwater everybody talks about it in their living rooms and jokes about it in the bars and in the little cafes, but nobody really knows, has an idea what it is really about. It has to be shown. How deep are the fingers of Scientology in this community? We can't come down town and just get a Starbuck's coffee if we want to drink, read the paper on a Sunday, especially if you are somebody like me, you are an enemy. You are everything bad. When they pull up here, when they assault me on the street corner, when their children in the presence of their parents hiss and spit at me. That's them telling their story about their own religion. You can't get any better than that.'

We said our goodbyes and headed for California. I had found him good company, and a sane and self-deprecating witness.

That was the last time I ever saw Shawn Lonsdale. His body was found by police in February, 2008. Shawn had his own demons, no doubt, but it seems difficult to see how the Church of Scientology can square its claim to be granted the respect due a religion with wallpapering Clearwater with posters dragging up a lone critic's past sexual indignities. Or, indeed, Tommy Davis demonizing him to the BBC by reading out his criminal record on camera.

Did the Church drive Shawn to suicide? I do not know. Did the Church act kindly towards a critic? It did not.

I broadcast a short obituary of Shawn on BBC Radio Four's *From Our Own Correspondent*: 'Clearwater got that little bit more creepy recently, with the death – the police are treating it as suicide – of Shawn. When alive a Scientology spokesman said of him: "He has no redeeming value to anyone, anywhere." Well, he was a bit of a hero to me. I, for one, mourn the loss of a brave and singular American.'

CHAPTER FIVE
'Your needle's floating, Tom'

B ack in the day, the story goes, four science fiction writers - Isaac Asimov, Robert Heinlein, Frank Herbert and L Ron Hubbard - were hanging out late at night in 1940 in LA, drinking and putting the world to rights. They made a bet, who could dream up the best religion? Asimov explained in a TV interview in the 1980s that it was more of a dare than a true bet, and the goal was not a religion proper but 'who can make the best religious story.' The results were *'Nightfall'* by Asimov, *'Dune'* by Herbert, *'Job'* by Heinlein and *'Dianetics'* by Hubbard. If the first version of the story is true, Hubbard won the bet.

They say L Ron also said: 'Writing for a penny a word is ridiculous. If a man really wants to make a million dollars, the best way would be to start his own religion.'

Asimov is long dead but his niece, Nanette, is alive and well and lives in San Francisco where she works as a reporter on the city's Chronicle newspaper. In 2004 she investigated the claims by Narconon – the anti-addiction programme promoted by the Church of Scientology – that it is an astonishingly successful drug therapy.

Narconon's enthusiasts assert that drug addicts can be cured by long spells in the sauna and lots of Vitamin B or Niacin. Mr Hubbard had worked out that addicts could sweat out drugs like heroin from their fat. Tommy Davis told me that Narconon enjoyed an 80% success rate and Charles Hendry MP praised its success in the House of Commons in 2005: 'I have seen for myself their project to take people away from drug addiction... Many of us have seen the good work that they do in those areas.'

Nanette Asimov's investigation suggested this was mumbo-jumbo. She reported one year prior to the British MP's endorsement and her series of stories was and is widely available on the internet for anyone to read. Nanette reported that addiction experts found Narconon 'pseudoscience' unsupported by scientific evidence; its drug education based on nonsense that drugs stay indefinitely in fat; its claim that drug residues produce a coloured ooze when exiting the body also nonsense; that sweating in a sauna helps you beat addiction, also nonsense.

On the trail of finding out more about Narconon, we flew from Florida to somewhere in the middle to somewhere on the West Coast. It took the rest of the day and much of the night. To someone who comes from a country where the sea is never further than 70 miles away, the United States of America is rather big. We had no sense that anyone was following us.

We woke in Oakland, on the other side of the bay from San Francisco. In Frisco, we popped along to the Scientology Org where I was not welcome. Later, we met Steve Heilig, a public health expert at the San Francisco Medical Society, who was asked by the San Francisco school board to review the Narconon drug education programme after Nanette's reporting. He worked with four physicians and another public health authority, so that his conclusion was based on the work of a spread of experts.

And his finding on Narconon? Heilig described it as 'outdated, non-evidence-based and sometimes factually inaccurate.'

Scientology's Narconon programme appears to be predicated on the belief that all drugs are fat-soluble, stay in the body long-term but can be flushed out by sweating. Science says that's rubbish. Drugs like heroin are flushed out of the body in a few days, cannabis in a month or so. Long term, they're not fat-soluble.

Heilig told me: 'The approach favoured by Narconon was not supported by science. So given that falsehood, to use a blunt term, we recommended they be removed from San Francisco's schools.'

I asked what struck him as being unusual about Narconon?

'The idea that if you could approach it properly, sweat this out, that you would have different colours of ooze coming out of your skin which represented the drugs. That struck our experts as quote unquote "science fiction"'.

Not science fact?

'Not science fact.'

The main purpose of our trip to San Francisco was to meet Bruce Hines, an ex-Scientologist who had 'audited' – that means heard the confessions of – stars such as Nicole Kidman, Kirstie Alley, Anne Archer, Tommy Davis's mother and, briefly, Tom Cruise. It is a confession. At the end, the confessor proclaims: 'By the power invested in me by the

Church of Scientology, anything you have truthfully divulged is hereby forgiven by Scientologists.'

Bruce was once a true believer, a devoted acolyte of the religion and so trusted by the high command that he heard the confessions of its most precious parishioners. He had joined Scientology in 1972 when he was a 22-year-old physics student, and left in 2003, after three decades. From 1979 to 2003 he had been in the Sea Org.

Now that he is out, he is back studying physics, in particular cryogenic dark matter search or CDMS. Bruce explained to me by email what this means: 'About 80% of the matter in the universe is made of something unknown. It can't be detected by usual means, because it does not emit nor reflect light or any electromagnetic radiation. So it is called dark matter. It is different than what composes stars, planets, atoms, people, etc. This is not to be confused with "dark energy", which is something else. It is definite that this dark matter exists, but to date no one knows for sure what it is made of. There are a few theories. I work as part of a collaboration that is testing one of these theories, the favored theory at the moment. I am with the University of Colorado, Denver. Some of the other institutions in the collaboration are MIT, Cal Tech, U of California Berkeley, Fermilab, NIST, Stanford, SLAC, U of Minnesota, U of Florida, Texas A&M, U of California Santa Barbara, U of British Columbia in Canada, Queen's U in Canada, a university in Madrid, the Universidad Autonoma de Madrid, and a few others. It is very competitive. There are some other international collaborations composed of major institutions racing to make the same discovery, i.e. exactly what it this dark matter made of. It is currently one of the most major unanswered questions in the world of physics. Most agree that it could lead to Nobel Prizes, not that I could possibly be awarded one.'

As I said at the start, none of the people who had been Scientologists were dumb. Bruce was a big man, still handsome, plainly massively intelligent but gentle and thoughtful, understated and modest.

We drove around San Francisco for a bit, admiring the pointy building which looks like a bishop's hat, and bumping into a George W. Bush cavalcade. We found a great background shot of San Francisco which framed the whole interview. The weather was ceaselessly sunny. It was weird listening to a man's story of being held in a prison of the mind against the back-drop of one of the most free-thinking, freewheeling cities on the planet.

Is it a cult?

'It is a cult. I would have violently disagreed with that, even five years ago.'

Bruce referred to the 1961 book by the American psychiatrist, Robert Lifton: *Thought Reform and the Psychology of Totalism: A Study of "Brainwashing" in China*, which I wrote about briefly in Chapter One. I've only got my head round Lifton's work while writing this book. Now I sleep with it under my pillow.

Lifton was one of the very first people to think hard about brainwashing, and his understanding grew over time. Later on, Lifton set out three simple definers for a cult in his foreword to Margaret Singer's book, *Cults In Our Midst*: that it has a charismatic leader who becomes a god; that it brainwashes; that it causes harm.

82

On Lifton's first definer, I think a reasonable person would say that if a 'religious' body allowed its Leader to abuse or even hit members of the Holy Order, repeatedly, with impunity, that would be close to treating them as a god.

'Most people, even Sea Organisation members and public Scientologists, have no idea what David Miscavige is like behind closed doors,' said Bruce. 'They have only seen him in these public gatherings, and there he's quite personable.'

The real Miscavige is rather different than the fluent man in the tuxedo, said Bruce, accusing him of being a 'very angry individual, he's violent'.

Bruce explained that in 1995 he had audited the wife of a senior Scientologist, and Miscavige was not happy with the results. The woman was in LA, but the husband was posted 90 miles away at the International Headquarters of the Church, often known as Int or Gold Base, 500 acres tucked away in the middle of nowhere on the edge of the Californian desert near a one-horse town called Hemet. Back in the day, in the late seventies, when Mr Hubbard was on the run from the FBI, Gold was top secret and for decades the Church sought to hide its existence from 'public' Scientologists. Today you can find it on Google Earth, snuggling the brown foothills of the San Jacinto mountains at Gilman Hot Springs, California. More than Clearwater or its complex in downtown LA, Gold is the headquarters of the Church, where David Miscavige is based. Bruce's task was to convince the unhappy wife through auditing that her objections to this 90-mile separation were misplaced. Unsurprisingly, he failed.

'I was in my office at Gold and I just heard out in the hallway, just outside my office, I heard him shouting, "where is that motherfucker?" and I go "uh-oh". He barged into my office, and he's always followed around by four, five, six people and they follow him in. And then he said, "there he is!" but he's talking more loudly than I am and with much more anger. He walked up and he swung and he hit me on the side of the head.'

To say the head of a religion, or, to be more exact, an organisation that claims to be a religion, goes round hitting people is a heavy accusation. Critically, the sources have to be credible and there has to more than one and this isn't the first time that someone has alleged that David Miscavige is violent. Back in 1987, Panorama reporter John Penycate interviewed Donald Larson, an ex-Scientologist who was described as being in the former 'financial police' of the Church. Larson told Panorama: 'It was my job to scare people.' What methods did you use? 'Extortion, force, threats, duress.' Larson described how, once Miscavige had taken over as leader of the Church, 15 Scientologists drove in three hired limos to the San Francisco Org to confront the head of the organization there. 'This is nothing to do with religion any more,' said Larson, 'this is "where's the money, Jack? I want the money. Where did you put the money?" The guy goes "I don't have the money. I don't know". So David Miscavige comes up, grabs him by the tie and starts bashing him on the filing cabinets. Then his tie is ripped off and he's thrown out onto the street.'

Ex-Scientologist Tom DeVocht used to be Miscavige's drinking buddy. The two men used to chew the fat over a bottle of Macallan's 12-year-old malt in the Chairman's den at Gold from around 2000 to 2005 when Tom got out. Tom is a builder by trade, a thoughtful and decent man, good company, and, I felt, a man who would be a good friend. He was so close to Dave that he became a car-shopper for him, picking out an Acura TL, a fancy Japanese model. Women readers may not quite get this, but for a man to franchise out the buying of a car to another man is no small thing.

Miscavige hit him twice, Tom told me in 2010.

'The first one, I was down at Gold, working on the renovations of compact disc manufacture and plant, and the next thing I knew all the international management, what they call "The Hall", had come running down from a good quarter of a mile away. Dave had come in and he'd called me and I was standing in front of everybody and I really can't recall exactly what he asked me. But I remember hesitating and thinking, what did he mean by that? The next thing I know, with an open hand, I got slapped, popped my ear pretty good. And pushed down to the ground and I think he might have hit me one more time in the chest.'

You are bigger than him?

'I would say most are, but yes I am bigger than him.'

If somebody hit me...

'...I was tempted to hit him back. This is where the cult aspect of it comes in. Here I have got the pope hitting me and I am thinking I have got 50-80 people behind him that I knew if I did anything to him, they would jump on me. I was outnumbered for sure. But that aside, you really do get into a mental state of...' Tom struggled to find the right words, '... you have got to understand for years these people up there have been hit. I've seen Dave hit people, 75 to a 100 times. No joke.'

'Second time,' – also at Gold – 'I was in the big castle, the studio. He was walking down the hall and I was there doing something, I forget. He walked by me and he just pushed me and banged my head into the concrete wall and he just kept walking.'

These are allegations that the Church of Scientology denies, I said.

'Yeah,' said Tom. And then he laughed.

These *are* allegations that the Church of Scientology denies.

Close up, Tom observed the slow accretion of power to Miscavige, how he switched from being on equal terms with other executives in the Church, when he addressed them by the first names and they called him Dave, to him insisting on them calling him 'Sir'. In the end, Tom said, Miscavige became, 'quite a monster, hitting people.'

Miscavige's abuse of his Holy Order's most senior figures was, at times, like a sadistic cocktail of the Theatre of the Absurd and the Theatre of Cruelty, according to Tom's description of it. Tom referred to a notorious game of 'Musical Chairs', the Scientology version, staged by Miscavige at Gold. Queen's Bohemian Rhapsody blared out. Too many believers, not enough chairs. The twist is: if you lose your chair, you face eternal damnation. So you have to win that chair. Musical chairs as directed by the thumping pope. Tom said: 'Everybody played the musical chairs game but with this mental anguish. And people were breaking down. It was unbelievable, a very eerie, strange thing.'

Like Bruce, Tom found the real Chairman to be unlike his official persona: 'Up front Miscavige is a very nice guy when you first meet him. You think, "Wow!" This is a genuinely nice guy, he cares about me, he cares about other people, this is what you would expect from the head of the Church of Scientology. The closer I got with him, I found out he is actually quite the opposite. That is all a facade. He is an evil person.'

Evil is a heavy word, I said.

'It is, and I am not using it lightly.'

The Church and David Miscavige deny allegations of abuse and violence in the strongest possible terms.

The Church's official organ, Freedom Magazine, is not uncritical of Tom. It says that he is 'a genuine pathological liar'; an incompetent who 'enlisted a convicted felon to broker a Church property acquisition', whose construction work for the Church led to 'cost overruns, blown budgets and inordinate project delays'; it alleges that he stole several hundred dollars from the purse of his wife's grandmother on their wedding day. It says that his ex-wife never saw any bruises on him: 'DeVocht's former wife, Jenny Linson: "I slept with Tom DeVocht for almost 20 years. I knew every inch of him. I never saw one scratch. I never saw one bruise. I never saw one black eye, nothing."'

We come across Jenny Linson later in our narrative.

Freedom Magazine goes on to quote Tom denying that he had ever claimed that he had been bruised. The magazine adds: 'DeVocht was so slow on the uptake he missed the logic train, i.e., that he *claimed* to have bruises or scars was not the point of his wife's refutation; it was that someone who was actually beaten would have obviously *exhibited* bruises and scars. Or to phrase it in terms of his own skewed thinking: it doesn't matter whether physical evidence "sort of" exists to prove what he's saying because he never claimed there was physical evidence in the first place. But, of course, if there is no physical evidence, doesn't that mean his allegations are "sort of" false, which in turn means DeVocht is "sort of" lying?'

Note the idiosyncratic, even peculiar, style of that rebuttal: pure denigration.

Claire Headley was born into the Church and signed the billion-year contract to join the Sea Org when she was still a teenager. She rose to work at the very top of the organisation at Gold base. Her recollection of Miscavige is not wholly favourable. Once, he ordered her, 'go and berate those people and say: "Suck my big fat cock."'

She is a beautiful woman, of poise and quality, the mother of two adored children, born in England, with a trace of her English accent still. Claire does not have a cock.

Did you do that?

'I did.'

Forgive me, I said, but that sounds crazy.

'It is.'

Her husband Marc joined in. Marc is a thick-set chap, a tekkie, self-assured, funny with a fast wit. You would not want to get on the wrong side of him, but he struck me as being a good man.

Marc tried to give me a flavour of how Scientology's pope thinks of himself: Miscavige 'went to some big celebrity dinner with Tom Cruise and John Travolta and a bunch of people and Bill Clinton was there and they shook hands or they talked or whatever, and when he got back to Gold someone said: "I heard you met President Bill Clinton", and he said: "No, Bill Clinton met me."'

Had Miscavige ever abused people in their presence?

Marc said: 'I've seen him beat many people up.' Claire said she had too. Marc had been beaten up by him once, too: 'I was in a production facility and I had made an offhand comment and he was already upset and he grabbed me and started punching me and I fell up against a wall unit like a shelf, desk type of thing and my glasses were broken. I was going to strike him back and I was escorted out of the building immediately.'

Marc has written a book on his time in the Church, *Blown For Good,* which is a shocking read. The book describes Miscavige's mass humiliation of the Sea Org staff: his version of Musical Chairs with people ripping chairs away from rivals and, on another occasion, when around a hundred of the Holy Order of the Church were made to clean out the sewage ponds at Gold by hand. Marc writes: 'As you picked up the waste, it would crumble in your hands and make dust. Multiply that times a hundred people, walking, handling and moving all that waste and that made a pretty big cloud... A giant cloud of dust made up of excrement was what I was breathing in.' The ordeal lasted two days. Eventually, Marc was allowed a shower. 'That night when I got to wash up, I took a two-hour shower to try and get the stench off me. It did not work. I think it took a week for all of the crap to work its way out of my pores, nose, throat, and ears. Even my eyes would tear crap mud. It was the most disgusting, humiliating experience of my entire life.'

One wonders at the mental state of anyone who allows himself to scrub clean a sewage pond thick with excrement crumble by hand in the service of what some say is a religion. If Marc is right, one hundred people did that.

The Church and David Miscavige deny the allegations of abuse and violence and describe the Headleys as members of a 'Posse of Lunatics'. The Church's Freedom magazine says that Marc is 'a fervid anti-Scientologist who never misses an opportunity to publicly denigrate the religion and its Founder.' It says he was about to be caught red-handed after teaming up with a criminal in a crooked concern, so he fled. It says he was then excommunicated. His wife Claire soon followed suit, making her unannounced exit shortly thereafter. Later, it says, Marc became a member of a cyber-terrorist group.

I thought the Headleys were a lovely couple with two great kids.

Steve Hall, Scientology's top scriptwriter until he left, described the following scene: 'I was called up to "Building 50". Everyone was made to sit in special chairs and told where to sit. It was about 15 or 20 people. Finally Miscavige came in and started walking up and down the aisles. Each chair was spaced out so he had plenty of room. No one knew what it was about, as per usual, but Miscavige was fuming, also as per usual. He glared at each person intently, then stopped in front of me. He shouted to the room that I was "out-ethics" but didn't say why. This was also usual. But this time he made a special point of it. After staring at me he finally moved on, went down three more people then suddenly attacked Marc Yager [a senior figure in the Church] without warning, striking him repeatedly on both sides of the head. Yager tried to deflect some of the blows but was not very successful because Miscavige was standing over him while Yager was sitting. Yager fell out of his chair and was visibly shaken.

'It was a bit like the scene from *The Untouchables* where

Al Capone walked around with a baseball bat. But without the bat.

'Later when Miscavige finally started talking, what he spoke about had nothing to do with Yager or me. I realized then that Miscavige, by suddenly starting to include me in his beatings, was actually grooving me in or grooming me up for the same treatment. It was obvious that I was the actual person he wanted to hit since he made the announcement, then hit someone else.

'A few weeks later, I think it was November, 2003, Mike Rinder and I were working on another script. Miscavige ordered something to be fixed. Although my IQ is over 150, I never could understand the guy or what he wanted because he had the knack of both telling you to do and not do something in the same meeting. Plus he would also say to do other things, making comprehending what he wanted nearly impossible.'

Remember, poor Naz, Tom Cruise's date who says she got dumped because she could not understand Miscavige's speed-talk? She was, it seems, not alone.

'So Miscavige ordered Mike Rinder to help me. Mike had known Miscavige longer and was able to decipher his gobbledy-gook orders a bit better perhaps. As per usual his orders were indecipherable. However, Mike thought he knew what to do. We made a minor fix of honestly just a few words. Miscavige came down to review the edit. For some peculiar reason, Miscavige ordered Mike and I to stand shoulder to shoulder while Miscavige stood just in front of us. Miscavige actually pressed us together so our shoulders were touching. Miscavige barked out orders to start the video then said "STOP!" He wheeled around and glared at me. As per usual I hadn't the foggiest idea what he was angry about. No one else knew either. His eyes held on me, then shifted to Mike for ten seconds. These stare-down sessions were part of how Miscavige rolls. He just stares at you and says nothing. Meanwhile, your mind is racing. Then he went back to staring at me. No-one in the room was even breathing. He looked back at Mike and suddenly launched at him. He was only about 12 inches away so he was at him lightning quick.

'Miscavige grabbed Mike's head with both hands and shoved him backwards so Mike lost his balance. Miscavige put his whole body into it, shoving from the legs up, and bashed Mike's head into the wall three times, solid cherry cabinets built into the wall. Miscavige's arms and whole body were shaking with the force and rage, as if he was trying to crush Mike's head, and Mike's head hit the wall HARD three times. Mike did not retaliate.

'After that, Miscavige left. Yager asked Mike, "What was that for?" and Mike who still seemed somewhat dazed said, "I guess he didn't like the edit."'

The Church, David Miscavige and Marc Yager deny the violence allegations against David Miscavige.

The Church's Freedom magazine suggests that Steve Hall was a fantasist, by claiming that in past lives he was variously Jesus, Buddha and the co-creator of the Universe. The Church mocks Steve's claim to be a 'scriptwriter' for the ecclesiastic leader of the religion, Mr Miscavige, saying the claim is 'patently false': 'By that definition, a person peeling potatoes in the army is "The President's Potato Peeler."'

I am looking forward to meeting Steve Hall and sharing a potato with him.

Amy Scobee was in for 27 years and rose to head the Celebrity Centre in LA, where she got to know Cruise, Travolta, Kirstie Alley, Anne Archer – Tommy's mum – Nancy Cartwright, Priscilla and Lisa Marie Presley, Juliette Lewis, Isaac Hayes and others. She is a lovely, bubbly woman, one of those people who wake up every morning as if they had already enjoyed a glass of champagne – not literally, of course. But Amy is fun to hang out with. She got out in 2005 and five years later told me that she had witnessed Miscavige beat people up seven, maybe eight times. On one occasion, she saw her pope attack a victim: 'He'd jumped across the table, grabbed him around the neck, knocked him unto the floor, jumped on top of him, grabbed the epaulette, pulled it off, grabbed the tag, pulled it off. Buttons flying, change falling out.'

Amy's book, *Abuse at The Top*, is a compelling read, setting out her evidence of grotesque physical, mental, sexual abuse of innocence. Her first contact with Scientology was at the age of 14. Once she turned 16, she signed the billion-year-contract, becoming a member of the Sea Org. Within months she was on the RPF, the Rehabilitation Project Force, which is a more extreme version of the Scientology boot camp in which Donna said she witnessed Tommy Davis having his hair pulled, an allegation Tommy and the Church deny.

Amy's crime? Having consensual sex with a man she was in love with and who she planned to marry. What kind of religion is it that places a sixteen-year-old on a punishment regime for slap and tickle? Amy spent two years on the RPF. Her account reads like torture. Inside the RPF, degradation was never far away. If you transgressed you were punished by being placed on 'rocks and shoals': made to run up 'laps' up and down stairs. A big 'lap' was running up and down 11 flights of stairs to the top of the Foot Harrison Hotel and back.

The cruellest feature of her experience on the RPF for her and her fellow 'convicts' was lack of sleep, making accidents, she says, grimly frequent. Her RPF unit was working full-time building a house for LRH at Gold, lest he ever return. In truth, Mr Hubbard was living – or rather dying – in hiding a few dozen miles away in an out-of-the-way ranch.

'Fatigue was constant,' wrote Amy. 'I recall in the middle of the night pushing a wheelbarrow up the hill and the next thing I knew I woke up in a ditch.' In her book, she writes that a fellow RPF-er cut his finger off on the table-saw; another cut open his leg with an angle grinder because he fell asleep while using it; a woman fell 20 feet off a scaffold and shattered her pelvis.

After all their efforts, the LRH was subsequently entirely demolished and rebuilt.

On Christmas Day, 1984, Amy's RPF was ordered to 'white-glove' clean the base galley for the crew. It being Christmas, the RPF were allowed to listen to the radio, a perk usually forbidden.

When LRH died in January 1986, the whole Sea Org was placed in a condition of mass mourning. Amy had no proper time to grieve her uncle, the NASA astronaut, Dick Scobee, one of seven killed in the Challenger space shuttle disaster, killed two days after the announcement of LRH's death. For a true Scientologist, the passing away of a man she had never met trumped the death of her uncle, the Commander of the space shuttle.

As she ascended in the ranks of the Church, Amy came

to know Miscavige well but not to admire him. One day Miscavige brought in a new executive, dressed in a black sweater with four gold Captain stripes on her epaulettes. The executive made a whimper when she saw Amy. Miscavige told her that the executive could sniff out crimes so she must have something 'pretty slimy' going on. The executive, she alleges, was Miscavige's dog, Jelly.

Violent beatings, sexual humiliation and psychotic behaviour were par for the course, she writes.

As Miscavige consolidated his grip on power, life at Gold became grim, grimmer than before. The little sweeteners of life – listening to the radio, having plants or pictures of your family in the office – came to be forbidden, she writes. Family time, an hour a day for parents to spend with their kids, was cancelled; pregnancies in the Sea Org were forbidden, meaning that anyone without children in Sea Org had to accept childlessness or the damnation that came with exit. Amy got out when she was 42, childless.

Amy reflects on her mindset, on why she allowed herself to be abused in this dreadful way: 'Unbelievably, I never blamed anyone for being put through these things. We were so indoctrinated or brainwashed into believing that we're not our bodies, the mission is more important than self and that anything personal could easily be sacrificed for the cause.'

After she left Amy read *Combating Cult Mind Control* by ex-Moonie Steven Hassan. One particular passage impressed Amy: 'Members are made to feel part of an elite corps of mankind. This feeling of being special, or participating in the most important acts of human history with a vanguard of committed believers, is strong emotional glue to keep people sacrificing and working hard.'

Amy reflects on her 27 years of what you could call '*mind-glue*': 'that makes a lot of sense to me as to why I could have possibly tolerated a fraction of what I did and still stick with the organisation.'

The Church and Miscavige deny Amy's allegations of abuse and violence. On Amy, the Church suggests that she is sexually voracious and grossly incompetent. Freedom Magazine says: 'Today, Scobee spends her days posting salacious drivel to cyber-terrorists on the lunatic fringe of the Internet. Although she has thus far escaped hate-crime scrutiny, she remains among the nastiest snipers and her snippets are filled with sexual tittle-tattle. So, yes, while Scobee may have never been a "celebrity queen," she at least now qualifies as a gossip maven...'

A simple test of a civilised human being is how they describe those who have treated them badly. An ancient but lovely Berliner called Wolfgang Von Leyden taught me philosophy when I was a student at LSE. He was brilliant, kind and good. He had had to run from Germany in the thirties. He described the Nazis as 'churlish and ill-bred'.

I thought Amy was smashing.

This list of ex-Scientologists who agree with Bruce Hines that Miscavige is angry and violent is not exhaustive. But I cannot include them all. My last witness on the issue of whether Scientology's pope abuses his adepts gave her testimony in open court in Texas in February 2012. Former Scientologist Debbie Cook told a court in San Antonio that she witnessed 'terror and tyranny' during the 17 years as head of the church in Florida.

Cook told the court: 'I witnessed Mr. Miscavige physically punching the face and wrestling to the ground another executive at Scientology International' – Gold. A colleague called Ginge Nelson, she said, objected to the violence and he was later made to lick the bathroom floor clean for half an hour. 'One time I was called into a conference room and asked some questions and he ordered his secretary to slap me. And she slapped me so hard I fell over into the chairs. One time Mr Miscavige ordered his Communicator to break my finger if I didn't answer his question. It was bent back very hard. It was not broken.'

Her lawyer asked: 'Getting ordered to have someone slap you down or throw water in your face or break your finger, what were the horrible crimes that you would commit that would cause these punishments to be inflicted?'

Debbie replied: 'Just not answer a question fast enough or maybe your expression displeased him. Maybe you were smiling or you shouldn't have been smiling.'

'Did you ever witness any incidents of violence or torture or degradation in England?'

'Yes, I did,' said Debbie. 'I was at a meeting with Mr Miscavige and with several top international executives. And then he ordered a man named Bob Keenan' – Fireman Bob – 'to take those other executives and throw them into the lake. At the time it was October and it was very cold in England... They were made to go into the cold lake.'

Was Debbie physically abused by Miscavige, her lawyer asked?

Once, she said, he 'grabbed my shoulders and shook me while he was yelling at me.'

Her lawyer asked her how she ended up in The Hole, a bizarre dungeon of the mind she described at Gold.

'In May 2007,' – the month our Panorama aired – 'I was at the International Base [Gold]. Mr Miscavige was not there, but I was supposed to be doing numerous things under his directions... I was on the phone to him every day, sometimes several times a day, and there were certain things that he was very unhappy... about, that weren't done to his satisfaction... I was on the phone to him. I was in an office. Someone was pounding on the door. Because I was on the phone to him, I didn't answer. I was trying to be on the phone and talk to him... The beating stopped and then someone pried the window open of the office that I was in and two big guys came in through the window. And Mr Miscavige said to me on the phone, "Are they there?" And I said, "Yes, they are." And he said, "Goodbye." And two men physically took me away to The Hole.'

The Hole, her evidence suggested, was a weird torture centre made out of two trailers on GOLD. Debbie told the court she was kept locked up in the trailers 'infested with ants' with other Scientologists for seven weeks as temperatures soared to 106 fahrenheit. Cook said: 'I was put in a trash can, cold water poured over me, slapped, things like that.'

The Church vehemently denied her claims, calling them 'outrageously false'.

It branded Cook a 'heretic' and withdrew its case to stop her using the court 'as a forum'.

David Miscavige and the Church of Scientology flatly deny all allegations of abuse and violence.

The allegations of abuse and violence by the Leader of the Church, conducted in full view of senior members of the Church hierarchy with impunity, suggest evidence that the Leader is treated as a god. If so, the Church passes the first definer for a cult according to Robert Lifton, the world's number one expert on mind control.

It is strange to think that Miscavige was Tom Cruise's best man. The chasm between what Cruise and the Church say about the Chairman of the Board and what the ex-Scientologists say is deep.

Lifton's next definer for a cult is brainwashing.

Back in 1961, Lifton in his book on brainwashing set out eight tests: 'where totalism exists, a religion, a political movement, or even a scientific organization becomes little more than an exclusive cult.' Lifton describes them as: 'Milieu Control', 'Mystical Manipulation', 'The Demand for Purity', 'The Cult of Confession', 'The Sacred Science', 'Loading the Language', 'Doctrine over Person' and 'The Dispensing of Existence'.

Lifton sums up his eight tests: 'The more clearly an environment expresses these eight psychological themes, the greater its resemblance to ideological totalism; and the more it utilizes such totalist devices to change people, the greater its resemblance to thought reform or "brainwashing"'.

Bruce Hines – auditor to the stars – reflected: 'Lifton had done some research into prison camps in China and mind control. It resonated with me when I read that. Those are methods that kept me in that mindset for thirty years.'

Let's take Lifton's tests for brainwashing one at a time. Together, they provide some kind of intellectual framework for assessing whether or not the Church brainwashes – a charge Tommy Davis vehemently denied to me in the Industry of Death exhibition and one it continues to deny in the strongest possible terms.

Test Number One is 'Milieu Control'. Lifton writes: 'The most basic feature of the thought reform environment, the psychological current upon which all else depends, is the control of human communication. Through this milieu control the totalist environment seeks to establish domain over not only the individual's communication with the outside (all that he sees and hears, reads and writes, experiences, and expresses), but also – in his penetration of his inner life – over what we may speak of as his communication with himself. It creates an atmosphere uncomfortably reminiscent of George Orwell's *1984*.' The most basic consequence of this information control, says Lifton, 'is the disruption of balance between self and outside world.'

Bruce told me: 'When I was in, if I heard someone say something negative about Scientology, I would instantly not listen to what the person was saying. I would think that person is a suppressive. You get into that sort of a mindset. And when I was in the Sea Organisation it would have been unthinkable for me to have a cell phone, to have a personal computer, to even get certain magazines. The mail I would receive would be read before I would receive it. Any mail that I would send out would be read before it could go out. And if there was anything wrong it would get kicked back. There are many, many ways where I believe it is a mind control organisation. A big one is to shut out any counter ideas, any critical ideas. When I was in, I was actually in the frame of mind where I would not listen to some critical thing about it. I would immediately dismiss it. I wouldn't even hear the words really.'

Test Number Two is 'Mystical Manipulation': adherents are, Lifton writes, 'impelled by a special kind of mystique which not only justifies such manipulations, but makes them mandatory. Included in this mystique is a sense of "higher purpose"... By thus becoming the instruments of their own mystique, they create a mystical aura around the manipulating institutions – the Party, the Government, the Organisation. They are the agents "chosen" (by history, by God, or by some other supernatural force) to carry out the "mystical imperative", the pursuit of which must supersede all considerations of decency or of immediate human welfare.'

Enter Lord Xenu. Can Scientology's struggle against the space alien Satan be classed as a 'mystical imperative'? What was Bruce's take on the 'Wall of Fire?'

'It's taught at the level of Operating Thetan III. OT3, it's a big deal, you hear about from the day you first get interested and then when you do this level you're going to have these great abilities. You'll be way above an average human being, and you have to undergo very strict security clearance to even get access to these materials. They're supposed to be very secret. The cosmology, the idea is that it goes back literally quadrillions of years. The current estimate on the Big Bang is fourteen billion, so this is orders of magnitude longer than you and I supposedly have existed. Relatively recently, seventy-five million years ago, there was this character named Xenu who was an emperor of a galactic federation and this is what... I read it and at the time I thought "oh cool!"'

What did Xenu do?

'There were twenty-six stars that are in this part of the galaxy, and so he had people killed and brought to earth and placed in or on volcanoes and blown up with hydrogen bombs, and then their souls are captured by an electronic ribbon he said, and then they are pulled down and given what is called an "implant" in Scientology, and this is basically pictures of forests to implant false ideas into the being.'

I didn't quite follow this, but Bruce wasn't finished.

'And the main part about OT3 and one of the things that is so secret about it is that a lot of these implanted souls are now stuck to our bodies, and they're here and there and there. Now supposedly I got rid of them on OT3. Although when you go onto the higher levels you find out that there are more of these body entheta they're called. And because they're implanted seventy-five million years ago, they influence the way you think and what you believe about things. A Scientologist who knew would say that you yourself, the fact that you're doing a story on Scientology, you're not really doing it out of your own freewill but you're like a robot carrying these evil things from the past to try to keep Scientology from succeeding.'

So a fundamental belief to Scientology is that we're actually contaminated by bits of space aliens?

'Very definitely so. It's patently false.'

Test Number Three, 'The Demand for Purity', sets out the goal of absolute purity, and reflects: 'thought reform bears witness to its more malignant consequences: for by defining and manipulating the criteria of purity, and then by conducting an all-out war upon impurity, the ideological totalists create a narrow world of guilt and shame. This is perpetuated by an ethos of continual reform, a demand that one strive permanently and painfully for something which not only does not exist but is in fact alien to the human condition... Once an individual person has experienced the totalist polarization of good and evil, he has great difficulty in regaining a more balanced inner sensitivity to the complexities of human morality.'

This test, 'The Demand For Purity', implies war against the impure. Was the Church in any way critical of Bruce? He is, says, Freedom Magazine, a liar and a religious bigot. 'In 2001,' while he was still inside, 'Hines wrote a 13-page public announcement in which he detailed the Suppressive Acts he had committed... Lying was a constant unchanging pattern with Hines.' Generating guilt and shame drip from virtually every line of Freedom Magazine.

To repeat, Bruce struck me as a painfully honest man.

Test Number Four is 'The Cult of Confession'. This, Lifton writes, 'is carried beyond its ordinary religious, legal and therapeutic expressions to the point of becoming a cult in itself. There is a demand that one confess to crimes one has not committed, to sinfulness that is artificially induced, in the name of a cure that is arbitrarily imposed... In totalist hands, confession becomes a means of exploiting, rather than offering solace for, these vulnerabilities.' Lifton identifies three special meanings of the totalist confession: first, a 'perpetual psychological purge of impurity'; second, it is an act of symbolic self-surrender; third, it is a policy of making public (or at least known to the Organisation) everything possible about the life experiences, thoughts, and passions of each individual, and especially those elements which might be regarded as derogatory.'

In the Church of Scientology, does confession become a means of exploitation?

Bruce audited Nicole Kidman and Kirstie Alley and, briefly, Tom Cruise.

Auditing is Scientology's version of confession, with the added element of the confessant holding two tin cans, or something like that, which connect to the E-meter, a kind of Bakelite box with a needle and dial. The E-meter works as a kind of crude lie or truth detector. The auditor asks questions. Quite different from the Catholic confession, the more the confessant confesses, the more the auditor probes the sins or crimes: what exactly did you think? Did you want to have sex with her? How did you have sex with her? It can be a probing and invasive investigation of sin, not just an admission. The question is – to what end? To help the person to lead a better life? Or to spy on them?

The Church has told the BBC that auditing sessions are routinely recorded for training purposes. What happens with that information is hotly disputed.

Ecclesiastically, when Bruce audited Cruise, he was the confessor and Cruise the lowly parishioner. But it didn't work out like that, he said. Bruce described a fateful session which ended badly for him. 'You're supposed to have what's called a floating needle, that's a certain motion that the needle is supposed to do, that's considered a good thing. And so I'm doing this exam on him and he's there and he has a big smile and he said something very brief like "that was a good session" or something, but I didn't see this floating needle immediately and so I was sort of waiting to see if one would happen.

And then I saw a floating needle and then I told him that, "Your needle's floating, Tom", but then later I was told he complained that I was too slow and so I wasn't allowed to do these exams on him anymore. In a regular organisation that wouldn't happen, but with the kid-glove treatment that Tom Cruise was getting, they would get someone who wouldn't imply in anyway that maybe he wasn't doing just great.'

He got kid-glove treatment?

'Aw, unbelievable, no other Scientologist got treatment like Tom Cruise.'

Other ex-members of the Sea Org suggest that Cruise's confessions were exploited by the Leader, Miscavige, his own best man.

Cruise's major confessor was Marty Rathbun, at one time an Inspector-General of the Church, and now out of the organisation, but still a believing Scientologist. His blog is the go-to running commentary for those Scientologists who hope for a Reformation of the Church. He is a tough man, no fool. Marty told me: 'There is a specific room for all the A-listers, John Travolta, Tom Cruise. And I audited Tom Cruise there. There is a shelf in there that has a false glass mirror panel and behind it there is a video camera.'

The Church's Freedom Magazine suggests that Marty is a mentally unstable and violent psychopath.

Audio-visual technician Marc Headley told me: 'When I was working for the Church of Scientology I installed over 100 rooms that had two cameras and a microphone in them where people would get auditing.'

The camera was not obvious but hidden, said Marc, 'inside of a smoke detector or inside of a picture frame. We're talking about pinhole cameras.'

The Church says it does film auditing, but that this is not a secret and has been announced publicly. Cameras are fitted within walls to stop them being intrusive and unsightly. The Church also says that auditing secrets are sacrosanct, protected by priest-penitent confidentiality and never revealed.

Claire Headley told me she watched a video of Cruise being audited: 'Marty, sitting in the chair. The E-meter and on the opposite side of the table Tom Cruise, holding the cans and the whole thing. I mean I saw those videos.'

And did they include personal things?

'Absolutely.'

Things that Cruise would not want people to know?

'Absolutely.'

The Church says recording is not a breach of confidentiality. Other Scientologists are authorised to listen in; selected staff are given access for the purposes of training and monitoring. The Church and David Miscavige deny that the sanctity of the confessional has ever been breached.

The idea that your most intimate, darkest sexual imaginings, the things that make you blush even thinking about them, could end up in the hands of the Church of Scientology frightened Tom DeVocht.

During auditing was it necessary to reveal intimate sexual details?

'Definitely,' he said. 'You couldn't in an auditing session say, "oh, I had an affair". You had to say what exactly did you do, how long did you do it.'

This is pornographic?

'Very much so.'

I took her clothes off, she did this....

'Yes,' said Tom.

'Exact details,' said Alison. 'I was Sec-Checked.' That's *SciSpeak* for Security-Checking. The devil lies in the detail. The Church makes a distinction between the sanctity of the priest-penitent confession and the Sec-Check, to defend the Church against attack. For the Sea Org member, holding the cans, being probed about his or her intimate secrets, the process would feel the same and the Church's distinction may seem one without a difference.

'They will ask you,' said Alison, 'what you have done and whatever comes up, maybe it is a sexual question, maybe it is to do with what you did at work, that they want to know exactly what you did. When you did it? How you did it?'

Tom cut in, saying the sexual end of it was far more important than if, as a staff member, you falsified your statistics. Miscavige appeared to enjoy, he said, bringing up staffers' sexual indignities in the hall at Gold Base in front of other Scientologists: 'First of all, what the hell has that got to do with him? Secondly, that poor guy is sitting there. And then you have got to think from a religious, from a Scientologist's point of view, it is a confession for god's sake.'

Not for publication?

'That's exactly right. But Dave would take a pleasure in just crushing... You can see the guy sitting there just sweating and going, oh my God, I can't believe this is being brought up.'

Tom recalled that Miscavige taunted one particular victim who had admitted taking pictures of himself with a camera phone, and that he called for the pictures to be downloaded and posted up on display. That never happened but by then everyone knew the poor man's secret.

The Chairman's old drinking partner also said that there was a warehouse full of the Pre-Clear folders, containing written reports and videos: 'You know he has got that information. It's a very scary but a very real thing.'

Miscavige's abuse of confessional secrets, Tom says, was common. He described a scene at Gold that he had witnessed. 'There was a break period where people were coming in, people coming out. And he goes, "watch this". And he calls at random, some people I knew, some people I didn't. He would call "Alison" over' – Tom gestured to his partner, giving her name to cover a real person – 'he would say, "Tom, this is Alison. Alison was thinking about committing suicide, she was thinking about killing me, she was masturbating, thinking about the captain of the organisation." I am thinking, OK, bye Alison. "Peter, here, was falsifying his statistics and had his finger up his ass on three different occasions."'

Tom said that Miscavige could bring up the dirt on 25 people instantly, like that – he clicked his fingers. He compared Miscavige's conduct to the Catholic confession: 'You go in as a Catholic and you say, look I have sinned, I have done this, that and the other thing. It is done, it is over for it. You don't have to worry about it.'

Absolution, I said. And the priest doesn't say anything to anyone, and that has been the rule since 1388.

'Right.'

The Church of Scientology and David Miscavige deny any such allegations that the sanctity of the confessional has even been breached and say that Tom DeVocht is a genuine pathological liar.

Tom described consistent violations of that priest-penitent relationship at Gold Base, how if a Sea Org member slighted Miscavige by looking 'at him wrong' or 'didn't stand to attention when he walked into a room' the person would be security-checked or 'sec-checked' in the jargon, and audited, aggressively, hour after hour. The auditor would get into trouble if he didn't come up with the goods, said Tom.

'So they had to sit there for hours and find out whatever the hell they could find out. If it was masturbation, if it was you thought about undressing somebody: I am giving you real life examples that I heard. You had sex with your wife when you were "down step"' – that is if demotion in the hierarchy made sexual relations with your higher-placed wife out-of-bounds.'

After the sec-checking came the public humiliation, Tom said. At a mass staff meeting on Friday night, Miscavige 'would go up there and say, "Peter, stand up. Yesterday Peter was masturbating in the bathroom." This is in front of the entire staff anywhere from 500 to 800 people. So dig it: you have taken this religious philosophy and he is using it to crush people. By the time I got there in 2001 there were people I knew for almost 30 years. They were cowed, you couldn't even talk to them. They were like different people.'

Amy Scobee in her book says that she witnessed the sanctity of the priest-penitent relationship abused: 'I have seen this trust violated on several occasions throughout the years – especially with staff members, but also with celebrities.' She describes how she was told that a man that she was uncomfortable around was appointed to be her boss, a decision she was personally unhappy with: 'I couldn't help but think that this was some sort of sick game Miscavige was playing.'

She was told she had no choice in the matter and was later given his confessional reports where he – in complete confidence – referred to his sexual infatuation with her. Then she was interrogated on the cans, asked repeatedly if she had had sex with the man who was infatuated with her. Her interrogator 'had an ear-piece in, and she was getting instructions about what to ask by whoever... was looking in on this confessional from the other room.' The confessional booths, she writes, are set up with LOOK-IN, LISTEN-IN and TALK-IN systems with video cameras positioned to be able to see the E-meter and the person confessing simultaneously on a split-screen monitor.

Amy said 'no' repeatedly to her interrogator, but was told that she would not be let out of the room until she confessed to having sex with the man or admitted to some other form of 'sexual perversion'. The E-meter interrogation lasted several gruelling hours, she said. This was, she writes, 'nothing short of sexual harassment.'

Her experience smacks of torture: prolonged physical and psychological abuse in order to extract information. In a BBC Radio Four documentary Torture in the 21st Century, the former Shadow Home Secretary Tory MP and ex-Territorial SAS trooper David Davis told me: 'Torture doesn't work.' The example he gave was of the CIA water-boarding a Libyan opponent of the Gaddafi regime and radical Islamicist, Sheikh al-Libi, a very large number of times, 'essentially until he worked out what it was his torturers wanted him to say, that there were weapons of mass destruction in Iraq and that there was some sort of cooperation between Al Qaeda and the then

Iraqi government. And that was a major part of the justification for the invasion of Iraq. So they got the information they wanted to hear.' But it was not true.

To end her E-meter interrogation, Amy confessed to the sexual perversion that they wanted to hear. She writes, that she admitted 'to a time that I put a finger in my rear end during sex with my husband.' Miscavige made a joke of this incident around the base, describing 'finger up the butt' for the type of transgressions the staff were making, she writes: 'Instead of coming clean on what we've done to "actively sabotage Scientology expansion"... This was not only embarrassing but a serious invasion of privacy and a violation of the priest-penitent relationship.'

After Amy left the Church and went public with her accusations, the Church went public against her, revealing details of her sex life. In its on-line magazine the Church labelled Amy 'The Adulteress' and accused her of 'wanton sexual behaviour' – something she denies. The Church also sent the St Petersburg Times the 'dirt', her intimate secrets that she had confessed in an auditing session or Sec-Check.

Amy told me: 'The details of how I had sex with my husband before I got married is not something that should go to a newspaper. They made it the world's business by issuing it on the internet and in a magazine that went to a hundred thousand or more people. It went to all my neighbours.'

The Church admits sending the newspaper material about Amy's sex life. It claims the information was from an affidavit signed by her and therefore not confidential.

Amy disputes this, saying the Church handed over handwritten confessions which she believed were confidential.

Lifton identified three facets to the totalist confession: a perpetual psychological purge of impurity; self-surrender; making public or at least known to the Organisation everything possible about the life experiences, thoughts, and passions of each individual, and especially those elements which might be regarded as derogatory.

Test Number Five: 'The Secret Science'. Lifton says the totalist milieu 'maintains an aura of sacredness around its basic dogma, holding it out as the ultimate moral vision for the ordering of human existence. This sacredness is evident in the prohibition (whether or not explicit) against the questioning of basic assumptions, and in the reverence which is demanded for the originators of the Word, the present bearers of the Word, and the Word itself. While thus transcending ordinary concerns of logic, however, the milieu makes an exaggerated claim of airtight logic, of absolute "scientific" precision.'

Bruce Hines reflected on the lure of Scientology's sacred "technology": 'There's always a carrot. From the beginning in my own case and I think maybe others, when you first get involved, the big carrot is that you can reach the state they call "Operating Thetan". This is a supposed state were you can leave your body at will and could do remote viewing and be totally certain of your own immortality, and not be afflicted by body troubles and things, some almost God-like state.

That carrot is always there.'

Are you an Operating Thetan?

'Well I was on OT7' – Operating Thetan Level 7, the second highest level inside Scientology.

So theoretically you're immortal?

'Yeah.'

Well, you used to be immortal and...?

Bruce started laughing.

The mood changed when he talked about his sister, a devout Scientologist. She completed OT8, the highest possible level, then suffered breast cancer. It was slow-moving and easily operable, but Scientology teaches its devotees that if you do the tech, you have cause – power, supremacy – over ill-health.

Bruce, fair-minded as ever, pointed out many Scientologists do take normal medical treatment. Was she treated medically?

'No, and she definitely should have been. She had breast cancer and it was a slow growing kind, and with...'

And easily operable?

'Yeah. The auditing would take care of it, but it just got worse and worse and then it was too late.'

She died, aged 55, in 1999.

'It had a profound effect on me,' said Bruce, 'although I wouldn't admit it at the time, because according to their ideology as you get up to those higher levels you should be more or less impervious to such things. In my sister's case, she was such a true believer, you're led to believe that as an Operating Thetan you are at cause over things that can go wrong with the body. She did believe that.'

Brainwashing Test Number Six: 'Loading the Language': 'The language of the totalist environment is characterized by the thought-terminating cliché. The most far-reaching and complex of human problems are compressed into brief, highly reductive, definitive-sounding phrases, easily memorized and easily expressed.' These clichés become, says Lifton, 'ultimate terms', either 'god terms' representing 'ultimate good' or 'devil terms' representing 'ultimate evil'. 'Totalist language, then, is repetitiously centred on all-encompassing jargon, prematurely abstract, highly categorical, relentlessly judging, and to anyone but its most devoted advocate, deadly dull.' For an individual, Lifton says, the effect of the language of ideological totalism can be summed up in one word: constriction. 'He is, so to speak, linguistically deprived; and since language is so central to all human experience, his capacities for thinking and feeling are immensely narrowed.'

Apply 'loading the language' to the following terms: 'auditing', 'covert hostility', 'disconnection', 'E-meter', 'ethics officer', 'floating needle', 'Int', "Operating Thetan', 'RPF', 'security check', 'Sea Organisation', 'upset', 'withhold' and 'Xenu'.

Brainwashing Test Number Seven: 'Doctrine over person': 'this sterile language,' says Lifton, 'reflects another characteristic feature of ideological totalism: the subordination of human experience to the claims of doctrine. This primacy of doctrine over person is evident in the continual shift between experience itself and the highly abstract interpretation of such experience – between genuine feelings and spurious cataloguings of feelings. It has much to do with the peculiar aura of half-reality which a totalist environment seems, at least to the outsider, to possess.' The consequence is that 'the human is thus subjugated to the ahuman… The underlying assumption is that the doctrine – including its mythological elements – is ultimately more valid, true, and real than is any aspect of actual human character or human experience.'

I asked Bruce about the effect of his commitment to Scientology on his family?

'I was in Scientology for about six years and then I decided to join the Sea Organisation, which is this sort of monastic type organization. You live in a paramilitary structure, you live communally, you eat communally and so you sort of move off and you give up any sort of normal life. It would be like joining a monastery if you were a Catholic. And at that point, although I told myself well it's all for the greater good, I rarely saw my family, my parents, my brother my sister, and I would maybe make a phone call every couple of years, and maybe write a letter. It's difficult to find time to write a letter because there's quite a lot of demands on your time. And it's something I really regret now, from their view, although they were very understanding, they would never say anything to criticise me. I went off and joined a cult and just left them.'

You've still got family in there?

'Yes I have.'

You talk to them?

'No, they will not talk to me, because I, since I left, and I have been officially declared in the eyes of Scientology as a Suppressive Person, and that means that my basic motivation is to stop Scientology because I want the world to go down, that's what they believe...'

Bruce continued: '...so I have two nieces who live in Clearwater who won't talk to me and formally sent me a letter saying that they love me and always will, but with the path that I've chosen they just cannot continue to have any communication or relationship with me.'

Disconnection. But that's a family smasher, I said.

115

'Well, yes.'

Brainwashing Test Number Eight is 'The Dispensing of Existence'. Lifton says: 'The totalist environment draws a sharp line between those whose right to existence can be recognized, and those who possess no such right... For the individual, the polar emotional conflict is the ultimate existential one of "being versus nothingness"... The totalist environment – even when it does not resort to physical abuse – thus stimulates in everyone a fear of extinction or annihilation.'

Why did Bruce, a brilliant physicist, stay in for so long? A big reason for him was his perceived fear of eternal damnation, chiming with Lifton's observation of fear of extinction or annihilation. 'The Scientologists I have known really believe that. You get on what they call, they have nice sounding marketing names, like "The bridge to total freedom" or whatnot. And you get your feet on the bridge and you have to walk and keep your next step, and you have to pay as you go. Particularly once you know about it, if you abandon it, you are going to have a horrible future. And your hopes of becoming an eternally free being are dashed. And so that is one aspect. You have got to toe the line or you are going to lose your chance.

'The other part is you are taught that anyone who is critical of Scientology, they say, that they have crimes for which they could be arrested. They [the critics] are part of this whole culture of evil and Scientology is the way out. When you try to suppress this force for good, because we are all implanted 75 million years ago, that we [the Scientologists] can't allow such a thing to happen. So the whole of society is going to try to suppress Scientology, and so you have to be tough to get through. And so people who are critical of it are evil.'

Bruce's intellectual and spiritual drift away from Scientology was gradual, but helped along by his incarceration in the RPF (Rehabilitation Project Force) for six years.

'It was out in the high desert of southern California, about ninety miles or so east of Los Angeles, and it's a very remote location. I understand they have now sold that property. You're about five miles or so from the nearest town, if you were going to leave you would either walk into the wilderness or have to go across an Indian reservation. It's in an environment where there are rattlesnakes, tarantulas, mountain lions, coyotes.'

Bruce did a stretch of three years on the RPF, was allowed to return to Gold Base, fell out with Miscavige again, or Miscavige fell out with him, he said, and then did a further three years. The second stretch was the most extreme, the RPF's RPF, 'as low as you can go in the Sea Organisation. I was not allowed to speak to other members. I had to work separately, had to eat separately. I would get the leftovers of the meals. I was with about four or five other guys. I had to sleep in a small shed, and this was in the summer in the desert, it was quite hot, on a concrete floor. I had very little space. There was a guard outside my door. And one time I said: "OK, I am leaving, I am out of here." It was the middle of the night and I came out and immediately the guard was there and people appeared and they kind of cajoled me and talked to me and get me to kind of go back to bed.

'And this went on for a couple of months. One time I was in a shed, just wooden sheds on concrete pads. And they closed the door and then they put a large baking pan against it, so that if I opened the door it would fall and make a noise to alert people that I was coming out.

'And I had to do pretty intense manual labour during that time. And it was July or August in the California desert and it could get 105, 110 even 115 degrees. And then I would spend a couple of hours at night having to read writings of L Ron Hubbard, and write up my misdeeds, I had to write them down my misdeeds until I had a realisation that I was a bad person and I needed to change my ways and get back into progressing towards my redemption.'

Bruce described a deep deprivation, lack of space, lack of ideas, lack of contact with people. 'So you feel very cut off. One or two people talk to you and tell you what to do and assign you jobs. There was a security guard, and he walked by and made sure I could go over to him. I said listen, "I want out of here, I want to leave." And so he was trained to say, "oh ok…I understand Bruce." The idea was that I continue over the days undergoing that sort of treatment that eventually my thinking would shift around, which it did.'

The physical abuse was extreme but it was trumped by Bruce's fear of annihilation according to Scientology dogma and his hunger to conform with the hive. He submitted to the ideology, which defeated his concern for his physical well-being. His self-surrender was complete; his brain had been washed.

How would you describe that time in your life? What they did to you?

'It wasn't the whole six years but definitely for those couple of months I would say it was torture. I hated every second of it. What is amazing to me though is that eventually I did swing around to the true believers' viewpoint again and for three years then worked to try to prove that I was OK. And eventually I was sent to New York City and I believe there was much less control there and so I had more contact with things outside. And I believe that helped me to free up from the mindset. Then I was able to walk out.'

The Big Apple ate away at the brainwashing?

'Yeah. New York City is a very vibrant place, there is lot's of creativity, lots of energy. And I just sort of like… "Wow, there is a whole world out there, there is a lot happening." After 30 years inside…'

Would you say you were brainwashed?

'I would call it brainwashing, particularly the Rehabilitation Project course.'

That would be a straight eight out of Lifton's eight tests for brainwashing.

Lifton's three broad definers for a cult were: a leader-cum-god; brainwashing; and harm. Do the adepts of the Church of Scientology suffer harm? One thinks of the series of allegations about cleaning out the sewage ponds and the RPF; about the many allegations of violence by the Leader, David Miscavige; about his use of abusive language; about the spying on the confessionals; about the humiliation of people by bringing up their sad sexual indignities in front of their peers. That could add up to harm.

All of the above are denied.

Back in March 2007, I had no idea of the number of people high up in the Church of Scientology who would subsequently say they were beaten or abused by its Chairman of the

Board, David Miscavige. At that time very few said anything at all, out in the open. But since then the growing use of the internet for lone dots of light to communicate with each other has changed the ability of the Church to constrict information. Back then I had also not read Lifton's superb book. But I made a judgment about Bruce and it was based on this: he'd volunteered to me that he'd once been ordered to scream his head off at another Scientologist and he had obeyed – and, now, looking back on it, he felt ashamed and that what he had done was cruel. That contrition suggested to me Bruce was telling the truth.

CHAPTER SIX
'This is the word of the Church of Scientology'

Were they shadowing us? So far, no. Or so we thought. We flew from 'Frisco to La-La Land, the city Raymond Chandler once described as having no more personality than a paper cup. Mole, Bill and I had been joined by our assistant producer, Patrick Barrie, a dry-witted, sceptical chap, the very opposite of paranoid.

This is Patrick's memory of what happened at the hire car place at LAX: 'There was a problem with the cars, as there was only one of them. During the wait to sort that out, one guy honed in on us and started asking questions about where we were staying on the pretext that he was looking for a good place and hadn't booked anything yet. Suspicious. We were very quickly wary of him and everything else besides.'

I like this because it makes Patrick sound like a paranoid fruitcake, and he really isn't.

Mole recalls: 'We were standing around at the hire car place out in the open and some guy took a shine to Bill. He asked where we were staying. All very suspicious. Bill told the guy which hotel we were staying in and the address. That was the point anyway – to see if they were spying on us.'

It was approaching dusk in LA. I was driving one car with Bill riding shotgun, camera on his lap, Mole and Patrick following in the second car. We left the hire car park.

Patrick takes up the narrative: 'Once we finally got the second car we knew to be on the lookout for vehicles tailing us. And lo and behold within a hundred yards of leaving the parking lot a vehicle parked on the right side of the road pulled out and was after us.'

You drive fast, slow, slow, fast. You turn left, then right, then left. If someone is following you, their evidently lunatic trail will soon become blindingly obvious.

Behind the wheel of the first BBC car, I spotted two vehicles tracking us, a Range Rover and a dark blue KIA Sidona people carrier. At one level I could not believe we were in a car chase in LA. But the evidence of my own eyes confirmed my suspicions. It was unbelievably exciting.

Bill's camera captured me giving a blow-by-blow account of the madness: 'The car in front – a Range Rover – seems to be following us. It's now taken a detour down a road and it's now going down an alleyway. Looks a bit creepy. I'm going to say goodbye to it. It's going quite fast down there.'

I drew ahead, fast, turned down a side road, did a very fast U-turn – hell, it's a hire car – and headed back towards the main road, parking up 20 yards from the junction. The essence of this game is patience. They want to trail you. You make them work at it – and then you can see them.

While waiting I knocked out a few pieces-to-camera, telly talk for the moment when Roger Smellie, The Man on The Telly, tells the viewer the bleeding obvious: 'We're being followed. I can't think the General Synod of the Church of England or the British Association of Muslims or whatever they are or the British Board of Deputies of Jews or the Hindus or the Sikhs would do this. It's crazy. Here's my prediction. Either – two cars, a Sidona or a Range Rover – will track along this road shortly.'

Bill repeated: 'Dark blue Sidona, black Range Rover.'

Nothing doing. No target car appeared. We were parked in a side road in Los Angeles, living out a million cop shows inside our minds. But in reality? Nothing. I tried to let myself down gently: 'Of course I might be completely paranoid.'

Yet I couldn't quite give up. We gave it another ten seconds. Another twenty.

'But I think we're being followed.'

A Blue Sidona drives past, slowly, clocks us, and accelerates away. Panorama gives chase.

'They're following us. The blue Sidona. I'm going to go and ask them a question.'

The Sidona is in front, changes lanes to go in front of a bus, turns right, races away. I stand on the accelerator.

'It would be really good to get the number plate. I'm driving circumspectly as my father would say.' That was for the fairies.

The Sidona turns right and comes to a dead stop at traffic lights. The number plate, ending: 'U204'. I get out of our car, run forward and politely but firmly tap on the driver's window of the Sidona.

'Hi, hello, are you Scientologists at all?'

The driver and passenger put their hands up to mask their faces and turn away from Bill's camera. In London, in Krasnoyarsk in the middle of Siberia, in Bucket, Arkansas, you tap

123

on the car window of an innocent party, and they wind the window down and say, 'can I help?' or 'what the bloody hell are you doing, mate?' You do that to the wrong people in parts of LA, I've heard, they shoot you. That the driver of the KIA put his hands up to hide his face was powerful evidence that we had chased the right people.

'My name's John Sweeney from the BBC. Are you from the Church of Scientology? I believe that you might be following us. Hi, John Sweeney from the BBC. Just wondering about your curious driving behaviour?'

The lights change, leaving us standing in the middle of a busy street in LA, having asked some blokes in a car their religious orientation, half-wondering whether we have gone entirely bonkers.

Some of the private investigators who work for the Church have a slightly foxed past. The most famous was a bent cop before he started working for the Church. Sgt. Eugene M. Ingram was dismissed from the LAPD in April, 1981 for misconduct, allegedly running a house of prostitution and also providing a suspected cocaine dealer with confidential police information and firearms in advance of a police raid. No criminal case ensued. Ingram had claimed to be wounded by a sniper in Elysian Park near the Police Academy in 1980 but an internal police investigation discovered that Ingram had inflicted the injury himself.

We had the chase on tape. The worry was – what would happen if our tapes, in TV jargon, the rushes, went missing?

Mole takes up the story: 'We got to the hotel on Sunset Boulelvard and in the lobby we saw Louis Theroux.' Ther-

124

oux, the British TV presenter and journalist, was in La-La Land to make a film about plastic surgeons. In real life, as on the telly, Louis sports a look of befuddled bemusement. But so did we all, and not without reason.

'In the background,' Mole continues, 'was a black guy with a cowboy hat on. It did cross my mind that he was a Scientology spy but I rejected it because he looked a bit dazed and so conspicuous with his cowboy hat on.'

Patrick recalls: 'When I came back into the hotel reception you were telling the whole story to Louis Theroux, who by chance was there. I was nervous as there was a black guy with a Stetson and possibly another person loitering in reception. They gave the impression of being both interested, but were also trying not to look interested. I remember wanting to try and find a way to cut in and end the conversation, because both of these guys didn't seem to have any reason for standing around in the lobby. By this stage there was a strange atmosphere, a mix of excitement after the car chase and a creeping paranoia about the goings on. That night we went for a meal across the road and had steaks and drank a lot. There was a rodeo ride in the restaurant which I think you wanted to go on, but you were talked out of it.'

I remember being frustrated as I was not allowed to go on the cowboy ride 'em thingy – my age at the time: 48. We went to another bar for one last drink where we drank green cocktails that gave us, well me, anyway, peculiar nightmares and viridescent poo. Patrick spent the night in a massive hotel room with the rushes – our tapes – safe under his pillow.

'The next morning,' Patrick recalls, 'because of my suspicions about the Stetson guy I came down for breakfast early and sat on my own. He was sitting in the far corner and was on the phone quite a lot. I distinctly remember hearing him something like "one of them is here now" in a not sufficiently quiet voice. I left breakfast and either told you and/or Mole and Bill that the Stetson man was there. I think that he left the breakfast room and then came back for a second time when you three were having breakfast and that Bill tried to get some shots of him.'

The paranoia grew and grew like a giant spider with hobnailed boots on acid and tequila.

Curious and curiouser: I got an email from Tommy, notwithstanding all the commotion at Plant City and on the roof of the car park back in Clearwater, inviting us to the Celebrity Centre in LA to interview a number of high profile Scientologists the following morning. They hated me. They loved me.

Cowboy Hat turned up at breakfast. Louis Theroux looked on quizzically – is that the only look he can do? – while Mole distracted the Hat and Bill shot him, hiding the small video camera behind a bowl of cornflakes. Later, I announced in my foghorn voice that I was going to pop down to the hotel garage to check on our car. Sure enough, there the Hat was, smooching around, hitching his trousers. On the surface, it was comic but, at a deeper level, existentially creepy, a malign, moronic presence watching over you. It helped generate not just mental discomfort but something darker and more animal: fear.

The Church of Scientology's Celebrity Centre is a perfect copy of a French chateau in the middle of Hollywood, all turrets and perpendicular Froggie-slated roofs and beautifully kept gardens and as real and true-to-life as Noddy's friend Big Ears sitting on a red and white-spotted mushroom with a

French beret on his bonce and a string of onions around his neck. Welcome to Ooh-La-La-Land.

Tommy Davis and Mike Rinder greeted us like old synthetic rubber friends and showed us around a kind of tea room, decorated with riotously beautiful Z-listers who I wondered might have been specially drafted in for the occasion of our visit. We were escorted to a lift, a faux-Victorian effort. I half-expected that the floor of the lift might disappear to drop us into a pool full of killer sharks, as in a James Bond film, but I was disappointed. We were led to a large room, decorated with fake Louis Quinze furniture, and a phrase of the late Kenny Everett in his transvestite mode came to mind: 'It's all done in the best possible taste.'

As Bill set up, Tommy and I went over old ground: I was a bigot, he was, some say, brainwashed; I had a preset agenda; some said they were a cult. Then I asked him about the creepy people following us around.

'We believe we were followed yesterday from L.A. airport,' I said.

I have a certain truculent physical style when I am not best pleased, like a bull beginning to take notice. Tommy registered it.

'Oh now you've taken it to a new level, wait a second. Let me try and get this right. I'm creepy because I show up at your hotel at 9.45 at night and call you on your cell phone and say that I'm there to see you. You hang up on me. Then…'

If this was a distraction technique, it worked pretty well.

'Hold on a second, you turned up at midnight.'

'No. It was at 9.45 at night when I arrived and then… I pull up to where you're doing an interview in a public place, and you refer to a perfectly normal rental car that I'm driving as a "creepy car" and then you repeatedly tell me the most obnoxious things about my organisation, describing it in horrifically pejorative terms and by the way I reviewed the tape, not always using the preface of "some people claim", there's a number of times when you actually just said it yourself, that Scientology is a cult in these disgusting terms you use and now…'

'Hold on a second…' I said, trying to staunch the Niagara of words from Tommy.

'…and when you….no, let me try and get this right, and now I'm having you *followed?*' Tommy stressed the final word, his handsome face puckering into a rictus of incredulity.

'Yeah.'

'It seems to me that you're the one who's gone a bit creepy.'

'It's a question. All right, so who followed us yesterday?'

'I have no idea!'

'When we arrived at L.A.?'

'I have no idea.'

'OK.'

'I mean you've done pieces all over the world with all kinds of somewhat notorious people. Is it possible that somebody else maybe was following you? I don't know. I don't even know what you're talking about or how you could characterise it as being followed.'

I challenged him to deny that the six people we thought had followed us so far in LA had nothing to do with Scientology. (The six were the first man at the hire car place who was unusually interested in our whereabouts, two men each in the Sidona and the Range Rover and the black guy in the cowboy hat.)

'I don't know who you're talking about,' said Tommy, all un-blushing innocence.

'There are no private eyes?'

'I don't know who you're talking about.'

'There are no Scientologists?'

'I don't know who you're talking about, and I'm happy to look into it but standing right here I don't know what you're talking about.'

'OK, all right,' I said, with the maximum amount of ungraciousness.

'It's easy to be a bit paranoid.'

'Nothing to do with you?'

'Anyway…'

'I understand.'

So did the Church of Scientology spy on the BBC?

Welcome to the strange world of Sci'gy-Leaks, an extraordinary cache of 25 pages of emails and BlackBerry messages which three years later fell into the wrong hands: mine. They appear to record in real-time a three-way conversation between Tommy Davis and Mike Rinder and the Leader's Communicator, Lou Stuckenbrock, about handling BBC Panorama. Taken together, Sci'gy-Leaks paint an extraordinarily weird picture of the Church.

The Church of Scientology strongly deny that the Sci'gy-Leaks are genuine.

The previous day, the Saturday, we had spent with the husband and wife heretics, Donna Shannon and Mike Henderson, the evening concluding with Tommy and Mike waiting for us at our hotel at midnight. The first Sci'gy-Leaks message is from Tommy to Lou on Sunday, March 18th, 2007 and is headed 'Hotel debrief': '*Last night Mike* [Zombie Mike Rinder, the hollow-cheeked Australian Scientologist and Tommy's deputy] *and I went to Sweeney's hotel around 10pm and called him and told him I was at his hotel and wanted to see him immediately. He hung up on me. I checked their rooms and found out that they were not at the hotel. We had Jesse Rad-strom'* – the black-clad cameraman - '*with us from Gold to shoot it. Sweeney, Mole and their camera man showed up around 12:30am.*

'*He* [Sweeney] *said that he had never told me what hotel he was staying in and that means that we are spying on the BBC and that he thinks that is very weird. I said that is ridiculous and that this is a small town and Englishman with TV cameras stand out like mad and we saw them interviewing the Shannons and walking around flag with them so that is utterly nuts.*

'*I then started tearing into him (not swearing as the cameras were rolling) and the hotel manager asked us to step outside. We continued out there.*

'*I told him that I was shocked at the unprofessional and juvenile way in which he was conducting himself and this program... I then said that he had come all the way here to Clearwater and was offered a tour of our facilities, the largest most significant Church facilities in the world and yet declined an offer to see or tour those facilities and instead was spending his entire day with Donna Shannon and Mike Henderson, two ex-Scientologists with a clear axe to grind.*

'*During the confrontation in front of Sweeney's hotel Sweeney said to me that Donna had told him that she did hard labor together with me when she was in the Sea Org and that she witnessed me get my hair pulled, my ears pulled and my face ripped off. This did not faze me at all and I calmly told him that I have no idea what she is talking about and that it is a complete and total lie and I could easily produce multiple witnesses to attest to that fact. He seemed somewhat shocked at hearing this.'*

I do remember being taken aback – shocked seems to be over-egging the pud somewhat – at the force of Tommy's denial that his hair and ears had been pulled and his immediate upgrading of the stakes, that he could provide multiple witnesses for his version of events against Donna's. The striking thing is that this is a fine detail I would not have recalled had I not seen Sci'gy-Leaks.

'I kept at him about how disingenuous and disgusting this all was...'

Tommy referred back to our meetings in England and the dispute over whether they had set three conditions or not: *'I told him that is not what I said and that he is again twisting what occurred in the meeting and that I would be happy to provide him with a transcript of what occurred as he may recall we recorded all of it. This seemed to shut him up.'*

Neither Tommy nor the Church of Scientology ever did provide a transcript of the meetings in England. I remain unshut up.

'At this point a CW [Clearwater] *Police car showed up having been called by the hotel manager (she overreacted to our dueling cameras and heated discussion).'*

The hotel manager was doing her job.

'The cop asked who we were. Sweeney said he was from the BBC and we never got a chance to say who we were... The officer came back out and said that the hotel would prefer that we disperse

and not continue. I thanked him and said that is not a problem and that we work and live around here and certainly don't want to disturb anyone. I turned to Sweeney and said "we are done" and walked away. He called after me repeating out loud the demands that he has mocked up we made of him "that we won't refer to you as a cult", "that we won't interview critics" and that was all.

'We continued surveilling them and saw that they did not leave for Vegas this morning.'

On the face of it, Tommy's repeated denials of the Church of Scientology spying on the BBC were not true. He was lying.

'However it was so down to the wire with so limited flights that we did not want to take the chance of them flying out later in the day and getting to Vegas ahead of us. For this reason Mike [Rinder] and Kevin Caetano went ahead to Vegas and will be landing there in the next few hours. Kirsten and I are still here in CW and are actually now at Plant City where the new Test Center in opening. Sweeney is here.'

The second message of the day comes from Mike Rinder: *'To: Lou, Dear Sir...'*

All of the messages from the Leader's Office come from Lou, the Communicator, but in an extremely masculine tone that suggests they are the direct word of the Leader. The Communicator is always addressed as 'Sir' but this is standard policy, set down by Hubbard, in Scientology, that all higher ranks are addressed as 'Sir' even if they are female.

Mike continues: *'I am now on Blackberry and saw the cc you sent. They are going to SFO [San Francisco] not LV [Las Vegas]. TD [Tommy Davis] is enroute now to SFO and I am going at 10pm and will know where they go. I am getting the debriefs put together and overall planning done in coordination with Bob and OSAI* [Office of Special Affairs International]. *Ml Mike.'*

The boss and/or his Communicator, Lou, is not a happy bunny: *'Why is Tommy going to SFO? Areb't they going to say you are following them. Are you this fing nuts (beyond just sp)? Please clarify. Please tell me he's not on their plane!'*

Fing nuts is short for fucking nuts – as the messages spool out abuse from the top becomes common. At no time do Tommy and Mike return the abuse. SP means Suppressive Person, a baddie.

Why does the Church's leader have his own personal Communicator, Lou Stuckenbrock? Why can't he communicate himself? In 1977 the FBI raided the Church of Scientology and the investigation got very close to Mr Hubbard. His wife, Mary Sue Hubbard, ended up going to jail, so ex-members of the Church say that the role of the Communicator is a deliberately constructed cut-out. Sci'gy-Leaks read as if Miscavige says something, his word is recorded and transcribed and put into the third person, so there is always a measure of deniability. This use of a private office cut-out so that politicians, for example, can have plausible deniability is common practice in Westminster and Washington DC.

It's conceivable that the Sci'gy-Leaks cache could be fake, an elaborate fraud. They are written, pitch-perfect, in Scientology-ese, which only someone immersed in the Church for decades could write. There are, of course, ex-members of the Church who could do that. What seems to me much more difficult to fake is the seemingly real-time reaction to events and actions that we took part in. Reality is imperfect, so it strikes me as evidence pointing to Sci'gy-Leaks being genuine that the BlackBerry machines are on different time settings and time zones, that the spelling is often grotesquely askew, and that real life panics and cock-ups do occur which strike me as beyond the imagination of even the cleverest fraudster. Still, both possibilities should be born in mind by the reader: that Sci'gy-Leaks are genuine; that they are fake.

The Church deny that they are genuine.

Twelve minutes later, Mike replies to the Communicator: *'Dear Sir He is definitely not on the same flight. He is going via Chicago to Oakland as the only available flight. There is no plan to do anything with them but to be available there in case (there may be internet chat on who they see) or they may try to go to one of the orgs there as we showed them SFO, SNC and Gatos. If not, then it is easy to get down to LA. ML Mike.'*

The next message is a terse thank you. That Monday we arrive in San Francisco. The Communicator demands of Mike at half past midnight: *'Well. Anything?'*

Mike replies: *'Dear Sir Nothing yet. My plane just landed in SFO. They arrive at 0130. TD arrives at 0900. Wont know anything other than where theyre staying until morning. Ml mike.'*

Tailing people is a sleep-killer. It was past midnight and Mike was at the airport, waiting for us.

A few minutes later the Communicator snaps back: *'What are you going to do? Act like you "guessed" they were there? Or, if you understand TD acronyms, BT?'*

TD stands for 'Technical Dictionary', Hubbard's very own version of *SciSpeak*; BT means, according to the Xenu-directory.com glossary: 'Body Thetan. Usually plural. Evil spirits which need to be exorcized, as in: "OT5 consists entirely of running out BTs; what a bore."' These are well known terms inside Scientology. The tone of this message is bullying.

At one am, Mike replies: *'Dear Sir. I am not planning to BT. Someone is speaking to them to find out their plans and whoever they plan on talking to is likely to say something on the internet thst wld become public knowledge. And of course if they show up at an org this will be known. No plan to contact them untll we have overt data. Will have moe data when they arrive. Ml mike'*

The phrase 'overt data' is a give-away: we were the subject of a covert investigation. The Communicator pings back at 0117am: *'Thank you. You realize this hasd gone totally out of control and you and Tommy have created the usual out of control sit - right down to Tommy wanting to ignore everything the boss said and just say "what's happening" (the ballroom).* [The ballroom? I have no idea that this means.] *'The boss view is that he spent 20 years doing this so others could get tech and orgs show on the rails and they did zero. And you thought the battles were the game, giving it all to him. He's not going to do it anymore as nobody will go free and there will be no orgs. Your contribution to LrHs birthday (a5 tommys) was to enturbulate. Period. He had a month to work on videos and refused it. He is you.'*

He is you? What on earth does the Communicator mean?

Five and a bit hours later – no-one seems to get much sleep in the Church – Mike replies: *'Dear Sir - I totally realize this and intend to deal with this so it doesnt create further enturbulation. I know we did nothing on March 13* [we met Mike and Tommy on that day] *and that this is the continuing treason. The people arrived sfo and drove to Berkeley and are in on on hotel.'*

This is a spying operation on a grand scale, conducted across 2,000 miles of the continental United States. Mike's admission of a continuing treason seems to be comically over-the-top and self-denigrating. But he knew roughly what we were planning to do in the morning: *'to interview two people tomorrow but we dont know their names yet though suspect one is the woman who stirred uo the SFO Chronicle earlier about NN* [Narconon] *in thhe schools as she lives nearby and was on on student of Margaret Singer. We have the DAs on her and Singer.'*

'DA' means 'Dead Agent', to spread malicious lies and rumours about an anti-Scientologist person or organization in an attempt to discredit them. LRH's policy on "dead agent-ing" appeared in a 1974 bulletin: 'The technique of proving utterances false is called "DEAD AGENTING". It's in the first book of Chinese espionage. When the enemy agent gives false data, those who believed him but now find it false kill him - or at least cease to believe him. So the PR slang for it is 'Dead Agenting.'"

Singer is a reference to Margaret Singer, a feisty academic who took on all manner of cults including the Moonies, Falun Gong, Hare Krishna and Heaven's Gate and wrote *Cults In Our Midst*. She suffered hate-mail, had live rats released into her house and travelled under an assumed name. She never backed down. Her view on cults was straightforward and una-pologetic: cults 'prey on the most lonely, vulnerable people they can find, cage you with your own mind through guilt and fear, cut you off from everyone...they don't need armed guards to keep you. Liars, tricksters, it's been the same ever since Eve got the apple, and I doubt it will ever change. They're all basi-cally, really the same, con men.'

At the age of 80, she frightened off a stalker – not from the Church of Scientology – who had been leaving menacing notes in her mailbox: 'I've got a 12-gauge shotgun up here, sonny, and you'd better get off my porch, or you'll be sorry!' she hollered out the window. 'And tell your handlers not to send you back!' By the time we landed in San Francisco, Singer had been dead for two years. Only the Church of Scientology would seek to 'Dead Agent' the dead.

Mike continued: '*We will ensure the orgs are briefed on them possibly trying to come in. TD arrives at 11am and will then have the full plan in coordination with Bob* [Fireman Bob, who, it seems, can do no wrong] *who is moving forward in UK. Ml*'

The Communicator replied nine hours after his previous message, presumably after a good night's sleep: '*Thanks. Still means nothing and I don't know why TD would take until 11 to get across country and why you are in sfo except if they try to ambush org (but org could have been briefed and told to chuck them) if they showed up. But that's my dub in as you and TD just are dangerous environ and REFUSE to give specifics (like maybe there is a reason you are there?)*'

Mike replied: '*Dear Sir. There were no other available flights and they had a 6hr wait In chicago. The original reason for going to sfo was to be there if we needed to confront them if needed. We did not know what their plans were. We now know they are planning to do two interviews today and catch a flight to la tomorrow morning.*'

How they knew our schedule, we do not know. We would have been wary about communicating our plans with anyone outside the team, and I trust everyone in the team, absolutely.

'*They have been meeting with bruce hines this morning.*'

More evidence, if it were needed, that they were spying on us.

'We are leaving people here to track their activities. The org DSAs have been briefed as well and are ready to handle them if they show up. we are going to la to prepare for them and get our complaint to the bbc prepared and coordinated with walsh' [Bill Walsh, the American lawyer we met at Saint Hill] *and uk counsel as they are way out of line. We have a 2:45 flight. Ml Mike'*

The Communicator replied: *'Tks. I hope they have all the dope on Hines. What's so bad is none of these people know anything happening anywhere in PT in the church.'*

PT stands for Present Time, the here and now. The Xenu directory gives a useful example: 'SPs are stuck in an incident in the past; they need to be brought up to PT.'

Mike replied: *'Dear Sir, we have the da [Dead Agent file] on hines and will get this to sweeney as he took him in front of sfo org to shoot shots of him so hines involvement is now overtly* [as opposed to covertly] *known. Clearly they are only interested in people who have allegations to make and no actual data and this is part of his gross bias.'*

Mike continued: *'We are in LA and now going through the transcripts of the statements made by js* [John Sweeney] *when he was confronted by tommy at the plant city opening and when he was interviewing shawn Lonsdale. I have never seen so many overtly bigoted and biased statements made by a reporter... We are going to lay out exactly how to further mess up his plans on wednesday as he expects us to refuse to show him anything. But we can force him to shoot our facilities. We can also line up interviews that he will likely refuse (on principal he is saying that anything we give him is just our propaganda) and we will use that against him. If he does interview them them they will da [Dead Agent] his lines.'*

And lo, exactly that came to pass: they bombarded us with interviewees. It seemed wrong to us to say no, so we interviewed all of the people they put in front of our cameras but the cumulative effect was boring telly and mind-shattering.

'*We are putting this together at osai*' – the Church's version of CIA HQ, Langley - '*and will send a complete report at the end of the nite as I know you hve only been getting bits and pieces on blackberry. This is ok ML Mike*'

The Communicator asks for the number where the two men are working. Then Tommy joins the conversation, messaging Lou: '*Dear Sir, I apologize for the generality.*'

Generality means waffle.

'*We are back in LA now and at OSA Int and going through everything – the transcripts from the UK, the BBC broadcasting guidelines, the legal data we have inn the invest results.*'

Tommy's mention of the 'invest results' suggests that there was an investigation into our team, perhaps by private eyes, on top of the tracking carried out by Mike and Tommy. Perhaps that investigation is the source of Tommy's remark at Plant City, which he swallowed in the next sentence, that 'I know where you live'.

They were working on a plan: '*to handle sweeney terminatedly. Ml, Tommy.*'

The '*terminatedly*' still makes my flesh creep.

The evidence from Sci'gy-Leaks seems compelling, describing in detail, in real-time, an elaborate spying operation by the Church of Scientology against the BBC, tracking us across the United States, from our hotel in Clearwater to identifying an important ex-Scientologist source we interviewed in San Francisco to LA. When Tommy Davis said he had no idea what I was talking about he was not, on the face of it, being honest.

On Wednesday, March 21st, we spent the day as Tommy's guest interviewing the stars at the Church's Celebrity Centre. An anxious message came from the Communicator in the evening: *'We are in LA now, are there any areas we should avoid? And is this guy's body now many new (torn worn to wall) assholes?'*

This is, some say, the word of the Church of Scientology.

CHAPTER SEVEN
'Do I look brainwashed to you?'

B ack in the Celebrity Centre I asked a question.
'That's insane,' said Tommy.

'That is nuts,' said Mike.

'That is insane,' repeated Tommy.

I tried to think of putting what Bruce Hines had told me about David Miscavige in the most diplomatic way I could think of. 'He's a thug,' I said, 'going around hitting people?'

'OK, good,' said Tommy. 'You broadcast that you're going to suffer the consequences because it's a gross, gross lie. And every time you come up with these lies I put you on warning and it's on tape.'

Could I interview Mr Miscavige? I asked, expecting the answer no.

Mike started talking, a rare event: 'John, that's the same allegation that they made in the 1987 Panorama programme, that took those allegations and laid them all out... Everyone on them was found completely and utterly not just untrue, totally without basis. The court threw that complaint out, the...'

Which complaint?

'The complaint that was the subject...' Mike was interrupted.

'From the 1987 Panorama show that you seem to be patterning this show after,' said Tommy.

'...it was exactly the same pattern,' continued Mike, 'there is a bunch of people who have these wild, outrageous, untrue allegations...'

'They found...' said Tommy.

'...comes along and says well, let's hear what you have to say...' said Mike.

'And it's thrown out,' said Tommy, 'and found to be frivolous, after five, it was thrown out five times!'

Did the BBC apologise, I asked.

'No,' said Tommy, 'even after the Internal Revenue Service investigated every single allegation made in that show there were all found to be unfounded and not true.'

I do not believe, I said, that the Internal Revenue Service of America has got any regulatory role whatsoever to do with the BBC, so that programme stood.

'We're not talking about regulatory role,' said Mike.

'We're talking about the facts,' said Tommy.

I get the point, I said.

'The facts are...' said Tommy.

So, no, the facts are... The fact was we were talking over each other.

'Wait, wait, so the point you...' said Tommy.

So David Miscavage is not a bully, I wondered, nonchalantly.

'Absolutely not!' said Tommy.

He doesn't hit people? I asked.

'Unequivocally not,' said Tommy. 'I've never seen him engage in any behaviour that could be remotely characterised as such, it's a bald-faced lie!'

Are you sure? I asked.

'One hundred percent! Without question. I have no doubt whatsoever. He's a personal friend of mine, I've known him for 16 years, I've worked with him closely for many and most of those years as has Mike and we know him and we couldn't even begin to conceive of anything that even remotely resemble what you've just described. It's such a disgusting mischaracterisation.'

He never hit Bruce Hines?

'Absolutely not, he's never hit anybody. Did Bruce tell you that?'

Tommy and Mike, according to Sci'gy-Leaks, knew full well that I'd spent time with Bruce Hines but I did not know that they knew. But Bruce had been happy to talk to us in public on camera so it was not a secret so I said: yes.

'Bruce Hines told you that?'

Yes.

'This is the Donna Shannon syndrome,' chipped in Mike.

Tell me about Bruce Hines. Is he a nice man? I asked.

They told me he was removed from the Church for gross dereliction of duty.

Bruce said there were a number of reasons why he left the church of his own volition, I said. One was that he had problems after falling out with Tom Cruise because it took him too long to say "your needle's floating, Tom".

'He never knew Tom Cruise, he's never met Tom Cruise,' said Tommy.

He has met Tom Cruise, he told me, I said.

'Oh really? Oh really? OK, good,' said Tommy.

You don't believe him?

'It's not a question of believing him,' said Tommy. 'He's just lying. I know it's not true.'

OK, I said. Bruce also said that Mr Miscavige fell out with him, Mr Miscavige came into the room and said 'where is the motherfucker?' and then hit him. That's what he says.

'You know John...' started Mike

Is that true? I asked.

'No,' said Mike, 'that's a lie and I know that it's a lie because I was already with Bruce Hines once before when I was on the TV show where that was brought up and similar type allegations were made and I asked Mr Miscavage. He never had that conversation, that incident, that run-in, whatever Bruce Hines claims, it never occurred. Now you think that this is very strange, this is what we are telling you John, we have seen these people for years, I have heard the most outrageous outlandish statements about myself, things I supposedly did that never happened, ever, ever happened and they will just make them up because what's the downside for someone like that? To make statements like that. What, are they going to get sued?'

That was probably the most thorough denial of an allegation I had ever heard. We carried on like Tweedledum and Tweedledee, for a bit, trying to bash each other's brains out, verbally I hasten to add, then Tommy introduced me to his mother.

I sat down opposite Anne Archer. Apart from having her bunny boiled in *'Fatal Attraction'*, Anne has appeared in the films '*Patriot Games*' and '*Clear and Present Danger*', and on TV in *Little House on the Prairie*, *Falcon Crest* and *Hawaii Five-0*. Outside, the Californian sun did its duty, but its light was shrouded by lace-effect drapes. She took one look at me and shuddered, a medieval martyr, about to be tormented by a witch-finder wielding a ret-hot poker. Or something like that. All of the celebrity interviewees the Church presented for me to interview were, as far as we were concerned, volunteers. They did not have to talk to me but elected to do so.

Bill and Mole filmed from our side. The Church's main cameraman was a tall, thin, German chap with a shock of white hair called Reinhardt; their number two camera woman was an exotic woman – Argentinian? – and I think they had a third plus a soundman, who looked Spanish or South American. They wore black and said next to nothing. Tommy and Mike settled down to watch from the sidelines, like line call umpires at Wimbledon or vultures waiting for a free carcase.

Anne told me she'd been a Scientologist for 30 years, and that it had helped her become a more able, sane, more responsible person with a very high sense of ethics, and that no-one she has been around with has ever been critical of Scientology, especially in Hollywood.

I took a deep breath. Some people say that Scientology is a sinister brainwashing cult.

Anne had no truck with that. It is, she said, a very intelligent, wonderful, highly ethical organisation, and the people in it have had wonderful success and wins in their life from utilising the Scientology technology. And then she went on to the attack: 'The thing I don't understand is why you are not talking to people who have benefited from it and why you are not giving a fair point of view to the other side.'

This was more than a little ironic. Four or was it five cameras – and who knows there might have been some hidden somewhere – were recording me doing exactly what she was complaining I was not doing.

She told me I was 'extremely bigoted' and not balanced as reporters are supposed to be. I told her that I had spoken to people who said that Scientology had ruined their lives, like Mike Henderson, and she told me that man had a criminal record. No, that was Shawn Lonsdale, I told her. She questioned why I talked to criminals, and I said Shawn's record was for sexual misdemeanours but the Church, he said, attacked and intimidated him and reacted out of all proportion. I didn't twig to the fact that she knew I had been spending time with a criminal.

'It is not out of all proportion. First of all, it doesn't happen,' Anne said, nonsensically. 'There aren't that many critics, and I have never come across those people in my life, it has never been my experience and you are putting on the air these very few who have whatever they have going on in their lives. Who are discreditable people and you are putting them on as credible people, and that to me is very offensive.'

I told her about Mike Henderson, who says that Scientology breaks up families.

'Scientology brings families together. Scientology, using L Ron Hubbard's technology, understanding, how to make relationships better, has without question saved more marriages, made more marriages happier, than any other technology or approach that I have ever seen in life. Otherwise I wouldn't be a Scientologist.'

Black and white; light and shade. There was no meeting of minds between us, whatsoever.

Had she ever been on a RPF course?

'An RPF course? No...'

Tommy interrupted: 'That's for Sea Org members.'

'No, I am public,' she said. The distinction is that 'public' means parishioner, Sea Org means a member of the Church's Holy Order, like a nun or a monk.

I put to her that the RPF is a dungeon of the mind.

'You know what? You are talking to the wrong person.'

Point to her. It was odd, though, that she had never heard of the complaints of ex-Scientologists: 'No. No. No... You have completely the wrong understanding of what Scientology is. Scientologists come and do courses, get auditing services because they are trying to grow as human beings. And the individuals that work within the organisation are the most ethical, fair, understanding and loving group of individuals I have ever met in my life. Who really care about helping people and not tearing them down, that has been my experience.'

I asked her about 'ripping your face off'.

'You are making me laugh. You know you so obviously have this bigoted point of view towards something, you are trying to drag that point home. And it is not reality. This is not truth for me.'

She had never heard of that phrase?

'No. Absolutely never heard of that phrase. It is ridiculous.'

No one has ever ripped her face off?

'Are you kidding me?'

You could have cut the atmosphere with a blunt implement.

I put to her stories of abuse and psychological torture. She denied it absolutely: 'There is certainly no mental torture, there is certainly no abuse, there's certainly nothing like that that exists in Scientology, believe me.'

I told her that we have spoken to somebody who said they had seen Tommy on one of these course being punished, humiliated, having his hair and his ear pulled about...

'I guarantee you that would never happen. And I happen to be back in Florida the time Tommy was there and we had many wonderful, lovely conversations and it is just not true.'

Some people say that David Miscavige is a bully, he goes round hitting people?

She laughed out loud.

Just for the record, is David Miscavige a bully? Does he go around hitting people?

'Of course not. He is a very intelligent and fair and kind, he is one of the kindest people I have ever met.'

Our relationship was not getting any better. 'You are a bigot,' she said.

Some people would say that she is brainwashed.

'Do I look brainwashed to you?'

I looked up to the heavens, but said nothing.

'How dare you!' she hissed. 'You know what? You are brainwashed.'

Is there any criticism that you would fairly level at your own organisation of the Church of Scientology?

'None whatsoever... You won't put that on the air.'

She was right about that, but for a different reason.

The verbal ping-pong carried on. She called me a bottom feeder, a tabloid reporter. More ping-pong or as Boris Johnson dubs it, wiff-waff.

'You obviously have an agenda here and this whole interview is kind of a waste of time.'

Indeed, why are you talking to us?

'Because you attacked my son.'

I didn't attack your son.

'Oh yes you have,' Anne said.

'Oh no I haven't,' I replied. 'Are you familiar with pantomime?'

And that pretty much was that.

Anne left, her place replaced with a strikingly attractive woman, I guess, in her early thirties. She sat down in front of me with an air of the lioness entering the den, the better to eat up the Christian. I liked her, or at least wanted her to like me. Bill attached the radio-mike to her, which always seems to involve asking people to slip this thingy through their undergarments. He was particularly charming with all the Scientologists, and all the Scientologists were charming back to him. I was beginning to suspect he was working for the other side, Traitor Bill.

My lack of charm did not help me resolve my immediate problem, which was embarrassing.

You have got to forgive me, I said, I am not a Hollywood reporter. I have been to all sorts of weird places but I don't know who you are. In LA there is no greater sin.

'Oh really?' She was actually quite sweet about it. 'My name is Leah Rimini and I am on a show called "The King of Queens"'. One of the biggest American sitcoms of recent times, the show often rated around 13 million viewers. The wreckage of our small talk out of the way, it was time for business. She told me that Scientology had offered her the ability to be a happy person, Scientology has given her those tools to try to be a good person.

I asked her about the auditing process, questions about all sorts of things, including your sex life, things that are embarrassing?

'It is confidential.'

But they record it, I said.

'Do they record it? No.'

Three years later we asked that very question of the Church. It said it does film auditing, but that this is not a secret and has been announced publicly.

Cameras are fitted within walls to stop them being intrusive and unsightly.

The Church also says that auditing secrets are sacrosanct, protected by priest-penitent confidentiality and never revealed.

I told Leah I have heard the allegation that David Miscavige has used some of the stuff which had been said in confidence. In Catholic terms, that would be a violation of the sanctity of the confessional?

'I mean that is so, so ridiculous because if that were true there would be a lot of law suits. There is nothing about me or about any Scientologist that I know has anything in their past that someone could use against them.'

There are stories out there, people say that they have been punished, in particular, on the Sea Org RPF. Have you ever heard that?

'Aha.'

What is RPF?

'I think Tommy has already explained that to you, right.'

Leah's interview took place immediately after Anne's. My deduction would be that Leah could have only known that Tommy had given me an answer on RPF if she had been watching a live feed of the interview in another room in the Celebrity Centre. I didn't work that out there and then, but just had a sense of an extra level to the game they hadn't told me about.

I pressed on. Are you aware of any criticisms that it punishes people?

'No, I haven't heard the criticism.'

We spoke to one guy who said that he has effectively spent six years in the RPF.

'I have to tell you that he has to be a complete idiot because the programme doesn't take six years.'

No, he was punished for six years.

'Well then, I think he is a complete idiot. Six years is a long time to try to get with it.'

Because he fell out with David Miscavige.

'Well, thank God. Six years is a long time. I'm glad we got rid of him.'

Have you met Mr Miscavige?

'Of course.'

Some people have said that he has hit them.

'That he has hit them?'

Yeah, physically.

She laughed: 'I don't know what to say about that, I mean it is so silly. That David physically hit them?'

Yeah.

'OK. I don't know what to say about that. He never hit

151

me. Should I consider myself insulted? I mean, I'm a friend of his and he's never hit me.'

I batted on.

He hasn't given a TV interview since 1992. What is he afraid of?

'What's he afraid of? Oh I think if you met Mr Miscavige you would see that he is really not afraid of anything. But I just think it is…'

Well, I said, he appears to be, because he is afraid of for example giving a TV interview.

'No, I don't think he is afraid.'

Some people would say that Scientology has got an unfortunate image.

'What?'

People out there, for example, on the internet.

'I don't go on the internet.'

As Bruce Hines had explained to me, the Church has an aversion to the internet, this, the single greatest expansion of human knowledge in modern times, and, if you watched the opening of the Olympics, invented by a Briton, for free.

Why not?

'But I just don't go to the internet for my source of information. I don't search the internet for any information on anything. This is a building you can walk in and you can see what Scientology is.'

Are there any down sides to Scientology?

'What?'

Apart from being interviewed by me.

'You seem quite pleasant.' She must have been kidding.

'Downsides, yeah? It's not easy to be a Scientologist

because the ethic level of this group is very, very high.' She made no criticism of the institution. Being an Operating Thetan Level Five, the ex-Scis say she would know about the 'Wall of Fire'.

You know about Xenu?

'I don't know... I have been in it for 25 years and I have no idea what you are talking about.'

So OT3, I heard, was Xenu, was the galactic war lord who 75 million years ago, sort of, put peoples, aliens...?

'I have already answered this,' interrupted Tommy. 'None of us know what you are talking about. It makes you look weird talking about it.'

Time froze. Donna Shannon and Bruce Hines had confirmed Xenu to be true.

So either Donna and Bruce and the Panorama 1987 team and everybody on the internet were mad, or the Church of Scientology, its representatives, Tommy and Mike, and this feisty, funny and beautiful actress sitting a few feet from me, were mad. This made my head hurt. Tommy had a simple solution to my dilemma.

'I think what the problem is,' said Tommy, helpfully, 'you must have talked to some lunatic... I mean I am not calling you a lunatic...'

I appreciate the distinction, I said. So it is wholly untrue, Xenu? 75 million years ago?

'Sweetheart,' said Leah, 'you are talking to me and it is like you are talking another language to me. It is, like, I have no idea of what you are talking about.'

I have spoken to a number of ex-Scientologists who have said yes, the Xenu story is part of the religion, I said.

'OK, so therein lies the problems. You are talking to ex-Scientologists and I don't know how much, I mean you are talking to crazy people, I mean I don't know. If that is what they told you then I go...'

'Yeah,' said Tommy. 'I mean here is the thing John, you are insisting on levelling to Scientologists things that you've heard, things that you find on the internet. We are the ones who are the Scientologists. We know what Scientology is. And what you are talking about plays no part in Scientology. It is just utterly bizarre. It is just bizarre.'

Is it possible you might be brainwashed, I asked Leah.

'What do you think?'

Oh, I ask the questions, I said.

'I know but you are sitting here looking at me. I mean what do you think?'

I don't know, I said.

'So I really couldn't really answer that question. "Are you brainwashed?" I could ask you the same thing.'

Of course she could. In 2012 I now realise that as an Operating Thetan Level Five she would have been taught that I have been brainwashed by Xenu into thinking that he doesn't exist. This is, then, a conversation between two people, one of whom suspects the other might be brainwashed; the other who knows the other has been brainwashed. The one who suspects doesn't know that the other who knows can't tell the first one he's been brainwashed because if she does he may die. Simples.

I don't think I am brainwashed, I said, weakly. I went on to say that was because my mind is open to stuff, for example, I read the internet, blah blah.

'It is not that I am not open to criticism,' she said. 'It is that there is so much crap in the world, why would I want to open myself up to being in a bad mood or why would I want to open myself up to reading nasty stuff about something that has helped me? We are not hurting anybody, we are doing just the opposite. We are helping people.'

Some people say that is not true.

'Well, that is bullshit, Baby-doll,' – I do wish she hadn't called me that.

She spoke about the success of Narconon, Scientology's drug treatment programme questioned by the doctors in San Francisco, and defended the Church to the utmost: 'We really don't give a crap. We know that we are helping people. Do you understand what I am saying to you? You don't have to say it is a brainwashing cult. Is there any other religion that would put up with this kind of talk? This kind of bigotry.'

I queried the number of Scientologists the Church claims, worldwide: 10 million people. I've looked through the windows of more Church of Scientology buildings than anyone else I know, and they always seem empty: a few souls, workers, hanging around the entrance. But no flood of people, coming to and fro.

'OK, there isn't 10 million in the building.'

I still looked sceptical.

'Oh, you caught us, you know, it's nine [million].'

She was playing with me. We batted on for a bit.

One last question, I said.

'OK, make it good. You haven't even got me riled up yet.'

I am not here to rile people up.

'I thought you were a little spicier,' she was taunting me.

155

I am very tame, I said. What is your view of L Ron Hubbard?

'As a man who cares. A man who cared about mankind. He has given me a gift.'

We carried on some more. I mentioned the c-word and she cut in, gently: 'Stop calling it a cult, it is just not nice. It is disrespectful you know.'

But they say it is, I said.

'I hear what you are saying. But as a journalist and as an Englishman I think it would do you better to stop using that word. It is just disrespectful. I would never say it to somebody. I would just hope that we as human beings would respect each other's beliefs. And it is just not something to say over and over again and it just pushes someone's buttons and that is really not the purpose of doing an interview.'

It is a criticism that the Church of Scientology does not want made, I said. It is a word you don't want the word used.

'Baby, it is not that. It is just about respect. You can call it whatever the hell you want. I personally don't give a shit. But what I am saying is it is about a respect. I would never say that to another person.'

Leah Rimini was the most subtle defender of the Church of Scientology I met.

They had filmed us continually. Mole, Bill and I were desperate to have some time to think alone, to work things out, to process stuff. But they never gave us a break. Somewhere in a gap between interviewees I set off towards the loo, but signalled for Bill and Mole to come with me. I sat down on the toilet seat and Bill and Mole crammed into the rest of the loo. Bill framed me perfectly, looking up from the toilet seat, whispering in fear, directly into the camera: 'We're just having an editorial conference in the loo because it's the only place where we can escape from them.'

That's all I had time to say because Tommy had sniffed us out: 'Are you guys OK in there?' He was up against the door, the proximity of his voice adding an extra dimension to our sense of dread. It was as if we were in *'Jurassic Park'* when the Velociraptor sniffs out the humans hiding in the kitchen.

'Yes,' I replied, quietly despairing.

'All three of you in the bathroom together?' To say his tone was mocking was an understatement. 'Is this like BBC policy or something?'

'It's a BBC requirement,' I said, po-faced. The Church of Scientology is the Church that hunts you down, even on the toilet. And then it was back to work.

Five million dollars is a bob or two in anyone's language. That's reportedly what Kirstie Alley gave to the Church of Scientology in 2007, the very same year I interviewed her at the Church's Celebrity Centre. Five minutes was the time, off-camera, Tommy said I could have with her. Kirstie sat down in the 'are you a member of a brain-washing cult?' hot seat opposite me, and treated me to a look of amused contempt, a tigress surveying a mouse dropping. She has a $1.5m waterfront property in Clearwater. Her fame rests on the hit TV series, *Cheers*, set in a bar in Boston. She is a big woman with big hair and big attitude and, had I encountered her in a different setting, we may have become big friends. But not that day.

Is Scientology a force for good? Or a brainwashing cult?

157

Her snort of derision could have been heard in Moosejaw, which I suspect is somewhere far away from Florida. 'I am just so glad you are asking me something other than why do I get so fat?' (The American media are obsessed with Kirstie's weight, which yo-yos around somewhat.) 'So I am glad you are asking me about religion. Here is the deal. I chose my religion because for me it gives me the most workable tools to handle life.'

The critics say that if you are a practising Scientologist then you must be brainwashed?

Enter the Nazis. 'They assassinated millions of Jews, and their view was that these Jews had horns, they told their children they have horns, they are spawns of the devil. And they created such chaos, and such hatred and such fear that camps were actually built to murder millions of people. So what a human society can do when it is under fear is mind-boggling...'

Fair enough. From there, she changed tack: 'People have the right to believe what they want to believe. And no matter how much you persecute them, no matter how much you beat them into submission, they will not give up what it is innately true to them.'

People who have been in Scientology say that there are effectively dungeons of the mind, I said, places where people that have annoyed the management, David Miscavige...

'...People say there are Martians. Look, I am the tabloid queen. It is....

It is not true, I asked?

'That there are no Martians?'

That Scientology has got punishment camps?

'John, I can't take you seriously...'

That is just not true, you have never heard of it?

'To my knowledge it is not true, but I can't take you seriously. It is like me asking you when was the last time you saw a Martian. Because I know some people in Oklahoma who told me they see Martians in their backyard. And there are those people. Not all Okeys.'

Kirstie is originally from Kansas, immediately due north of Oklahoma. I'm guessing, but presumably Okeys are a byword for credulity and foolishness in Kansas.

Let's talk about aliens, I said. Her first film role back in 1982 was *Star Trek II: The Wrath of Khan*, playing the half-Vulcan/half-Romulan Starfleet officer Lieutenant Saavika, but that wasn't what was on my mind.

Which level are you on?

'Scientology level or which alien level?'

Operating Thetan...?

'Thetan... Does the audience know what Thetan means? Because it means a spirit.'

I am worried that we have only got five minutes, I said. So Operating Thetan...?

'You are not really worried, we can help you with your anxiety.'

Thank you. What level are you?

'I am on OT7, which is an upper level in Scientology.'

So let's talk about aliens, I said. Is it true that Scientologists are told at OT3 that Xenu, the galactic warlord banished souls, alien souls, banished them to earth and then blew them up next to volcanoes?

'That would be not true, John, that would be not true.

Now I have heard other interviews because I have been sitting upstairs and everyone has told you that is not true.'

It was good of Kirstie to confirm that the celebrities had been able to watch the previous interviews. Nothing wrong with that, but until now, no-one had explained that was what was going on.

Kirstie continued, echoing my question: '"But is it true?" This is what I am asking you, this is why I find this fascinating. You guys as journalists keep doing the same story. You have the same ten Scientology defectors and I know their names. They are like the ten Scientology celebrity defectors. They run around the world, they probably make money off it, they certainly get all the attention that they would ever get in their life off it. It is not like there is millions...'

What is not true?

'It's not true. I have already told you it is not true. Leah told you it is not true. Every person is telling you it is not true. Do you still beat your wife, John? Do you still believe in aliens? Do you still keep slaves in your basement, John? Because I heard people say you do. It is not hard to poison people's minds and make them afraid of things. It is the easiest thing in the world. And as far as religion goes it is the super, the easiest thing in the world. All you have to do is to say something sort of freaky about somebody's religion and suddenly you can get people up in arms, oh my God, we are so fearful. And then you have things happen like the Holocaust.'

I had, if you recall, asked her a question about Lord Xenu. With great energy and passion, Kirstie seemed to me to be suggesting that I might have a penchant for singing the *Horst Vessel* song and heel-clicking my shiny black boots. I don't think being sceptical about Xenu makes me a Nazi, but that seemed to be the implication. Still, she was on a roll.

'...I could go on and on about religion through history and show you where people like to incite fear so that people will attack. So I can't say that I see that you are doing anything other than trying to incite fear. Because if you wanted a real story, that's Scientology. Look if I wanted a real story about what Christianity was, I would read the Bible. And then I would go talk to ministers, and I would talk to parishioners. I would not go interview Judas.'

Well, I would you see, I said. Because it [an interview with Judas – Why I Betrayed My Friend Jesus] is a good story.

Tommy: 'Seven minutes.'

Kirstie: (to Tommy) 'I'm fine.' She turned her attention back to me: 'It is not a good story, John. I tell you what, a thousand people have done it.'

I would interview Judas.

'You might and you might fall in love with Judas but if you want to find the upside of Judas, would you be trying to find the upside of Judas because he doesn't exist.'

Never mind Judas, I said, thoroughly confused. I would like to interview David Miscavige. You are an actress. You are happy to talk to me. Why can't the leader of Scientology talk to a journalist on camera. Not since 1992?

'Because they see crazy things like you. You may not be a bigot but the question is, would you ever ask a Jewish person, would you ever sit with a Jew and say what was...?' We were talking over each other.

'... less than half a century ago there was a whole group of people and you would have been over there interviewing.

161

Right now, you would be researching the Nazis to find out about Judaism instead of reading the Torah.'

Are you saying that I am an equivalent of...

'I am saying you are the equivalent of a bigot yes. Because this is what bigots do.'

Are you calling me a Nazi?

'I am calling you a bigot. Did you not hear me? I am calling you a bigot. You are a bigot. Would you ever sit with a Jew and tell them that their religion was a cult?'

She sounded very angry. I did not raise my voice, but I found what she seemed to be implying offensive.

No.

'Why?'

Because Judaism, I said, is bigger than that.

I went on to raise with Kirstie the case of the Kabbalah Centre, which critics say is a sinister religious cult, a kind of 'Jewish Scientology', a charge it strongly denies. Kabbalah's most famous adherent is Madonna. In 2005 a TV investigation found the Kabbalah Centre selling Zohar books and bottled water at very high prices. They claimed they could cure cancer with their water. One undercover investigator was told how the Kabbalah water worked, with a devotee explaining: 'We start with the purest artesian water and then we do the various meditations, injecting energy into it.' The Kabbalah Centre website explained that a process called Quantum Resonance Technology 'restructures the intermolecular binding of spring water'. The investigation discovered the water actually comes from CJC Bottling, a bottling plant in Ontario, Canada, which was the subject of a public health investigation in 2002 into how its water was tested. CJC was ordered to improve manufacturing techniques, though there was no suggestion that they ever sold polluted water. The investigation was shown in a BBC documentary called *Sweeney Investigates: The Kabbalah Centre,* directed by Nobel prize nominee Callum Macrae. One of our undercover investigators was Mole, allowing me to broadcast the following line: 'so we decided to send in a Mole...'

I left all of that out, but I did put to Kirstie that the Kabbalah Centre was, its critics said, a cult.

'I am not a Kabbalist,' she said, 'but I can tell you it is not, and I can tell you some of the finest people I know are Kabbalists. So why do you think it is a story? Journalism isn't about the finding the most hideous things in life. You should go to prison,' – I guess that was a verbal slip – 'you should go into a prison and you should interview people of different religions and ask them if they have anything to do with why they are in prison, that would be a better story.'

My job is to ask questions, I said. People who spent many years of their lives in Scientology have told me that it is a rip-off, it tells people rubbish and it warps their minds.

'Are you really concerned about that, does that bother you?'

And I am asking you as a public face of Scientology why is it that the leader of Scientology, David Miscavige is so terrified of that question that he won't give an interview?

'See the way you say this, this is how bigots...'

It is a question, I said.

'No, it isn't a question. It is like: "do you still beat your wife?" Listen John, "I know that you molested children for three years, is that still going on?" Is that a question? No. It is a loaded gun, and you know exactly what you are doing.'

The argy-bargy continued. We did brainwashing cult; Miscavige's reluctance to be interviewed and then we got onto the Scientology critic with the sign in Florida.

What is his name, I asked her.

'The guy from Clearwater? Dennis…'

She had not been paying proper attention. No, I was thinking of Shawn. It was like a mad, mad parlour game.

Why are you so terrified of criticism, I asked?

'Do I look terrified to you?'

She did not. I had meant the Church as a whole, but never mind.

We did the Church's Volunteer Ministers at Hurricane Katrina, her admiration for British people, the BBC and *The Vicar of Dibley* – she was prepping up to do the American version of the BBC comedy about an Anglican woman vicar; the series was never broadcast – and then it was back to me: 'talk about immoral, and talk about creepy…this is creepy.'

Talk about creepy? I hadn't talked about creepy with Kirstie at all. The last mention of the word 'creepy', I think, had occurred much earlier when I had challenged Tommy about the car chase and he had flung the 'creepy' word back at me. Kirstie could only have picked up on 'talk about creepy' from the celebrity real-time screening upstairs, so when Tommy had a go at me earlier he was very much on display mode. At the time I was so punch-drunk I didn't properly understand the game they were playing with me and just carried on.

OK, I said. What is the RPF?

'I don't know.'

You haven't heard of it? Do you use the internet?

'No, I don't because I am a little bit stupid on the internet. I am a little bit in the 1940s. I can't do the internet.'

Had I known about it then, I would have ticked Lifton's test number one for information control.

We did Narconon; she thought it was great and had seen the real effect it had on improving people's lives; I reported what the doubting doctor had told me, that heroin was not fat-soluble, that there was no scientific basis to Narconon's claims. Then we discussed the founder of the Church. To Kirstie, Mr Hubbard was 'a very intelligent man who really cared a lot about mankind and really wanted to help people and I believe that his goals were, which are the goals of the Church of Scientology, a world without insanity, a world without criminality, and a world without war.'

There is stuff on the internet...

'I am not on the internet, John remember?'

Scientology in my experience, I told her, is the first ever 'religion' that I have ever dealt with which the moment I am talking to a critic rushes out, finds me, hands over a copy of a criminal record. The Church of Scientology seems to be uniquely a religion – or it claims to be a religion – that is so incredibly damning of people who criticise it.

'Where did you get that?'

My own observation.

'Your own observation. I am probably damning of you because you are calling it a cult. You are doing nice polite things like calling it a cult, money-mongering, I don't remember your other terminology. You have called me brainwashed. So am I supposed to sit here with manners? I don't know, do brainwashed people behave like this? I always thought that brainwashed people behaved like sort of like zombies. That's what I thought. Because I thought actually if you read that research on brainwashing which they used during wars, they deprive people of sleep, food and they administer torture. Isn't that how you brainwash somebody?'

And that is exactly what some ex-Scientologists say happened to them inside Scientology.

'Is it possible that those ten people who do this as a living, is it possible that they are the nuts? And not the millions of people who just go on about their lives and try and do better in their lives and then the ten dudes are the weird asses? Isn't that possible?'

Yes, it is possible. So if that is possible, then why spend so much energy attacking them?

'I don't spend one ounce of time in my life attacking or vilifying them. You are doing a show for the BBC. If this shows airs in front of millions of people, so if you decide to take a slant which I think you already have that this is a whatever it is, a mind-warping thing that you have got going, I would just love the opportunity to say to the British people y'know that is not me, and if you care to know about my religion, read a damn book, read a book. That will teach you what Scientology is and you can decide to do it or not do it, I don't care.'

I brought up Xenu, again.

'The guys that are telling you these crazy alien things, they are nuts. Do you think the guys who see the aliens in their backyard... Look, John, I wish there were aliens. I wish we had an ET or two around. I would hope that some place in all of the stars and all of the planets and all the galaxies there is some other form of life, because we are destroying this planet. And I would love to have another planet to go to.'

Money came up. It is a pay as you go religion?

'No. You can do a lot of things in Scientology for free. You can't build churches for free. And I don't know any other religion where you can. Do you?'

The difference is that say, for example, Christianity, the scriptures are open and freely available. Not with yours. Your religion is different.

'I don't know that Christianity that they are all open and available. I don't know that.'

The bible is.

'I know the bible is.'

If you don't hand over the cash, you don't get to know, you don't go up a level?

'That is a lie... You are so loving the gossip and the bad news and the creepy little things of life, don't you? It makes me wonder about you personally because you love such creepy little creepy things that I wonder what you are up to really on your weekend off.'

Her implication hinted at some inner darkness I might possess. On my weekend off, I go to the pub, walk the dog, watch Dr Who, spend time with my family, snooze over the Sunday papers, go to the pub.

Why should the rest of the world think that Scientology is a religion, I asked?

'Because the IRS does.'

The American tax man?

'Because it acknowledges the religion in most countries in the world. Because it deals with the spiritual being, because

167

it deals with the here and now and the hereafter and faith, I don't know. I think that is the definition of a religion, John. So I think it is a religion. It doesn't have one element to it that does not make it a religion.'

Then the tape ran out. Alleluia. The interview with Kirstie was supposed to have lasted five minutes. It felt like five years.

They fielded four more celebrity Scientologists that day, Megan Shields, Bob Adams, Bobby Wiggins and Michael Duff, none of whom I'd ever heard of, all of whom said nothing different in substance from what Anne, Leah and Kirstie had told me. It was as if I had spoken to not Scientology's Magnificent Seven but one person alone.

Of the four also-rans Bobby Wiggins stood out a bit as an expert on Narconon. He asked me whether I had any problems with addictive drugs. I told him alcohol. Knowing how the Church works, I reckoned that telling them something everyone who knows me knows was the better policy than absolute denial or a blank refusal to discuss the matter. He suggested I take up Narconon to solve my problems with alcohol, advice which, I fear, I have yet to heed.

Interviews over, it was time to get out of there. It wasn't just a question of feeling mentally exhausted, although I was, deeply. There was an extra dimension to how I felt, a kind of spiritual exhaustion, too. My soul, if I have one, was burnt out. Tommy had different ideas. He launched at me, yet again: 'And that you sit in this room across from these esteemed women and treat them disgustingly.'

'I don't think you understand the nature of journalism, with respect,' I said.

'No, no, no. I understand the nature of you as a person.'

'Very good, thank you,' I said.

'You have no objectivity whatsoever - zero. Because Shawn Lonsdale, convicted sexual pervert, is your pal that you are chauffering around Clearwater?'

I told Tommy that Shawn was not my pal. He attacked me for asking the interviewees whether they were in a brainwashing cult. I told him that I am a reporter, and we interview people who are critical of things, and I will talk to anybody on the planet about anything if I think it necessary.

'Have I ever complained about you talking to them?' asked Tommy with a mind-warping lack of self-knowledge. He had done nothing but complain about them.

He told me that I had been far more 'lenient and forgiving' with Shawn than with their celebrities. I batted that away politely, and told him, yet again, that we were making our film on our terms.

'No, you are making this film with no objectivity, from a bigoted, slanted, pre-conceived already determined idea of exactly how it is going to go because you decided what Scientology was the day, long before you ever even called us.'

'OK, that's it. We need to go.'

As we took the lift down – I can't be sure this happened at this moment or another time at the Celebrity Centre – Tommy carried the camera tripod. In the lift, with no cameras running, he was charming, polite, chatty, convivial. The switch from Tommy Nasty, ranting, preposterously in-yer-face thug, to Tommy Nice, was mind-bending. Is this the same person? Am I really seeing this? Is this happening? Am I going mad?

We got in our car and drove away. One block, two blocks, three, four, five. And then I started to scream, a long roar of frustration, fuelled by fear that I was losing my grip on reality. Collectively and cumulatively, they were doing my head in.

And them? How had our day at the Celebrity Centre gone for the Church? According to the Sci'gy-Leaks messages between Tommy Davis and Mike Rinder and the Leader's Communicator, Lou Stuckenbrock, who speaks on his behalf, rather well. Last time we looked inside the mind of the organization it was the evening of Wednesday, 21st March, after I had interviewed Anne Archer, Leah Rimini and Kirstie Alley and the other chaps I had never heard of. The Communicator had wanted to know whether there were any areas they should avoid and how many '*new (torn wall to wall) assholes*' my body now had.

Mike answered: '*Dear Sir. They are staying in best western hotel on sunset at sunset plaza.*'

The location of our hotel was information we did not share with the Church.

'*They definitely have many new assholes and more to come tmro… Kirstie, anne, leah, bobby wiggins, bob adams, michael duff, megan shields all went after him today. He was repeatedly exposed as a bigot and tabloid bottomfeeder. Anne and kirstie in particular went for the jugular on his bias.*'

What is so striking is that those two phrases, bigot and tabloid bottom-feeder, were thrown at me again and again. Were the Scientology seven rehearsed in their responses to me? Who knows?

'*He was demolished on NN* [Narconon] *and didnt know how to handle the facts when confronted with them as had been relying on assertion that heroin doesnt lodge in fatty tissues. We are right now briefing CCHR* [The Citizens Commission on Human

Rights, a Scientology front group that campaigns against psychiatry] *ppl for tmro. They headed west on sunset from their hotel. Ml Mike.'*

It wasn't a good enough answer for the Leader's Communicator.

'The only specific you give is on Heroin in fatty tissue. Screw that. Not that it doesn't, but people get off drugs!!!!!!!! I guess he doesn't care about that????

Were these ass rippings on camera? What did he think when Anne went after him for saying her son is brainwashed. Any other details you Generality infested CSMF?'

The 'ass rippings' Miscavige's Communicator was concerned about were filmed on five cameras. Generality means waffle. CSMF stands for 'Cock Sucking Mother Fucker', not a phrase normally associated with say, His Grace, The Archbishop of Canterbury.

Mike replied: *'He got flustered when anne said he was a bigot and had accused her son of being brainwashed. he even said that 'some ppl say u (anne) r brainwashed... He was v upset and tried to argue with her that he isnt a bigot.'*

'Kirstie derided him... Leah disarmed him entirely as she was very polite...

'He asked anne, kirstie and leah why we were afraid of critics in general and why wld david miscavige be afraid of being interviewed by the BBC. This was stuck up his ass that this was ridiculous and that cob [Chairman of the Board: Miscavige] *fear's nothing...*

The Leader's office even got to hear about our team trip to the toilet: *'Sweeney, Sarah* [Mole] *and the cameraman all going into the bathroom together to talk (which we have on. Video with tommy at the door asking why they are hiding in the bathroom together).'*

How this can be written us as victory for the Church I do not understand. It was an elephant trap of a joke at the Church's expense, and they fell for it, tuskers and all.

'Throughout the day we hammered him with the majority of the 120+ questions we had put together...'

It felt like 120,000.

'Bobby got sweeney talking so much that he told bobby that he is an alcoholic and does himself abuse alcohol and that it is a problem for him. Bobby told him how narconon cld help him with that.'

I like a drink but I'm not an alcoholic. But as far as Narconon goes, I'd rather drown, like the poor Duke of Clarence in Shakespeare's *Richard III*, in a butt of malmsey.

CHAPTER EIGHT
'They want you to be afraid.'

I t's hard to get across just how weird all of this was. I had spent the whole day inside a mock-French chateau in Hollywood talking to seven people all of whom denied being in a cult and passed the evening with a man who said oh yes they were. It was like being trapped inside a cosmological panto, *Xenu in Boots*. Black is white! *Oh no it's not.* Xenu doesn't exist. *Oh yes he does.* Is Scientology's a cult? *Oh no it's not.* Oh yes it is.

Rick Ross is probably the leading expert on cults in the western world. His mentor was Margaret Singer, the gutsy psychologist who in her 80s once scared a cult member off her property with a shotgun and believed that cults were con tricks. Singer was on the board of the Rick A. Ross Institute. Rick's website is one of the most extensive archives of cult activity on the planet. As Kentucky Fried Chicken is to Colonel Saunders, then counter-cults is to Rick Ross, if you get my breaded chicken leg.

Or, if you believe the Church, Rick is nothing more than a convicted felon with 'an extensive history of mental instability and dangerous conduct dating back to childhood, which psychiatrists concluded stems from his anti-social, manipulative behaviour and his sexual problems.' I found him to be a rock of common sense.

We'd first met Rick when we made the film about the Kabbalah Centre. His view on Madonna's 'religion' was a world apart from that of Kirstie Alley: 'The Kabbalah Centre caters to the narcissism of many celebrities. They want to have enlightenment, they want to be happy and they want people to cater it. Just like the catering trucks on location for their movies.'

Is Scientology a force for good as they say, I asked Rick.

'I don't see anything wrong with respecting Scientology's right to practice their religion. The problem is the harm that they have done over the years to people. It is expensive, and it can be harmful to people and it can cause a great deal of distress.'

What harm?

'First, Scientology is very expensive, so when people take courses or they go through auditing or through the purification run down or whatever they do, it costs money. I receive complaints from families that say, unlike some of the movie stars who can easily afford Scientology, they can't. It has caused them financial distress. And I would say that the basis for Scientology, specifically some of the claims made by L Ron Hubbard, just don't bear any close scrutiny. They are just not factually based.'

Ross gave the Narconon programme as an example: 'Hubbard said that you needed to do the purification run down because toxins or poisons are stored indefinitely within the fatty tissues of the body. That's just not true, according to medical science. That's why the Narconon programme was asked here in California to leave the public school system because their programme was not scientifically or factually based.'

They told me that is not true, I said.

'They don't have the support of the school system as they once did. But for them it was a matter of faith. The faith that when L Ron Hubbard says something it is true, whether the science supports it or not. The problem is with many of the things that L Ron Hubbard taught that there is no scientific basis for it. He was a science fiction writer, not a scientist.'

They denied Xenu. Is that right?

'Well, they are not really answering you. They may give you a kind of evasive answer, they may say it is ridiculous, they may say it is preposterous, "who told you that?" But the point is, if they have reached Operating Thetan Level III, OT3, they have been told about the incident, which includes a galactic overlord named Xenu, it includes space-ships coming to earth. It includes a residue of space aliens that remain, on you, on me, and we need Scientology to get rid of them. Now if you are in OT3 or higher in Scientology, you know that. But according to the church if you are not an OT3 you are not prepared to hear it. And so they may withhold that information because John, they think you are not ready yet.'

But that means that their theology requires them to lie to people?

'Well they may parse their language and talk in circles. But if you ask them: "Is it true that if you have reached OT3, you were told about an incident? And that incident involved aliens from outer space coming to a planet called Teegeeack now

175

known as Earth, and that that incident had a direct impact upon the world then and continues to have an impact upon humanity today?" they would have to either stonewall you or admit well yes, there are bits and pieces of that that are true. And in some interviews Scientologists have admitted bits and pieces.'

Is it a cult?

'They seem to fit the criteria that most people that examine cults would attribute to a cult: that the group is personality driven, and that personality would be L Ron Hubbard. He is dead now, but he has been replaced by David Miscavige. So the group has an absolute totalitarian leader that has no meaningful accountability. Ask Tom Cruise when the last time was that David Miscavige ran for re-election. He won't have an answer for you.'

Rick moved on to brainwashing: 'Second, that the group uses a process that can be seen as thought reform or what is popularly called brainwashing. That is a control of information, of the environment and a manipulation of people in such a way as to gain undue influence over them psychologically and emotionally. Third, that the group does harm. That they take advantage of people in one way or another. Now Scientology appears to fit those three criteria in my opinion. And that is why many people have called the group a cult.'

Rick's three definers of a cult mirror Lifton's.

What about David Miscavige, I asked Rick? I put to him the allegations that he thumps people. I summarised what Bruce Hines had told me, that Miscavige had come into his office and said where is the mother-fucker? and then hit him. Did Rick find that story astonishing?

'I don't know if that story is true or untrue. But what I do know is that David Miscavige is an absolute authoritarian leader, that he has no meaningful accountability to the general membership through democratic, elected church government, and that he pretty much is in a position of leader for life, the same role, in many ways, that L Ron Hubbard once held. In that sense, he can pretty much do what he wants.'

I asked Rick why Miscavige last gave an interview to TV in 1992.

'He appears at Scientology events. He does photo ops for Scientology publications. But he is not a person that is very friendly or forthcoming with the media.'

What about the money?

'Scientology is a very rich church. When L Ron Hubbard died [in 1986] his fortune was estimated at about $600 million. So Hubbard amassed assets, cash and Scientology remains a very visibly wealthy organisation. Look at all their building projects just in the last two or three years in cities across the United States and around the world. They have been on a kind of building marathon. Spending millions and millions to refurbish buildings, to build new branches and so on. But I wonder how many members there really are to support all that structure. There is no doubt that it is a very rich organisation.'

A billion dollars?

'I think conservatively they are certainly over a billion dollars in net assets.'

It is hard to work out a reliable number in the absence of any disclosed figures but if you tot up the real estate assets of the Church in Florida and California you could hit a billion dollars pretty quickly. Add the rest of its assets in the United States in cities such as New York, Washington DC, San Francisco and Europe – there are ten Scientology centres in Britain, including four in prime-sites in London, on the Tottenham Court Road, on Victoria Street near Blackfriars, on Fitzroy Street and New Cavendish Street and 50 acres in Sussex – and that number could easily be two or three billion dollars.

They say 10 million members?

'I don't think there is anywhere near the millions of members that Scientology has claimed. In fact some people estimate the membership may actually be below 100,000, based on their fund raising, and people that show up for events and mailings. When Scientology says they have millions of members, I think, what they mean is over the years, from the 1950s, millions of people have at one time or another been on a mailing list. Whether they are really true supporters, take courses, give money to the Church, that's another question entirely.'

That would chime with my own observation. For example, someone who used to live at our house in London years ago is still sent mail shots and magazines from the Church. I wonder, then, if our house is listed as a Scientology one. For the avoidance of doubt, no Scientologists live in my house, at least, not yet.

What about the private eyes? I told him about the chase when we arrived in LA.

'That is what Scientology would call a noisy investigation. They want you to know that they are following you. They want you to be afraid. To be very afraid of them, to be intimidated. And the idea of following you all around is to create that kind of fear that they are watching you and it will affect your reporting.'

That seemed to me a terrifyingly perceptive observation.

'Many people that have been critical of Scientology have experienced a noisy investigation. The objective is intimidation. To get you to stop doing whatever it is that they want you to stop doing. They want control of the public perception of their organisation. And they want their image to be a certain way and if they feel a critical report is coming out they are concerned about that.'

Every critic we have spoken to, Scientology has got an instant label for them. What have they got on you?

'A 19-page pdf document exists on me on the internet. They have traced back my childhood all the way to the age of eight. I got counselling, I got in trouble as a youth, all of it is in Scientology's pdf file. I mean that is part of what it is all about. If you criticise them, expect them to literally go through your garbage.'

Have they gone through your garbage?

'I have reason to think that they have gone through my garbage. And not only Scientology, a couple of other groups. There have been incidents where private investigators have gone door to door in a neighbourhood I used to live in, asking questions about me. This was just a couple of years ago. I think that was a private investigator hired and paid for by the church of Scientology. There were efforts to have my phone number forwarded to another number. And my fax number forwarded to another number some years ago. The phone company called to tell me, they didn't have my passwords on my account, they failed. I believe that was someone working for Scientology. So I have been stalked, I have had private investigators harass me and my neighbours. And I have experienced quite a bit at the hands of Scientology. But that just comes with the territory. If you want to look at them and examine them critically, they will do that.'

The private eyes, the constant filming, people dressed in black. The intense aggression to any kind of open criticism. Is this an organisation steeped in mass paranoia?

'Organisations like Scientology that have been called cults are mirrors of their founder or leader's personality. L Ron Hubbard was often described by his critics as paranoid. Even delusional. Some people thought he was mad. Hubbard is the assumed prototype of the most perfected human being that Scientology can offer. He is their model. And they mimic him. You could even say that the whole auditing process of Scientology and its courses are a way to make you more Hubbardist or Hubbard-like. So in that sense what you perceive as paranoia may just be a kind of cloning of Hubbard's personality.'

We wanted to interview Miscavige and Tom Cruise, the leader and the chief apostle of Scientology. Do you think we are going to succeed?

'Doubtful. They probably have established that you are not going to do a puff piece, a friendly report that they approve of. And I don't know that they will give you access to David Miscavige. And Tom Cruise is in a very vulnerable point in his career, and I would think that at this point he is not really happy to do an interview with someone like you that might be critical of his Church.'

His needle is floating?

'Some people think his career is sinking because of his

constant preaching and proselytising regarding Scientology. People here in the States see Tom Cruise increasingly as a weird and a bizarre character. And I think that is largely because of him going on and on about Scientology.'

What is in it for the celebrities?

'Celebrities are very specially treated and catered to in Scientology. They have these Celebrity Centres where they go. They are waited on hand and foot. They are pampered, they are just treated in a way that some would argue that they feel entitled to, accustomed to, through their celebrity status. And this carries over even into their Church life. So being a celebrity in Scientology is a lot different than being a grunt, being a Sea Organisation member and waiting on celebrities in the Celebrity Centre. And that is why celebrities, they really don't see the tough stuff compared to the regular rank and file. Certainly not treated like Sea Org members.'

But Cruise, Travolta, the others, because they live in the public world, because they are public figures, they must know that out there, there are people who are deeply critical of Scientology. They must know about these stories of people talking about mental torture. Why don't they act on that?

'Scientology celebrities like Tom Cruise, John Travolta and others, they don't believe the stories that are critical about Scientology. They see it as somehow part of a larger conspiracy by drug companies, psychiatrists and media to lynch them. To persecute them. And they don't believe those stories. They think that they are false, that they are propaganda and they dismiss them.'

I asked Rick about our two minders, Mike Rinder and Tommy Davis? He didn't know much about Tommy but Mike had crossed his radar – and in Rick's view held a higher position that his current lowly status suggested.

'Mike Rinder is often talked about as number two in Scientology. If you will, Miscavige is leader for life and Mike Rinder is something of the enforcer. He deals with Scientology's perceived enemies and he can be a pretty tough customer. He is associated with the Office of Special Affairs. That is the area of Scientology that is responsible for dealing with the outside world, threats to the church, perceived enemies and so on. So Rinder is the cutting edge of Scientology's machine that it uses to deal with anyone and everyone outside.'

People have told me that he has a reputation for ripping people's faces off. Well, what the hell does that mean?

'Mike Rinder can be very harsh. He can describe Scientology's enemies in a very harsh way. And you know it is important to understand how that all evolved. It was all part of L Ron Hubbard's teachings. That is go after those that are your enemies before they can get you, get them first. And get them better. And find out what their vulnerable areas are and exploit them. It is all part of Scientology's teachings. The teaching of their prophet Hubbard.'

Why do celebrities get involved in Scientology?

'Because L Ron Hubbard said so. L Ron Hubbard taught that by recruiting celebrities or important people, VIPs, that you could garner the attention that you wanted in order to recruit other people. So Hubbard taught his followers that they should specifically target notable people, celebrities, movie stars. And they have done exactly that. The creation of the Celebrity Centres is dedicated to that principle. That if you can get someone like Tom Cruise to join Scientology, or

John Travolta, these people are icons in pop culture. And you can influence the public, and then you can garner attention and use that to recruit even more people.'

Rick reflected on how the Church deals with critics: 'Scientology has used litigation at times almost like an article of faith. They have sued anyone that criticised them. They sued Time magazine and they sued an organisation called the Cult Awareness Network here in the United States more than 70 times until they bankrupted the organisation and then they bought its name, its files, its phone number and even I think its post office box, whatever assets it had, in a bankruptcy liquidation sale. They literally took over their former enemy. It would kind of be like the Anti Defamation League of the United States which is run by Jews being taken over by Neo-Nazis.'

The Church's celebrities dissed the internet. What did he make of that?

'So Scientology has – probably more than any other single organisation that I can think of that has been called a cult – fought a kind of war on the internet to silence their critics, to purge them from the net, and to keep information that they don't want their members to read, from appearing on the internet.'

I asked Rick about auditing, the intimate questions about your sex life. Is it possible that that could open you to blackmail?

'When you are being audited, John, they are taking copious notes. That goes into what is called your pre-clear file or folder. And whatever you say can become part of that file. And many people that become involved in auditing sign a release in which they give Scientology rights over that file that they relinquish. So what that means is that your innermost secrets, the darkest things that you have in your history, in your life, may be revealed and brought out and examined through auditing, which I would see more like interrogation. And the E-meter as a kind of apparatus similar to a lie detector.'

That raises the possibility that you could be blackmailed?

'Persistent rumours that have come out about Scientology and in particular about celebrities is that they are reluctant to leave the Church because they are afraid. They are afraid of what Scientology knows about their personal life. And I have had calls from former members of Scientology who are not only afraid of what the organisation has on them, but they are afraid that they will no longer be able to communicate with family members that are still in the church. So that is a concern. There are many ways that they can retaliate against someone who has left the organisation.'

That was the gist of the verdict given by Judge Breckenridge in 1984. Rick Ross was saying that nothing much had changed. We left Rick to his lonely war, and went for a bite, wondering what on earth the morrow would bring.

CHAPTER NINE
The Industry of Death

At 6616 Sunset Boulevard you can find the 'Psychiatry: An Industry of Death' exhibition. Tommy led me along the line of greeters: Jan Eastman, a blond, middle-aged Australian lady, President of the Citizens Commission on Human Rights International (CCHR), Bruce Wiseman, President CCHR for the USA, Marla Filidei, a blond American and the Vice President of the CCHR, Fran Andrews, the executive director, and Rick Moxam, General Counsel for the CCHR – fancy talk for a lawyer. Someone handed me a cup of tea and I stared at the entrance to the exhibition, a great black steel door, suggesting the entrance to a gas chamber or a totalitarian torture chamber, or, to be more precise, a Hollywood set designer's idea of the above.

Tommy kicked off by introducing me to the lawyer, Moxam: 'You may recall from the event' – I think he was referring to one of the ultra-long videos they showed us at Saint Hill what seemed a trillion years ago – 'Rick was the one who did the brief that went to the Supreme Court on the admissibility, on psychiatrists being no more valid to give testimony on someone's sanity in a case than anybody else. Do you remember that from the event?'

I did not.

'Sure thing,' I told Tommy.

'OK, good,' he said.

The CCHR claims to be wholly separate from the Church of Scientology. Ex- Scientologists say the CCHR is its creature. Tommy just so happened to address what was on my mind. He indicated Team CCHR: 'They also happen to be Scientologists. Jan is OT5, Bruce is 7, Marla is Clear, Fran is Clear and Rick is 7.'

Clear is where?

'Before you start the OT levels,' said Tommy.

Very good.

'Makes sense? Any questions?'

What is your level? I asked Tommy.

'Clear.'

That was weird. Tommy was clearly a senior figure in the Church presiding over this unprecedented access and yet he was low down in the pecking order, almost at the bottom rung of LRH's Road to Total Freedom.

Good. I turned to Mike. And…?

Mike: 'I am not telling you.'

Well, everybody else has…

Mike: 'OT5.'

Very good.

Remember: OT3 is the 'Wall of Fire', when you find out about the space alien Satan, Xenu. The different OT levels mean that of the seven Scientologists present, Bruce, Rick, Jan and Mike knew about Xenu, but Marla, Fran and Tommy did not; nor could Bruce, Rick, Jan and Mike tell Marla, Fran and Tommy about Xenu lest they kill them by telling them the secret their minds were not ready for. During the previous day at the Celebrity Centre, Tommy professed not to know about Xenu – so if the Xenu story is correct he did not lie, but his mum, Leah, Kirstie and Mike did. The Scientologists were not just lying to me; they were lying to each other. This is the hard-wiring problem which results from a 'religion' which keeps its Holiest Writ secret from the lower levels. In Lifton's book, he tells the story of a Catholic bishop unsuccessfully brainwashed by the Chinese Communists who, upon his release, summed up his admiration-tinged condemnation of his captors in the simple statement: 'They lie so truly.'

Is the CCHR separate from the Church? Jan told me that it included non-Scientologists and was set up 'independently by the Church' which didn't sound very independent to me. Very good, I said, and asked, what was the ratio of non-Scientologists to Scientologists?

'Wouldn't have a clue,' said Jan.

Are you sure?

'Absolutely.'

As of that moment outside the CCHR, the organisation's ratio of non-Scientologists to Scientologists was zero-to-seven.

Very good, smashing, lovely cup of tea, thank you. Shall we go into Dante's gates of hell?

The great steel door swung open to reveal an interior of Stygian gloom.

From the early 1950s, psychiatrists blew the whistle on the Church. In return, L Ron demonised the doctors of the mad, accusing 'psychs' of 'extortion, mayhem and murder'. Hubbard believed that psychiatrists were plotting a conspiracy to take over the world on behalf of the Soviet Union: 'Our enemies are less than twelve men. They are members of the Bank of England and other higher financial circles. They own and control newspaper chains and they, oddly enough, run all the mental health groups in the world... Their apparent programme was to use mental health, which is to say psychiatric electric shock and pre-frontal lobotomy, to remove from their path any political dissenters. These fellows have gotten nearly every government in the world to owe them considerable quantities of money through various chicaneries and they control, of course, income tax, government finance. [Harold] Wilson, for instance, the current Premier of England, is totally involved with these fellows and talks about nothing else.'

Harold Wilson, for all his many faults, did no such thing. Hubbard's hatred of psychiatry spawned a novel *Battlefield Earth*, which John Travolta turned into a film of the same name in 2000. The plot of both turns on the war between the evil Catrists, which is, perhaps, a pun on the back-end of the word 'psychiatrists', and the alien Psychlo species. Critics say the wretched Psychlos of *Battlefield Earth* are L Ron's prophecy of how humanity would end up under the thumb of psychiatry were it not for Scientology.

Critical reception of *Battlefield Earth* the movie was something of a curate's egg: 'a cross between *Star Wars* and the smell of ass' cracked Jon Stewart; the *Washington Post* said: 'A million monkeys with a million crayons would be hard-pressed in a million years to create anything as cretinous as *Battlefield Earth*... so breathtakingly awful in concept and execution, it wouldn't tax the smarts of a troglodyte'; the *New*

York Times said it 'may well turn out to be the worst movie of this century' and even Jonathan Ross, who sticks up for Scientology in his biography, said: 'Everything about *Battlefield Earth* sucks. Everything. The over-the-top music, the unbelievable sets, the terrible dialogue, the hammy acting, the lousy special effects, the beginning, the middle and especially the end.'

The Industry of Death museum flows from the same creative spring. My guide was Jan Eastman. The very first thing that hits you in the exhibition is a quote from a gent in eighteenth century get-up, Benjamin Rush, talking about how terror acts powerfully upon the body through the medium of the mind and should be employed in the cure of madness.

That is evil nonsense, I said.

Jan said: 'Benjamin Rush is the father of American psychiatry.'

I did not know anything about Benjamin Rush, then.

'That's a psychiatrist that has actually said that.'

That man was talking evil nonsense, I said. But that doesn't knock out the whole of modern psychiatry.

'Well, why don't we actually go through the museum, because you are actually jumping to conclusions.'

The exhibition was organized chronologically, starting with medieval abuses of the mad, moving up to twenty first century torture. I was staring at a medley of pictures of Bedlam, the old London lunatic asylum, where the mentally ill were put on public show and treated cruelly.

They used to poke people with a stick, didn't they? I said.

'Yes, so you essentially have that concept that if you use pain, terror, punishment in order to change a person's behaviour. You seem to have a pre-disposition to talking about brainwashing.'

I hadn't mentioned brainwashing. How did she know I had brainwashing on the brain?

'Oh, because I have watched some of your stuff.'

You have already watched the Scientology tapes of me?

'Absolutely.'

Very good. Has everybody, just out of interest?

'No,' said Jan. 'I personally wanted to see who I was doing an interview with. So if you look at the 1500s you had Bedlam, that actually used again pain, terror in order to change a person's belief system. And if a psychiatrist or a person or even a relative didn't like your behaviour this was used in order to change a person's behaviour or to incarcerate them. So rather than just go into a whole interview about it now, what I want you to see is the first documentary which sets up the whole biological model of psychiatry.'

So long as they are not three hours, that's fine, I said. I had spoken too soon.

The first video started, illustrated by paintings and drawings of 18th century wretches suffering revolting treatments at Bethlehem Royal Hospital in London, one of the world's first psychiatric institutions, commonly known as Bedlam. The tone of the voiceover was grim: 'The hospital was little more than a warehouse for those deemed mad. Inmates were confined to cages, closets, and animal stalls, chained to walls and flogged while the asylum charged admission for public viewers. In the 18th century, William Battie was the first to promote that his institutions could cure the mentally ill. Battie's madhouses made him one of the richest men in England.

But his treatments were every bit as inhumane as those prac-
tised in Bedlam with not a single patient cured. His financial success triggered a boom in the asylum business, and an
opportunity for psychiatrists to cash in on this new growth
industry.'

I knew precious little about the history of the treatment
of the mad, then. I do now. This is junk history. Some of the
grim material, audio and visual, was true and historically correct. Much of it was not. I was being indoctrinated with facts
which, once you study them, are not facts; assertions which
either cannot be born out or are obviously untrue. All of it
was manufactured to make one hate the idea of psychiatry,
which is nothing more than the study of how to cure people
with sick minds. No doubt, the early doctors of the mad made
terrible mistakes. But they were grappling with the unknown,
and some of them did good.

Take William Battie, demonized by the Church as a
money-grubber who grew rich out of madness. Born in 1703,
history tells us that Battie was, for his time, an enlightened
doctor, who challenged the conventional wisdom that lunatics should be chained and kept in dungeons. The man who
ran Bedlam disliked Battie greatly because of his open criticisms of the very cruelties that are exhibited in the Scientology museum. Battie's book 'Treatise on Madness' – which
now, if you dare to use the internet, you can read – sets out in
eighteenth century English why a series of cruel and abusive
treatments of the mad do not work. There is much wrong in
this book, we now know, but it strikes me as an honest attempt
to think about the mentally ill rationally and with kindness.

Back to the video, the voiceover still banging away, 'while

those who ran the institutions were getting rich, psychiatrists yet lacked the credibility to maximise their cash flow…'

Our ignorance of history makes us slander our own times, wrote Gustave Flaubert. Treating the mentally ill, in the eighteenth century or today, is not a route to making money, and to suggest that it is seems foolish.

'In order to justify their profession they needed to come with these biological solutions… In essence, torture… For example, one device involved putting the patient into a coffin, closing the lid, and dumping it into a bath of water.'

Again, junk history. True, the mentally ill were ill-treated for centuries. True, they were long thought to be possessed by demons or evil spirits. True, they suffered vile and abusive practices in lunatic asylums. But in 1790 an English Quaker woman, Hannah Mills, fell mentally ill and was admitted to the York Asylum. She died a few weeks after she had been admitted. Her loved ones investigated, and discovered foul conditions where the patients were treated worse than animals. A Quaker, William Tuke, set up a model mental hospital in York, known as the York Retreat, where the mentally ill were treated decently, as human beings. No bars on the windows, no patients manacled. Psychiatrists around the world took note and things began to change for the better.

Higher up the social order, the king of England lost America and then went stark, staring raving bonkers. The madness of King George III was a personal tragedy for him and a harbinger of the future. The radical poet Shelley wrote: 'An old, mad, blind, despised, and dying King.' But George III's ministers and court noted that his mental agonies came and went and, when not foaming at the mouth, in his periods of lucidity, George could be sweet and kind and sensible.

From the monarchy down, a new sympathy for the mentally ill grew. It was only with the publication of *George III and The Mad Business* by Ida Macalpine and Richard Hunter in 1969 that the king's malady was explained by intermittent attacks of a hereditary disease, porphyria. The Quakers in York and the king's illness both changed the climate in which mentally ill people were treated – one century and a half before the birth of the Church of Scientology and an unsung revolution not reflected in their exhibition.

The video had still not finished: 'Pushing the biological theory of mental illness a step further an American, Benjamin Rush... He bled his patients for madness... He was so revered that in 1965 Rush was enshrined as the father of American psychiatry on the seal of the American Psychiatric Association...'

The video hammered on, pile-driving images of horror and cruelty into my brain.

Junk history, again. The exhibition's take on Rush is unfair and ahistorical. Rush may have written that terror can treat madness, and that is wrong; Rush may have believed in bloodletting, and, that, too is wrong, but that was a common medical view in the late eighteenth century and early nineteenth. History sees Rush as a great and humane doctor. Born in 1745, he became a signatory of the American Declaration of Independence, the greatest single political document ever written, and was an early opponent of the slave trade and capital punishment. In the field of mental health, he was revolted at the grim conditions mental patients were held in the Pennsylvania Hospital. In 1792 – two years after the Quakers in York started their movement for proper psychiatric care in England – he campaigned for the state to build a separate ward where mental patients could be treated more humanely. He opposed the reigning practice of chaining mental patients in dungeons, noted that patients given decent work recovered much better than those kept locked up and is considered a pioneer of occupational therapy. In his book, *Diseases of the Mind,* he wrote: 'It has been remarked, that the maniacs of the male sex in all hospitals, who assist in cutting wood, making fires, and digging in a garden, and the females who are employed in washing, ironing, and scrubbing floors, often recover, while persons, whose rank exempts them from performing such services, languish away their lives within the walls of the hospital'.

Rush was one of the first doctors to identify alcoholism as a form of medical disease not a sin, and one of the first to identify Savant Syndrome, in which autistic patients, as we now call them, can be brilliant mathematicians. Tom Cruise starred in a film about a sufferer of the syndrome, *Rain Man,* in 1988, having already enjoyed his first contact with the Church through his then girlfriend, Mimi Rogers, which makes Scientology's demonization of Rush all the more peculiar.

Had I been less ignorant of the true history of Rush, I would not have accepted Scientology's version of him uncritically. Yet again, the Church says x is bad; on critical examination of the evidence, there is some fragment of truth to what the Church says, but it is partial, unfair and untrue to the whole picture.

The video had not finished: 'As the 1800s wore on psychiatry.… In curing madness threatened their financial… forcing them to invent a new medical model. The cure that was promised wasn't delivered. So by the 1860s and 70s the growing pessimism was covering Europe and North America, and if that didn't... The new institutions were ever growing in size but not growing in their effectiveness. The 20th century brought more medical models. American psychiatrist Henry Cotton mutilated his patients by removing their body parts, declaring this a breakthrough in the treatment of mental illness. The earliest target was the teeth, and then the tonsils, and the sinuses... so stomachs need to go, spleens need to go, colons need to go as public outcry escalated over torture and maiming of patients, psychiatrists would have been... Each one hailed as the miracle of cure. But each one was ultimately proven no more effective nor less brutal than the last.'

I watched dumb-struck as I saw up on the video screen a big close-up of a mouth. Historically, it is true that New Jersey psychiatrist Henry Cotton did great harm, killing hundreds of his patients with wholly unnecessary operations before his death in 1933. It was a classic case of one charismatic man wielding power without checks and balances, without scrutiny.

The video still hadn't finished: 'a huge part of what psychiatry has done really comes down to torture...'

Very good, very high production values, I said. This is 'Telly Twaddle' for the 'look' of a film, leaving any comment as to its content unsaid. I was trying to be polite.

'Yes, isn't it?' said Jan.

'We are quite good at making documentaries,' said Tommy.

I was commending you for your production values, I said, silently leaving the matter of editorial judgment on the tiles, waiting for the cat to sniff it. I turned to Tommy, and asked: when is your film coming out by the way?

'I am not going to tell you,' said Tommy.

Well, you will know when ours is coming out.

'You will get it in the post,' he said.

But we would like to have your film so we can put a bit of your film in our film, I said. It will make our film more fun. Nothing doing.

'OK,' said Jan, seizing hold of the conch, as it were: 'So this is where we start off the Pavlovian conditioning and it goes into brainwashing.' She quoted some German psychiatrist - Wilhelm... Ho??? Who? ' I didn't quite catch the name – 'who said the soul does not exist...' My brain cells were dying, hand over fist... '...which is something that we are philosophically opposed to...'

A word-picture of the scene: we're in a big gloomy box on Sunset Boulevard, being filmed by two black-clad Scientology camera people, Reinhardt and Sylviana, plus a black-clad soundman, watched over by seven Scientologists, four of whom know about their space alien Satan and three of whom do not, looking at ghastly pictures of human beings being tortured, brains being drilled into, slack-jawed wretches being bled, helpless figures electrocuted. The Natural History Museum in South Kensington it is not.

I absorbed some of the exhibition display reading material. I see, I said, that on the stuff on Pavlov you say this is the basis of behavioural psychology, the inhuman brainwashing methods used by the former Soviet Union, China, and the infamous CIA mind control experiments of the 1950s. You are aware that the irony is that some people say that Scientology is a brainwashing cult?

'Well,' said Jan, 'I have worked in CCHR for 30 years. And if you want to know about brainwashing, our organisation has been investigating brainwashing at least since 1969. There is an entire section in this museum about brainwashing.'

OK, I said, congenially. Shall we have this argument in the brainwashing section?

'Yes, we can.'

Very good. Let's get to the brainwashing section.

'Well, we are going to do this first.' She motioned to another video, lurking in the dark, waiting to be played.

How long is this video?

'It is five minutes. I am not going to show all of them to you.'

The second video was grim, grimmer than the first.

I was watching a screen full of babies screaming.

I was watching electric-blue sparks flash inside a see-through skull.

I was watching monsters in gowns drill into a wretch's brain.

The tone of the commentary becomes more manic, the words more difficult to understand. It was like eating a dish of parboiled madness, with a side salad of lunacy: 'For nearly a year Skinner isolated his daughter in a box similar to those he had built for rats. The child was stimulated...like a chicken or a rat in a cage ...they are given this electric shock therapy for no other reason but for them to have pain...Other techniques include administering electric shock to treat sexual... shooting high voltage through surgically implanted electrodes... And while this science without soul... billions in research...

psychiatric... the death of millions.'

That was the end of the second video. During my time as a war reporter I have seen a man with his eyeballs blown in by the pressure wave from heavy artillery in former Yugoslavia, I have seen a man with a slice hacked out of the back of his head by a machete in Rwanda and I have listened to Chechen resistance fighters describe how they were tortured by the Russian secret police. But this stuff in the Industry of Death was sickening, twice over. Sickening one, because of what it reflected was real. Real people had endured this suffering. Sickening twice, because of what I felt to be the twisting of half-facts and quarter-truths into their attack on the doctors of the mad. This was like watching a video of the history of heart surgery only told through the lens of botched operations, dead patients and greedy heart surgeons.

'That is contemporary modern psychiatry that's using pain and torture against children to try and change their behaviour,' said Jan. 'And it is our organisation...'

She was talking wicked gibberish. Jan moved on to eugenics, the idea that 'genetically inferior' people should be castrated or killed. It enjoyed some popularity in the 1920s, and was chiefly practiced in the Deep South of the United States against mainly black victims, and in Nazi Germany.

'The establishment of eugenics,' said Jan. 'That was used throughout America. It led to y'know tens of thousands of people being sterilised... British psychologists that actually came up with that theory. And it spread throughout, not just America, throughout Britain, but also through Nazi Germany.'

Am I correct in thinking, I asked, that there were psychologists and psychiatrists who believed that eugenics was wrong?

'But it was a theory that was still being used throughout Britain,' said Jan. 'It was a theory that was being propagated to the public and people were sterilised in the UK.'

Ping-pong, we went, pong-ping. She was utterly confident of her side of the argument. I was scraping away at my memory.

What I am trying to say, I said, is that there are [and were] many British psychiatrists and American psychiatrists that would have absolutely nothing to do with eugenics.

Jan carried on, relentless: 'If you have a look at the policy of eugenics, whether it is an official policy from the government, it still permeates throughout psychiatry.'

What was so unbearable and exasperating about this argument was that I didn't know my facts. The facts are: many doctors and psychiatrists opposed eugenics, then. One such was a man who is now another hero of mine, Dr Hyacinth Morgan MP, a man of rare courage despite his silly name. After graduating as a doctor in 1909 he worked in a Glasgow mental hospital before becoming an army medic in the First World War. He then became a Labour MP and stood up in the House of Commons in 1931 to oppose a proposed eugenics bill. Dr Morgan said the case for eugenics was 'moonshine' and concluded: 'I ask this House to refuse to give leave to introduce this pagan, anti-democratic, anti-Christian, unethical Bill.'

The House divided: Ayes, 89; Noes, 167. 'Moonshine' is a fair summary of the Church of Scientology, some say. But I didn't know about Dr Hyacinth Morgan back in the Industry of Death.

Jan carried on, now talking about psychiatry and eugenics: 'So it is all hidden. It is not out in the open.'

No, that's nonsense, I said. It is not all hidden. There was a huge argument in the scientific world.

Jan brought up ASBOs being a consequence of eugenics. An ASBO is an Anti-Social Behaviour Order, introduced by the Blair government in Britain to crack down on anti-social misconduct. In 2007 some were concerned that the powers used were unfair and disproportionate. The argument that eugenics leads to ASBOs is rubbish. Then Jan said something that that made my head hurt as if she had hit it with an axe.

'The psychiatrists set up the whole euthanasia campaign in the concentration camps. They went into the concentration camps and they set it up, and they decided who was going to be killed.'

I struggled to get my head round the meaning of what Jan had just said, effectively that psychiatry paved the way for the Holocaust, that it is a Nazi pseudo-science. It was no slip of the tongue. Tom Cruise thinks along the same lines. Cruise was challenged by a reporter from *Entertainment Weekly* in 2005 that 'Scientology textbooks sometimes refer to psychiatry as a ''Nazi science'''. Far from disputing that, Cruise effectively endorsed the notion, replying: 'Look at the history. Jung was an editor for the Nazi papers during World War II.'

This is not true.

A Swiss national of Christian stock, Jung was never an editor of Nazi papers. He maintained friendships with Jews and helped Jewish psychotherapists retain membership of an international body in flat defiance of Nazism. In his 1936 essay *Wotan* Jung described Germany as 'infected' by 'one man who is obviously "possessed"...rolling towards perdition.' Hardly Zeig Heil.

Cruise continued: 'Look at the drug methadone. That was originally called Adolophine. It was named after Adolf Hitler...'

This is not true.

Intensity and nice teeth do not of themselves prove historical knowledge or intellectual rigour or common sense. Cruise is spouting a modern myth. Methadone was invented in Nazi Germany in the late 1930s but it was never called 'adolphine' or 'adolophine' or 'Dolphamine'. At the end of the Second World War, the Western Allies expropriated many German genuine scientific advances, for example those in rocketry and medicines. In 1947 pharmaceutical company Eli Lilly in the United States introduced methadone as 'dolophine' – from the Latin for 'dolor' = pain and 'fin' = end. The nonsense term 'adolphine' first surfaced in the United States in the early 1970s. If you think about it for two seconds, the Nazis were picky about what they allowed to be named after Adolf Hitler. An SS division was fine and dandy but no-one would name a chemical substitute for opium desperately needed by the growing number of wounded German soldiers in Adolf's honour. That would have been foolish. Cruise is talking poppycock.

Cruise's bigger point – regurgitated to me by Jan – that psychiatric drugs and psychiatry itself are bad because they were the product of the Nazi mind is not just not true. It is *bonkers*. A number of racist German psychiatrists did take part in the Nazi euthanasia, true. But Hitler and Himmler set up the Holocaust, not psychiatry. Many psychiatrists were Jewish and were murdered by the Nazis. Jewish psychiatrists who could, fled Nazi Germany, among them Ida Macalpine and Richard Hunter – the mother-and-son team of psychiatrists who diagnosed George III's porphyria. Many non-Jewish psychiatrists also fled. To blame psychiatry for the Holocaust is nonsense with a capital N. It is to tell a lie about history and that is not good.

Bearing in mind the Church's proclaimed hatred for psychiatry, I should point out that I'm not an advocate for psychiatrists. They strike me as being like bin men or pest control officers. Society needs them. They can make mistakes. But they are not inherently bad. Once I went to see a psycho-therapist after I had returned from Algeria where the stories I had investigated about torture by the junta against so-called Muslim extremists were unutterably depressing. The therapist asked some weird questions so I stopped going and bought a toaster instead which seemed to do the trick. But psychiatry, which is medicine's honest attempt to treat mental illness, is not evil.

'And they' – the psychiatrists – 'decided' – Jan's words echoed in my mind – 'who was going to be killed.'

I fear they are brainwashing me. I fear that if I put up with anymore of this I will go quite mad.

The pressure never ceased. Jan moved into the shadows and Marla took over – Scientology's version of brain-tag-wrestling. A tall, beautiful woman in her late 40s or early 50s with long blond hair, Marla was one of a number of high profile Scientologists who had demonstrated on the streets of Washington DC in 1999, along with Juliette Lewis and Kirstie Alley, holding placards warning that psychiatrists were, 'hooking kids on drugs'. Marla's script was exactly the same as Jan's: psychiatry and its heinous crimes. When Marla stopped, Jan took over, then back to Marla, and on and on...

So, I said, for example, why would Jewish psychiatrists endorse a Nazi policy?

'Which Jewish psychiatrists, and what period?'

I didn't know the answer to her question. The three of us stopped in front of a display showing, guess who? A Nazi psychiatrist.

'He became a Nazi psychiatrist. You can watch the documentary but there is something like more than 30% of psychiatrists were part of the National Socialism. Even before the Nazi party was in full fledge and the whole Holocaust section happened in this horrible...'

But Jan, I said, you see the mind trap here? There were also Nazi bus conductors. Because there were Nazi bus conductors does not mean that all bus conductors were Nazis.

'Bus conductors,' said Jan, 'didn't come out with an ideology that led to six million Jews being murdered and 11 million people being killed. They didn't actually turn on the gas, they didn't do the first experiment in a psychiatric hospital where 18 people were actually murdered while psychiatrists watched and went yeah give it a thumbs up. Now let's put it into mass production.'

I struggled on: because there were Nazi bus conductors, does not mean all bus conductors were Nazis. There were many psychiatrists who at the time said eugenics is wrong, this Nazi rubbish is wrong...

'You keep going back to Germany... name the psychiatrist... So are you saying that Nazis?' Both women seemed to be attacking me. 'Less than a handful of psychiatrists in

Germany said "whoa this is…" while the rest of them go and murder…'

You only need one psychiatrist, I said, to expose the flaw in your logic.

'One psychiatrist? So if one psychiatrists disagrees with the Holocaust that means that psychiatry is actually OK?'

Listen, I said, I am not an expert on pre-war British psychiatry, or pre-war American psychiatry. But what I am spotting is a very, very simple but massive flaw in your logic. Because there were some psychiatrists who were Nazis does not mean that psychiatry is Nazi.

'It is not the logic…'

Well, what is the logic then? Because this man, he is a Nazi psychiatrist therefore psychiatry…

'He wasn't a Nazi psychiatrist when he came up with this theory. This came up in the 1890s. Now listen. Have you actually studied this? Have you studied this?'

Are you addressing my bus conductor point?

'Are you looking at the fact that the bus conductors taken aside, this was a…. No this is a psychiatric period…'

There were Nazi bus conductors. Therefore all bus conductors are Nazis?

'That is irrelevant.'

In front of me, horrible pictures of children, suffering, emaciated faces, half-lives in Hitler's death camps.

Jan and Marla kept up, in rotation, until, in my mind's eye, they mutated into one another. I found the joint attack from the two women hard to deal with. Tommy and Mike watched on, expressionless.

'OK, so you have 65,000 people a year who are still given

electro shocks. We want to watch this one.'

It was time for yet another horror video. I sat down on a bench and someone pressed play.

The video voice-over began on a grim note: 'In 1938 two Italian psychiatrists decided to observe that before slaughtering pigs in order to make the pigs more docile they were applying electrodes to their temples... This stunned the pigs but it didn't kill them and they could then slaughter them. Well, this gave them the encouragement to try inducing convulsion with electricity. You will see teeth falling out, broken spines, bones knocked out of joint, broken bones and people with internal organ damage from being restrained while they were having this uncontrolled writhing...'

I have seen a river in Rwanda full of bloated corpses, victims of a massacre.

I have seen a morgue in Osijek full of zipped open thoraxes of freshly dead.

I have seen an old Chechen lady gibber with fear after the Russians had bombed her home.

But watching Scientology's electro-shock horror video was more unsettling because of the ill-logic driving the horror. It was like watching a horror movie of great cruelty and being told this is not a horror movie, this is true.

'It jump started in 1848,' the video was just getting into its stride, 'when an explosion blew a steel rod straight through the head of the railway worker Phileas Gage. While Gage survived, his personality was dramatically altered.'

The photograph of this hideous accident, in which a metal spike speared through Phileas's brain, shot up on screen.

'Seventy years later Portuguese neurologist Egaz Moniz...'

Reinhardt, the black-clad Sea-Org cameraman was crouching on the floor with his camera pointing up. Not to be outdone, Sylviana did the same. They looked like two great black bug-eyed creepie-crawlies.

'…and pouring pure alcohol directly into the brain killing the tissue of the brain lobes. Moniz called this new procedure a lobotomy…'

At Barton Peveril Grammar School, my friend Gaz Lovelace liked to say: 'I'd rather have a bottle in front of me than a frontal lobotomy…'

'…Dr Walter J Freeman who became the most infamous practitioner he discovered he could do it faster without having to drill through the skull …and he would just lift up the eye and stick nothing more than an ice pick right into the brain … and then just rake the thing back and forth until he was satisfied this would cause a massive disruption of brain tissue and then pull it out…'

Mike Rinder and Tommy Davis were staring at me, chewing gum in sync.

'…travelled the country in his loboto-mobile hacking apart his patients brains on stage or sometimes right there in the vehicle. They lobotomised a million people in the 40s and the 50s and the beginning of the 60s…'

The video stopped, thank God. Lobotomies are now discredited, thank God.

I did not know this at the time, but not one million people suffered lobotomies. Around 70,000 did, worldwide. That is, of course, 70,000 victims too many but it is hard to see why anything is gained by multiplying the number of victims by 14. A major cause of its fall was the rise in effective anti-psychosis drugs in the 1950s. I did not know it for a fact then, but the very first scientific criticism of lobotomy was made in 1944 in the *Journal of Nervous and Mental Disease*: 'The history of prefrontal lobotomy has been brief and stormy. Its course has been dotted with both violent opposition and with slavish, unquestioning acceptance.' One of the very first people to question the practice from 1947 onwards was Swedish psychiatrist Snorre Wohlfahrt, who called it 'rather crude and hazardous in many respects.' Cybernetics inventor and brilliant US mathematician Norbert Wiener said in 1948: 'Lobotomy... has recently been having a certain vogue, probably not unconnected with the fact that it makes the custodial care of many patients easier. Let me remark in passing that killing them makes their custodial care still easier.' It should be noted that these criticisms were made before the birth of the Church of Scientology.

The moment the tape stopped, Jan was at me again. This absence of time to reflect, to weigh up, to think things through, is the woof and warp of what some say is the black magic of the Church of Scientology; it certainly was a constant in the minds of ex-Scientologists.

'... surgery is still being performed in the UK as well,' she said, 'so do you think that that is a valid form of therapy to be damaging the brain, cutting it open to try and change behaviour? That is Psychiatry. 110,000 Americans are subjected to it each year, 65,000 British. That is the wave of shock. So the older you are the more shock you get. So if you are a ten year old, and ten years olds have been given electro shock except that we had that practice banned in California in 1975.... that's how... How old are you?'

I am 48, I said.

I was staring at the model of a head suffering an electric shock: plasma lightning strikes in see-through plastic.

'That is how long the shock is coursing through your body. If we go to 80…'

I wanted to run away; I had had enough; more than enough.

I think, I said, you have made your one-sided point in a very one-sided way, and what you are saying is that psychiatry does this, therefore psychiatry is inherently evil. Now I believe that there are some psychiatrists who don't agree with this.

Marla opened up: 'What is the other point? You said there was one side of our… What is the other point?'

It is annoying me, I said, I can't remember his name, but there was a psychiatrist during the First World War in 1917 in Netley in Hampshire and he treated a whole bunch of the Tommies who had war shock, including I think the poet…

'Oh, don't tell me, it is William Sargent.' It wasn't.

No, all I know is he treated the poet Siegfried Sassoon. But he didn't believe, if my memory is correct, in any of this. He believed in sitting down and talking to people. But he is a famous psychiatrist and he didn't believe in this.

The name of the heroic psychiatrist I'd forgotten was William Rivers, who fought the military mind-set that said shell-shock was a kind of cowardice, and treated Sassoon, Wilfred Owen and others.

Marla banged on: 'But that is not our point. Our point is "don't you think ECT and electro shock treatment is barbaric?"'

It looks barbaric, yes.

'Exactly,' said Marla. 'And that's our point, the study we have done today…'

But I am not a psychiatrist.

'But you will have to be to understand. If a child puts his finger in a light socket we know that is bad, same premise. There is no more science to psychiatry than sticking your finger in a light socket and having up to 450 volts of electricity coursed through your brain. Don't you think that's bad?'

I, well, it looks horrific, it looks barbaric.

'That's right. That is our point.'

Jan took up the cudgel: 'There is a lot of literature that the Royal College of Psychiatrists, the American Psychiatric Association puts out about electro shock that is one sided. They will actually diminish the amount of memory loss. One of the most, greatest advocates of electro shock for 30 years has been saying that it doesn't cause memory loss…'

Somewhere around here I just wanted it to stop. Perhaps it was Jan's relentless tone. This may sound ungallant, but I found there was something especially strident about Jan's voice, a chain-saw cutting into a Eucalyptus tree while the resident Koala bear squealed its head off.

'But if we today are still using electro shock treatment, and we are still using psycho-surgery, if we are damaging the brain and driving people in order to change their behaviour? And the number of people who are becoming mentally ill is escalating rather than going down. There is a serious problem with psychiatry.'

Very good, I said.

Next, it was the story of the drugs industry killing children. Yet again, there was some truth in what they were telling me. Over-prescription and over-use of drugs like Ritalin is a huge worry and a story reported by my colleagues on Panorama. But, yet again, those real worries morphed into a general, unhinged assault on all of psychiatry and psychiatric drugs.

After that, the state's abuse of children. More graphic photos, but more grim evidence of wrong-doing, extrapolated into a general assault on treating the mentally ill.

Hold on a second, Jan. I… these pictures are terrible. No civilised person could possibly endorse what has happened here, it is plainly wrong. And the state abuse of children is wrong and must be challenged wherever it happens.

'And that's why you have an organisation like CCHR. It is there to protect the rights of individuals, to give parents like this grieving mother information to stand up for their rights…'

Time to enter the brainwashing or Mind Control section of the exhibition which was dominated by images of victims of brainwashing. Perhaps the most striking was a colour photograph of black smoke belching from including the Twin Towers on 9/11. For the avoidance of doubt there was a sign saying 'Mind Control' in big letters above my head. Tommy swung into view. I was beyond punch-drunk.

He called me a bigot, again.

'And because you are. See there's a difference here because what I'm saying is true.'

What's the time?

'…and what you're saying about me being brain washed isn't.'

No, hold on, what's the time?

'It's 12 o'clock.'

That's the first bigot of the morning, I told him.

'And they'll keep coming.'

It was now three against one. Tommy did his usual riffs – the time he'd spent with me, my lack of respect, my bigotry blah blah – but standing right next to him were Jan and Marla, who would take a bite out of my brain, as it were, the moment he paused for breath. I was firing back, a brainwashing cult here, a brainwashing cult there, but there was something about the accumulated sediment of all that had happened that was sticking to my boots. I didn't have a moment to reflect what was going on, what they were doing to my head.

'I want her to explain to you what brainwashing is,' said Tommy.

'Do you know what the definition of brain washing is?' asked Jan.

No. I am not an expert on brain washing.

Jan gave me a book. I read out loud: 'Brainwashing is the use of isolation deprivation, torture and indoctrination to break the human will. OK.'

'Torture,' said Jan.

We knocked around brainwashing for a long time. They said they first uncovered CIA brainwashing; I said hadn't the Soviets and the Chinese Communists done it too? We got into the Catholic Church and paedophilia. I told them there is a huge problem with the Catholic Church because of the unmarried priesthood, and that is one of the problems I personally have with the Catholic Church because I do not believe in a non-married priesthood.

211

And then I said: so that aside, what people who used to be Scientologists say, is that I now realise having left the Church, that it is a sinister brainwashing cult.

Tommy stepped in close: 'We can just bring this down a couple of notches for a second? You keep accusing my religion, my faith, OK, my faith and the faith of a lot of people in this room, and a faith of millions of people the world over, OK, of engaging in something which by definition involves torture, drugs, sleep deprivation…'

Not necessarily drugs, I said.

'Of inflicting bodily harm. OK. And what is the methodology? It is a methodology which is widely considered by many people who are not even Scientologists to be one of the most heinous and barbaric things you could ever do to another human being: brainwashing.'

Tommy was calm, smooth, perfectly fluent: 'And you throw that term around with every Scientologist that you meet and you do it under the cloak of your preface "some people claim". You claim to be an investigative journalist, which means you investigate things, you get to the bottom of them, and you find out the truth, OK? When you were interviewing and I quote your friend, Shawn Lonsdale, a convicted sex pervert…'

Shawn was the lone videographer, who filmed them filming him filming them. When I had interviewed him in Clearwater a zillion years ago – it was, in fact, only four days before – Tommy had interrupted our interview by reading out his criminal record for having consenting sex with men in a public place.

Hold on a second, I said, I want to say he is not my friend.

He is not my friend.

'I have you on camera…'

OK, I said, I am English, I use irony. Some of the words I use you should not take a literal meaning. It may be a cultural difference between us. But when I would say…

'Some words you use you should watch what you use, because you are the one who says them.'

OK, I said. But I just think that you have a cultural problem with my use of irony. I am English. Sometimes I say 'my friend' when I actually mean, I don't like this person. But actually that is a subtlety. But when Lonsdale…

'Well, we'll put a little endnote on our documentary.'

I turned to Reinhardt's camera, and addressed it directly: hold on a second, have we got that? When I called Shawn Lonsdale a friend, I could well have been using English irony, and I didn't actually mean those words.

'So when you say you're not friends that actually means that you're enemies so I'll remember that now.'

Looking back with the benefit of hindsight, I suspect that I might have been falling into a trap that Tommy had made for me. Shawn was not my friend, and, as a BBC reporter, I did not want to appear overly close to him. But at the same time, as a human being, I felt, then and now, that Shawn was a singular and brave man and Tommy succeeded in thrusting this dichotomy at me so forcefully that I felt I had betrayed Shawn in some way, and I felt guilty about it. It is only on reading Lifton's book on brainwashing, that I realise how successfully the Chinese Communists used guilt as a weapon to brainwash westerners. For example, an extraordinary brave Dutch priest, Fr Vechten, was racked with guilt generated by his captors long after his release. Tommy succeeded in making me feel guilty that I had betrayed Shawn. For the first time in my direct contact with the Church, I was in serious trouble. Keen to show proper distance from Shawn I now felt guilty that I had disowned him too much. Tommy smoked out my confusion, and went after it like a terrier.

'When you interviewed him you didn't once ask him, because he did also use that term brainwashing. And you say OK Shawn, what evidence do you have of that? Because I have investigated and the term brainwashing and the definition of brainwashing almost invariably involves sleep deprivation, lack of food, and things which by all definitions amount to torture. So what evidence, Shawn, do you have that people are tortured?'

I'm John, I pointed out, helpfully.

'I am saying this is what you should have said to him. Ok what evidence, Shawn, do you have that people have been tortured?

Me: 'No, hold a second Tommy…'

Tommy: 'No, no, no I am not stopping you listen to me for a second. You are accusing members of my religion in engaging in brainwashing!'

His voice was raised, just shy of shouting at me.

I wish I had not done what I did next, but I could not help it. Had my father's death had anything to do with it? I don't think so. The previous evening's session with Rick Ross may have had a paradoxical effect, of reinforcing and reawakening the fundamental reasonableness and common sense of objections to the Church and its teachings. I feared I was going to lose my mind, my sanity, my grip on reality. I feared they were out to brainwash me. If I didn't fight it, then soon I would be saying that psychiatry was responsible for the Holocaust, that I had not been followed by sinister strangers in a Kia Sidona, that the man with the cowboy hat was just passing by the reception desk, that Tommy and Mike were not at our hotel at midnight, that I had made it all up. For the past hour – it felt like an eternity – my brain had been assailed by some of the darkest and cruellest images I have ever seen, and I have seen bad things. But these images were constructed and pressed home by fanatics, members of an organization which people who used to belong to it say is literally maddening; an entity so crazy that half of them didn't know about the space alien Satan that threatens us all, and half of them did. Worst, for me, was the sense that I didn't know enough about the history of psychiatry to be able to say clearly and with authority that they were not telling the truth. But about Shawn Lonsdale I knew what Tommy was implying was not true. I had asked Shawn a tough question at the very beginning of the interview. I had asked him: 'You are a social outcast, a menace, a fruitcake, a nutter. Why would Scientology make those kinds of suggestions about you?'

That was a solid fact, and I could stand by it full square. They were not going to brainwash me. I saw red, my face turned into an exploding tomato. Our two faces were inches apart, back-lit in the curious sulphuric red light of the exhibition, set against the background of a huge blow-up picture of the Twin Towers burning. I had had enough of the Church of Scientology; more than enough; and I fought back, jet-engine loud, screaming my head off as loud as I could holler.

Me: 'NO TOMMY YOU STOP!'

Tommy: 'BRAINWASHING! BRAINWASHING IS A CRIME!'

Me: 'YOU LISTEN TO ME!'

Tommy: 'Brainwashing is a crime.'

Me: 'YOU WERE NOT THERE AT THE BEGINNING OF THE INTERVIEW. YOU WERE NOT THERE.'

Tommy: 'Brainwashing is a crime.'

Me: 'YOU DID NOT HEAR OR RECORD ALL OF THE INTERVIEW.'

Tommy: 'Brainwashing is a crime.'

Tommy's repeated mantra adds to the utter weirdness of the scene: it's as if he had been trained to repeat a phrase over and over again, so that it gives the other party no break or opportunity to return to calmness. What I was driving at was that Tommy couldn't say for a fact that I was cosy with Shawn because he wasn't there at the beginning of the interview. Tommy only invaded it half way through – and our tape could prove that. Frankly, it was a very minor point to lose one's temper over, as is often the case when you chuck your toys out of the pram.

Me: 'Do you understand? Did you understand?' Suddenly, weirdly, my voice drops in volume.

Tommy: 'Brainwashing is a crime against humanity.'

Me: 'YOU ARE QUOTING THE SECOND HALF OF THE INTERVIEW.'

I am back to yelling again: quite why I stopped shouting and then started again is inexplicable. Perhaps I should see a psychiatrist.

Tommy: 'You are accusing my organisation of engaging

in a crime.'

Me: 'NOT THE FIRST HALF. YOU CANNOT ASSERT WHAT YOU'RE SAYING. Now will you listen to me?'

I shot a quick look at Mole, who flicked her eyes at me, once. Oh, dear, what had I done?

I apologised then and I apologise now.

CHAPTER TEN
The Tethered Goat

I t was Mole's fault. Sweeney's iron law of TV: if things go well, the reporter picks up the awards. If they go badly, it's the producer's fault. For the record, it was, of course, my fault I lost my temper. Mole could do nothing to stop me once I'd gone tomato. But what happened was a wholly unplanned, unintended consequence of Mole's cunning plan.

Back in 1971, journalist Paulette Cooper had written *The Scandal of Scientology*. This led to 'Operation Freak-Out' whose goal, according to Church documents, was to get Cooper 'incarcerated in a mental institution or jail.' The Church of Scientology sent bomb threats to itself, but faked them as if they had come from Cooper. She was indicted in 1973 for threatening to bomb the Church. Cooper endured 19 lawsuits by the Church but was finally exonerated in 1977 after FBI raids on the Church offices in Los Angeles and Washington uncovered documents proving the Church was behind the bomb plot. No Scientologists were ever tried over this scandal. Cooper's blood parents were both killed at Auschwitz and she was adopted by American parents at the age of six – so the Church ended up trying to jail a child victim of the Nazis, an irony which its Nazi-obsessed museum neglects to mention.

In 1987, the Church did its best to stop the BBC Panorama team making the documentary, *The Road to Total Freedom?* Reporter John Penycate and producer Peter Malloy were spied on, filmed, lied to and faced preposterous legal threats.

Around the same time, L Ron's biographer, Russell Miller, faced Scientology's inquisition. He told me: 'When we were researching the book in Los Angeles we were followed by a bright red sports car with huge wing mirrors so they obviously wanted me to know that I was followed. I was told my phone was tapped and the mail was intercepted. I was accused of various crimes. They said I was responsible for the murder of a private detective in south London, and I was an arsonist and I had set fire to a helicopter factory somewhere in the north.'

Are you a murderer and arsonist, I asked Russell?

'No,' he said.

What did they accuse you of?

'I got a call from the police saying "what was I doing on this particular day?" and I said "why do you want to know?" and they said "we have had information that you were involved in the killing of a private detective in a car park pub in south London". I said, obviously, I wasn't. It became so frequent that I had a special number I could call every time I was accused of something. I said to the police, OK, don't worry about this, the Scientologists are doing this, so call this number in a police station and that took the heat off me.'

Russell was also accused of the assassination of a Cold War defector. 'They found out that I was in East Berlin at a time when an American rock star called Dean Reed who was a Communist and had defected to the east, killed himself in 1986. I was there to interview him but that weekend he killed himself. And they discovered that my wife had been born in East Germany and put two and two together and made five and were convinced that I had murdered Dean Reed. They fielded a lot of private detectives, one of them was Eugene Ingram. They tracked down all the friends that I have in the United States and here in Britain. I found out where this guy was staying and called him and said: "What are you doing?" He said: "We are pretty sure you killed Dean Reed and we are going to prove it."'

Had Russell killed Dean?

'No, I hadn't.'

Stasi files, released after the Wall came down, show that Reed committed suicide.

Russell was asked by the first ex-Scientologist he interviewed in LA: '"Are you being followed?" And I said no, I have never been followed in my whole life. So that alerted me and then I realised that I was being followed. They had a different car every day. The car would be at the end of the street. The car would pick me as I went off to do my job. It was distressing. You think, this is madness, this is paranoia gone crazy. What are these people doing? They obviously wanted to know what I was doing and who I was interviewing.'

He summed up his experience of the Church of Scientology: 'These people are so brainwashed that they don't understand what is happening to them. It is only when they get out of the organisation that they understand what is happening.'

In 1991 it was the turn of Richard Behar of *TIME* magazine to be the centre of the Church's attention. He was followed so regularly that he started commuting by roller-blade, so that he could spin around, and roll along against the traffic on Fifth Avenue in New York to lose the vehicles tailing him.

Behar wrote: 'Strange things seem to happen to people who write about Scientology. For the *TIME* story, at least 10 attorneys and six private detectives were unleashed by Scientology and its followers in an effort to threaten, harass and discredit me.'

One of them was ex-cop and private eye, Eugene Ingram.

'A copy of my personal credit report, with detailed information about my bank accounts, home mortgage, credit-card payments, home address and Social Security number, had been illegally retrieved from a national credit bureau called Trans Union. The sham company that received it, "Educational Funding Services" of Los Angeles, gave as its address a mail drop a few blocks from Scientology's headquarters. The owner of the mail drop is a private eye named Fred Wolfson, who admits that an Ingram associate retained him to retrieve credit reports on several individuals. Wolfson says he was told that Scientology's attorneys "had judgments against these people and were trying to collect on them." He says now, "These are vicious people. These are vipers." Ingram, through a lawyer, denies any involvement in the scam.'

Behar hadn't finished: 'During the past five months, private investigators have been contacting acquaintances of mine, ranging from neighbours to a former colleague, to inquire about subjects such as my health (like my credit rating, it's excellent) and whether I've ever had trouble with the IRS (unlike Scientology, I haven't). One neighbour was greeted at dawn outside my Manhattan apartment building by two men who wanted to know whether I lived there.'

Behar still hadn't finished: 'An attorney subpoenaed me, while another falsely suggested that I might own shares in a company I was reporting about that had been taken over by Scientologists (he also threatened to contact the Securities and Exchange Commission). A close friend in Los Angeles received a disturbing telephone call from a Scientology staff member seeking data about me, an indication that the cult may have illegally obtained my personal phone records. Two detectives contacted me, posing as a friend and a relative of a so-called cult victim, to elicit negative statements from me about Scientology. Some of my conversations with them were taped, transcribed and presented by the Church in affidavits to TIME's lawyers as "proof" of my bias against Scientology.'

In 1997 it was the turn of Channel Four producers Jill Robinson and Simon Berthon, making a film for the *Secret Lives* series about L Ron Hubbard. Jill told the *Independent* and the *Daily Telegraph* how the Church of Scientology had reacted to their scrutiny. Jill went to the States on a research trip. Within days of her arrival, her production company started receiving messages from the Church's headquarters saying they knew she was in LA. When she left her hotel room at 5am to go to Phoenix the man next door came out of his room at exactly the same time.

Jill's brother worked in the US. When she dropped by his house, the phone went: it was the Church of Scientology, asking for Jill. When she went to a friend's dinner party, a woman knocked at the door at 10.30 at night saying she needed water for her car radiator. Jill did not go to the door but she could hear the woman's voice: she claims it was that of the guide who had led a group of visitors, including Jill, around the LA museum dedicated to Hubbard's life. Her friend gave the woman the water but could see no sign of a car. Jill believes there wasn't one at all. 'It was their way of saying: "We're here, we know you're there,"' she told the *Independent*.

When filming began, everywhere Channel Four went, the Church of Scientology, like Mary's little lamb, was sure to go. They got hold of a copy of Jill's shooting schedule. Cars tailed them. Weird phone calls bugged the crew in the middle of the night. In Denver, Jill and her crew took a wrong turning and ended up in an industrial wasteland; so did the tailing car. In San Francisco, her cameraman challenged the driver of a car watching them filming. He hid his face and sped off. In Florida, she and her crew went to a mall to do some shopping. They stopped a Volvo and asked the driver why he was following them. He said he was from New York and there were three of them on the job, getting paid to follow her around.

Back in England, while Jill was editing the film, her neighbour in Kent spotted a man loitering outside her house and called the police. He had not committed any offence and they let him go. His reason for being there was unconvincing. He did, however, tell police he was a Scientologist. Eugene Ingram came over to Kent to probe the horse riding stables where she kept her horse. That was not all. They even tracked down her parents and her hairdresser. 'It's a bit spooky,' she told the *Telegraph*. 'I just don't see what it is they hope to achieve, except they seek to intimidate me.'

Jill's exec, Simon Berthon, told the Telegraph that when friends began to complain that they had been visited by

Ingram, the Church's favourite private eye, he checked with 12 friends and relations whom he had recently telephoned from home. He said: 'Out of 12 calls made, I have discovered that nine have been telephoned by a woman offering a free magazine if they take part in a TV viewing-habit survey and give their name and address.' Three of those nine had subsequently been visited by Ingram. 'This is well beyond coincidence,' said Mr Berthon.

The Telegraph reported that among them was a friend and neighbour, Charlotte Joll, whom he had telephoned recently to accept a children's-party invitation for his daughter. Charlotte said: 'Last Friday afternoon a man rang on the doorbell showing me his private investigator's licence and then asked me if I knew someone he was trying to get in touch with. He showed me three photographs of a man I had never seen before and said this guy was wanted for some kind of offence to do with getting money fraudulently. I had no idea what it was about. Then he mentioned Simon Berthon's name. Did I know him? I said "Yes, our children are friends." I then remembered that our au pair had told me a couple of days earlier that she had been rung by someone purporting to be doing research on our television viewing habits, offering her a year's subscription to her favourite magazine and asking for our address.'

Another of Mr Berthon's friends who was asked to take part in a telephone survey was Dorothy Byrne, the then editor of ITV's The Big Story. She said that Ingram had telephoned her at her office, saying that he was a private detective investigating extortion, and asking for information about Simon and Jill.

Dorothy said: 'I told him that Simon was one of the most highly regarded people in television. I also told him that in Britain we don't really appreciate private detectives hanging around outside people's houses. Then on Friday I received a phone call from a woman saying that she was doing a survey of TV viewing habits.'

In all, Jill Robinson, Simon Berthon, the associate producer, the cameraman, the sound recordist, the picture editor, the assistant cameraman and the composer of the music had visits from Ingram and his colleagues.

The Independent got in touch with Mike Rinder, who told the paper that documentary evidence about Hubbard had been provided to Channel 4. It was not true, Mike maintained, that the Church had refused to co-operate - quite the contrary. The programme-makers had ignored the Church's offers of access.

Mike Rinder said that behind Jill's sources 'were repeated threats against the church and demands for payments of tens of millions of dollars'. Channel 4, alleged Mike, had missed the real Hubbard story - of his 'solutions to the social ills of drugs, illiteracy and crime' and the 'more than 40 million who have been touched by his non-religious moral code; and the many millions who hold his work to be the cornerstone of their lives.'

Mole had studied what had happened to our journalist colleagues who had gone down the same path ahead of us. She predicted that the Church of Scientology would attack me and attack me and attack me. Before we flew out to the United States Mole had said: 'You're going to be like the tethered goat in *Jurassic Park*, bleating as the Tyrannosaurus Rex

225

comes to get you. All you have to do is bleat. You can bleat, can't you?' I told her I could.

Everything had gone to plan. Every time Tommy and Mike turned up, at the hotel at midnight, at Plant City, at the top of the car park in Clearwater with Shawn Lonsdale, every time we were followed, every time the private eye in the cowboy hat turned up – it was all part of Mole's brilliant tethered goat plan. The Church of Scientology had fallen into her trap, again and again and again. Our only goal was to film every attack. The one thing she did not predict was the behaviour of the tethered goat. I did not bleat. Or perhaps I did, but after too much of them, I ended up lowering my head and charging. Not, then, a Tethered Goat. An Un-Tethered Rhino, more like.

So what happened in the Mind Control section was, I think, that two traps went off at exactly the same time. I fell into Tommy's trap. But he – and they – fell into Mole's, again.

Incredibly, weirdly, madly everything continued as though nothing had happened. After losing it, I felt nervous and jumpy, and you can clearly see me on the rushes, appearing strained, anxious, worried. In the grammar of television I had made a career-killing mistake. I was almost certainly finished at the BBC; our whole documentary could be killed by BBC management, hugely embarrassed by their fruitcake reporter who could not interview anyone without screaming at them. What the Church's agents described in Sci'gy-Leaks as my usual 'arrogance' was gone. I was, of course, in the wrong. I do believe that. People in the public eye should hold their temper. I had lasted, what, six or seven days (I couldn't be sure) with them. It felt like six or seven years. I wanted to run away, to talk through my catastrophic loss of control with Mole and Bill. But Tommy and Mike wouldn't let me.

Weirdly – and I am sorry for the repetition of the adverb, but no other will suffice – Tommy and Mike helped me get my composure back because they carried on attacking me, calling me a bigoted reporter. I carried on telling them that some say they belonged to a brainwashing cult. It was as if I had never done my rhino impersonation at all.

Of course, they knew that we were making a long-form documentary, and it would take us at least a month to cut, edit and legal our film. And therefore it made good tactical sense for them to keep their powder dry. But still, it was beyond strange.

So, after the shout, it was back to the same old battle. Tommy said: 'So you, John Sweeney, are a bigot, and you are biased and you are incapable of objective reporting, and you have no leg to stand on.'

I have two legs to stand on, I replied. The BBC will fairly and accurately report your view.

An ocean of argy-bargy later, I put to Tommy the stories on the internet that David Miscavige spits at people.

Tommy replied: 'That is disgusting. It couldn't even be further from the truth. David Miscavige is a personal friend of mine, I have known him for over 16 years, my entire adult life. He is the kindest, most humane, most caring, most generous, hardest working person I have ever met or had the privilege to know.'

Has he ever thumped anyone?

'Absolutely not,' said Tommy, before committing a very rare slip of the tongue: 'And you continue with these gross allegations I will go after you for slibel...for libel and slander.'

For slibel?

'I am just combining the two. It is a good one we will put it in the dictionary. Anyway the point is it is libellous and it is slanderous for you to level such accusations that the leader of the Church of Scientology is anything other than a genuine honest and straightforward person. And you know what every accusation that you are levelling has been investigated at enormous length whether it is courts of law or the Internal Revenue Service for the purpose of determining the charitable status and religious nature of Scientology and every single one of them was found to be utterly and completely false.'

We carried on bashing each other for a bit. I asked to interview Miscavige, again.

Tommy replied: 'He won't give an interview to you John Sweeney. Do you know why? Because I wouldn't ever in a million years put him anywhere near your presence. You are bigoted, unobjective, biased, disgustingly despicable bottom feeding tabloid issues, slanderous libellous presence.'

I understand, thank you, I said.

Mole pressed Tommy for an interview with Miscavige. Normally, this kind of conversation is not filmed, but the Church of Scientology is not normal.

'Where is he? Is he in LA?' asked Mole.

'You are assuming he is in LA,' said Tommy.

'You don't want to tell me where he is,' said Mole. 'Phone him. Ask him has he heard of our interview approach? Does he know about this programme?'

'Absolutely,' said Tommy.

'Surely the man's got 30 minutes. Ask him.'

Tommy blocked her, waffling on about this and that.

'How high are you?' asked Mole.

'Well, I report to Mr Miscavige. Is that high enough?'

'So are you number two in the organisation? Or is that Mike?'

'We don't really operate in that regard of number one and number two,' said Tommy. 'This isn't *Austin Powers*.'

It felt like *Austin Powers*.

I wondered aloud to Tommy and Mike: are you Brother Number Two or Brother Number Three?

'Yeah, precisely. Anyway that is not how we operate. But as far as public relations and media relations...'

'...you are number one, OK. Well if you could pass on our request again that would be great and give him a call and ask him?'

'Gladly.'

'Can you ring him now?'

'Right here? On camera?'

'Yeah, why not? Go on, ring him now,' said Mole.

'A nice guy called John Sweeney wants to interview him?' Tommy looked doubtful, adding to the implied negative, 'I think that is kind of obvious.'

'Why? What is wrong? Why won't you call him?'

'Because that is ridiculous.'

'How is it ridiculous?'

'The head of a major organisation? I am just going to call him up...' said Tommy.

Marla cut in: 'A president of an organisation? You are so juvenile.'

Mole says that she found Marla hard to deal with, and

229

might have lost it with them, too, eventually.

I asked Mike: What would your recommendation be?

Mike: 'That you're an asshole.'

Mole seemed to find Mike's remark exceptionally funny: 'That you're an asshole. That is the recommendation from Mike.'

Mike repeated himself: 'An asshole.' Mole carried on smirking.

Marla: 'You're the one screaming. I have worked with journalists for the past ten years, I have worked with *60 Minutes*, I have worked with journalists...'

I was trying to make a point, I said. I've apologised.

'I have never witnessed that type of a reaction from any member of the media in ten years working with them on a direct basis,' said Marla. 'Why on earth would we recommend you with that type of behaviour? I wouldn't even recommend that to my enemies, or maybe a few psychiatrists I would. But I certainly would not recommend you to be in the same room with anyone who I held in high regard after that type of behaviour.'

Funnily enough, one year before I lost it Marla said much the same to another reporter who had toured the *Industry of Death*. She complained of Andrew Gumbel of *Los Angeles City Beat* that his behaviour amounted to "the most bizarre encounter I have had with a reporter in 10 years." Perhaps she says that to all the reporters.

I got the feeling that Tommy didn't want Marla to raise the subject of my exploding tomato performance. Suddenly, she switched off.

Marla: 'That's it. I am done. That is my comment.'

Are there any...?

'I am done,' said Marla.

I am glad that you are done, I said. I am just replying to your point that there are some sort of slightly strange things that go on when you start investigating Scientology. We have been followed throughout by investigators.

'It's boring. It's boring. I'm bored,' said Marla.

We went to lunch, on our own, to a burger bar called Tommy's. I apologised, again. Mole told me to shut up. Bill, our cameraman, tendered his resignation. He was going to leave the BBC and start anew. He was going to join Gold, the Church's camera team based in the Californian desert, to work with Reinhardt and co. I started gulping in terror. The only reason stopping him was that he didn't fancy wearing black all the time. I called him a traitor. We started laughing, and couldn't stop.

CHAPTER ELEVEN
The Concrete Angel

L ike a pitiless concrete angel, the vast two-winged Scientology building stands in downtown LA proclaiming its power to the city of dreams. The building, the old Cedars of Lebanon hospital the Church acquired in the 1970s, is painted a deep space blue and on top of it a great white sign proclaims 'Scientology'. At night, it lights up, piercing the night sky. Welcome to L Ron Hubbard Way. This street, and the area around it, is dominated by the Church of the Stars. White-shirted, black-trousered adepts hurry across the street, hither and yon.

After lunch we met Tommy and Mike at the far end of the complex from the old hospital. The car park was packed, a sea of windscreens flashing in the sun. It hadn't drizzled the whole time I was in America. Odd. When I walked through the doors, the strangest thing happened. I stepped into the building about ten feet ahead of the camera teams and Tommy and Mike, and I saw an entire film set, frozen in space and time, as if waiting for a signal from on high, from the Director. One beat, and then as if by unspoken command, everyone started moving, criss-crossing paths, hurrying slightly too fast for real life. I had walked inside a Church of Scientology video. Creepy.

Tommy and Mike were the soul of politeness. It was walk this way, see this, can I answer your question? What had they got up to over lunch? Shown Miscavige the tape of me doing an impression of John Cleese in *Fawlty Towers* going nuts? I guess so.

We came to a stop in front of a bust of L Ron Hubbard. There is a brilliant *Dr Who* episode, *Blink*, about stone statues that are in reality space aliens that move when you blink. Since watching that, I have always felt uneasy in front of statues or busts of any kind.

All of Mr Hubbard's lectures on compact discs, said Tommy, tantalisingly, pointing at a wall of CDs.

The same thing that we saw at Saint Hill, I said. I didn't say it then, but the Church of Scientology's centre in LA is the least religious religious building I have ever been in, in the whole world. It looks and feels like a shop.

A fancy plasma screen caught my eye. Mr Hubbard, said Tommy, gave over 3,000 lectures…

Inside a wood-lined study was a desk, decorated by a naval white cap, as if the captain of the Isle of Wight ferry had just popped out for a pint.

Every Church of Scientology, said Tommy, has an office for L Ron Hubbard.

Other religions have shrines to their dead founders. Scientology, in keeping with its weird mix of corporate Americana, dollar signs and religiosity, has an office. Tommy went on to explain that LRH wasn't a prophet, guru or a god.

Smashing, I said. What is the naval hat for?

Tommy waxed lyrical about Mr Hubbard's mastery of the sea, a master mariner licensed to captain any ship on any ocean of any tonnage, sail or motor. The heretic biographer Russell Miller gave me a somewhat different version of Hubbard's career in the US Navy: 'He fired on Mexico by mistake. He fought a battle with a submarine that never existed on the Pacific coast. He was not a war hero. He stumbled from courts martial to investigations to unpaid bills. His war career was a disaster.'

Our tour continued. Outwardly, I appeared interested. Inwardly, I was wondering, when would I get fired? We came across a grown man playing with plasticine. Mr Hubbard worked out, said Tommy, that playing with clay figures helps Scientologists.

The man lumped his figures into a ball...

'...And the supervisor will be able to see...'

...then rolled out his clay.

We walked past a couple sitting at a table facing each other, an E-meter on the table. In real life, it was an unimpressive piece of kit, whiffing of Bakelite and 1950s valves. The needle, floating or not, would not look out of place on the dashboard of a Spitfire. Hi-tech, Scientology is not.

Tommy explained how the Scientologists were training how to become an auditor: 'And so that involves how to use the E-meter and various drills for that.'

Drill is a military word.

'...and that they know their tools, they know their trade perfectly and exactly...'

We were watching a display of auditing, not the real thing.

What are the wood bricks for? I asked.

'Similar to the clay,' said Tommy.

More auditing was going on.

'The auditor does not ever validate, evaluate or anything like that. The auditor is fully there to assist the person receiving the auditing and finding out for himself what it is that's troubling him.'

There were more grown-ups playing with clay, people studying, people auditing with E-meters in rooms off the main corridors. In one long room there were dozens of people, bent over their studies or their clay, none of whom paid any attention whatsoever to the two agents, the reporter, the four separate people behind cameras and the sound person with the very long boom. And that is weird. It is a simple constant of working for TV, everywhere on the planet, that people come up to you and ask, 'what are you filming?' and 'what's it for?' and 'when does it go out?' and 'hello, Mum.' When people not only don't do that, but do the opposite and entirely ignore the cameras, one can reasonably deduce that they been commanded to behave in that peculiar way, beforehand. It was like wandering around inside the set of *The Truman Show*.

'Was that satisfactory?'

Very, very good, I said. More than satisfactory.

We were out in the fresh air.

'If you wouldn't mind,' asked Tommy, 'letting me know where you are going to go? The only reason literally is that when you show up, people are going to call me and say "there is a camera crew here, do you know who they are?"… So just let me know and I will just… even if you just tell me on the day I will tell everyone here there is a crew from the BBC… OK?'

235

I couldn't be bothered answering that.

'Do you have any questions John?'

How much is the Church worth?

'To be honest with you, I have actually no idea.'

After our tour, it was back to 'The Some Say Brainwashing Cult' suite at the Celebrity Centre. Juliette Lewis walked in, the goofy yet very beautiful star of *Natural Born Killers* and former girlfriend of Brad Pitt. In 2007, she was a musician with her own rock band.

The Sci'gy Leaks messages had predicted: '*Juliette will go off on him about narconon and that she wld be dead if it wasnt for the program and how dare he criticize it.*' And lo, it came to pass.

You're a Scientologist, why?

'Well, thirteen years ago I had a little drug problem that was horrible and I did the Narconon programme and it's the only drug rehab I ever did and then never looked back, never did drugs again, so I'm kind of happy about that.'

What does Scientology do for you? Has it made you a better person?

'Well, what I think about Hubbard just as a writer is he's like just really interesting and I find his writing compelling and makes me think about things all the like courses I've done in Scientology's made me able to understand communication better so that I could connect with people because as an artist first and foremost that's like the most important thing to me is this connection with people. And also to understand each other, to resolve differences, because when I was like more of an introverted teen who couldn't articulate my feelings to save my life, it was really an uncomfortable place to be so now just being able to be more comfortable in my own skin, eh, has allowed me to do live rock and roll shows as well so it's good, good things. I've only had good things.'

It felt like *Groundhog Day*. Still I had to go through the motions.

Which level of Scientology are you at, I asked?

'I don't like to speak in mysteric, you know, mysterious terms that people don't understand so first and foremost I would just say I'm Juliette, I am an artist, I am female, those are the things I'm sure you understand. So as far as levels in Scientology I've done lots of courses, I've had the auditing which is the equivalent to what counselling might, you might know as counselling and stuff like that.'

Some people say that it's a sinister brainwashing cult. What would you say to that?

'Some people have also said that women are really stupid and shouldn't vote!'

Well, the people who said that it's a sinister brainwashing cult used to be in Scientology.

'I did movies for fifteen years and I still do movies, and I've been sort of in the public eye, I guess, since I was twenty, so I'm kind of used to stereotypes, clichés, rumours, even my best of friends, you know who, they're just hilarious stories, so, the point is the brainwashing thing I just think is funny because anybody who knows me that's like really funny, I don't know.'

Who's Xenu?

'Who's who?'

Xenu.

She did a weird kind of, 'I have no idea what you're talking

237

about' look. Not terribly convincing. Hardly Oscar winning.

'I don't know. Is that, what? Off the internet?'

The Church seeks to mock the utility of the internet and net-nanny its parishioners and Juliette's response fitted in nicely within this picture.

I told Juliette about the evil galactic warlord who blew up bits of aliens, having flown them to earth, next to volcanoes.

'Really? I don't...' She burst into infectious giggles. 'It sounds like great science fiction!'

Has it anything to do with your religion?

'I've never heard of it. I don't know. Xenu? I don't go on the internet a lot for like conspiracy theories and research so I don't know that that theory, the aliens...'

But you've never heard it?

'Xenu? No! Never heard it. It sounds like a good movie.'

But nothing to do with Scientology?

'No. That's the thing, the reason, you have to know why I came here today, is because I have a little rock and roll band and we tour the world and I have to do phone interviews and in-person interviews for hours and hours and hours, and a lot of times like I'll go to Denmark, Sweden, Germany, UK and I get asked about Scientology, and a lot of the times the journalists will have really funny questions, they're funny, depending on what mood I'm in, other times they're annoying or aggravating.'

Funny ha-ha? Or funny peculiar?

'Yes, exactly,' she laughed again, 'either one depending on the mood I'm in. But no, my point is to come here is to do, give, do whatever I can to clear the air and I can only talk from personal experience and I, just as a purely selfish reason, would love to not be asked some of the very peculiar rumour questions that I'm asked a lot about Scientology. I'm also asked really funny questions about Hollywood because people have a lot of stereotypes about being an actress, you know, that I own a Rolls Royce or I have a team of stylists. I do yoga, and so I do do some alternative medicine just not the stereotype and this is from you know, all these little funny magazines, on being a Hollywood actress. So I'm used to sort of rumour and stereotype. But the Xenu and the brainwashing and the thing and aliens and blah-de-blah, this is the stellar imagination of people which I think is really creative.'

Nothing whatsoever to do with reality of the Church of Scientology as you've experienced it?

'As I have experienced... That is there are tall tales dreamed up by bored people, maybe people who are on the internet a lot, who do lots of blogging, maybe they don't do blogging, maybe they just read conspiracy theories.'

Other than your mum and dad, is LRH the greatest influence in your life?

'I'm sort of influenced, like a lot of artists, we're very kind of led by our imaginations and creativity and daydreams and stuff like that so right now I'm sort of this single minded rock and roll singer so my biggest influence right now is rock music. Next week it might be something else, but I have to sing Neil Young...'

Good answer.

'Naw, I'm just kidding. But to answer your question. Influence? Influence about things that I find strengthen and seriously L Ron Hubbard... I do hate when things are said, they're so negative and so wrong, they're so far-fetched off somebody that that I find extremely compassionate, intelligent and helpful to me, yeah. So it really, you know you get like that, you want to stick up for somebody that's, you think, is a decent person, humanitarian.'

When you do the Narconon thing, in the sauna, you drank the corn oil or whatever it was?

'The oil at the end of the programme, not in the sauna, cos it needs sweated out, but at the end to put back in the oils you lose in, in or eh go into your, to replace, give your body good fat eh and get out… Out with the old, in with the new.'

It worked for you?

'Yeah, not only did it work, it's friggin' genius, can I say genius?'

Yeah.

They gave me some more Scientologists to interview, and I asked them my usual questions, but I had no idea who they were, and they all stayed on script, and none were as lucid as Juliette.

Reflecting on my four encounters with Anne Archer, Leah Rimini, Kirstie Alley and Juliette Lewis while writing this book, I set what they had to say against the tests for brainwashing set out in Lifton's book. This is a wholly subjective exercise. Lifton's first test, milieu control, was passed with flying colours. They either did not use the internet at all or kept well away of anti-Scientology sites; they only referred to critics of Scientology in wholly negative terms. Normal, everyday sources of information for the rest of us – journalism, newspapers, TV – were also derided.

On mystical manipulation: Leah, Kirstie and Juliette all

denied the existence of Xenu who has, by the way, 2,240,000 hits on Google. I did not ask Anne about the space alien Satan. The women spoke reverently of the 'technology' or the assistance offered by the Church, but critics say the E-meter and the auditing process is a form of brainwashing. Lifton's third test, the demand for purity, requiring the elimination of 'taints' and 'poisons' was evidenced in their reactions to critics in general and me in particular: uniformly negative. The fourth test, the cult of confession, is virtually impossible to score if the adherents are still inside the cult. One can only apply it to people who have left. The fifth test, the sacred science, is similar to the second, mystical manipulation: again, the results would be positive. The sixth test, loading the language, generates an interesting observation: none of the women got very far with me into the brain-hurting maze of linguistic spaghetti which ex-Scientologists like Donna Shannon, Mike Henderson and Bruce Hines say they routinely used when inside the Sea Org. On the contrary, they blocked me. Likewise Tom Cruise and John Travolta, on the very rare occasions when they are asked probing questions about Scientology, block, and talk in general terms about technology and improved communication skills. The sixth, seventh and eighth tests seem impossible to score, even subjectively, if the adherents are still inside the cult, if cult it be.

Rick Ross's simpler three definers of a cult are, first, does the group have an absolute totalitarian leader who has no meaningful accountability? Second, does the group have a process that can be seen as brainwashing: control of information, a manipulation of people in such a way as to gain undue influence over them psychologically and emotionally? Third, does the group do harm? You decide.

That evening we drove to Santa Barbara to meet another defector, one who was happy to talk to us, but not willing to be filmed. I zig-zagged from side to side of the freeways, watching for cars tailing us. I remember driving off the highway into a long, empty car park overlooking the Pacific Ocean, and parking, waiting, watching, to double check that we were not being followed. Had the BBC given us a sea-going car, I would have driven off into the Pacific all the way to Hawaii, to test if we were being followed, but unfortunately the bean-counters vetoed it.

But, according to Sci'gy-Leaks, they were on our tail although not sure who we were going to see. The Communicator was told by Mike: '*Dear Sir. SG is confirmed in the Bay area not STB [*Santa Barbara*] ml Mike.*'

Who is the mysterious SG? We have no idea. The only SG that pops up on the pro-Church 'Religious Freedom Watch' website is Scott Goehring, the founder of an internet newsgroup called 'alt.religion.scientology' (often abbreviated **a.r.s** or **ARS**) which the Church strongly dislikes because it encourages Scientologists to defect. However, we had no plans to talk to any SG.

The Sci'gy-Leaks message traffic takes up the story. On Friday morning the Communicator asks: '*Who were they seeing at STB then?*' Mike replies: '*Dear sir Jeff Hawkins.*'

Dead right. So they followed us successfully all the way to Santa Barbara and smoked out our source, without us ever realising that we were being tailed. This was an impressive achievement. One ex-member of the Church explained to me: 'The most likely ways are: 1. There was a plant who talked to

Jeff or someone who talked to Jeff and he mentioned it or 2. His phone records were gotten and it became known he was in touch with you and the deduction went from there. There is a data base, both hard copy and computerized on Suppressive Persons and reporters at OSA Int. It is maintained in the Investigations (Intelligence) Bureau (division).'

So perhaps all the agents did was track us on the freeway heading to Santa Barbara, make a phonecall to check on SPs in the Santa Barbara area and come up with Jeff's name. If we did succeed in losing them, all they had to do was to discreetly tail Jeff from his home – and he would have led them to us. But it is equally possible that we never succeeded in shaking them.

Jeff Hawkins joined the Church in 1967 and left 38 years later, taking my tally in 2007 of people who had been inside Scientology past a century: 108 years, combined, to be exact. Jeff is a brilliant graphic designer who was responsible for the volcano logo on Scientology books and TV ad campaigns in the 1980s and 1990s. He had only recently left the Church and he was not yet ready to go on TV, but the picture he described of life inside was somewhat different from what I had just heard from Juliette Lewis and all. He is a compact, quietly spoken, seemingly diffident man. He said he had been beaten by David Miscavige.

Once? I asked.

'Five times,' he said. 'The first time was in February, 2002. I was doing writing in the Marketing area. I was called to a meeting with Miscavige to go over a script. There were 30 or 40 people there, all of the top execs of Scientology. He proceeded to disparage the script completely and denigrate me. He was talking about me in the third person, as if I wasn't there. At one point he started saying "Look how he looks at me!" He was pointing to my face and getting himself worked up into a fury. Then all of a sudden he pumped up on the table and launched himself at me, beating me about the head and knocking me down on the ground, scratching my face and tearing my shirt. I was then sent to do "deck" work, physical labour, for two months.

'In 2003, while we were taking a break from a meeting with him, he was talking to me and suddenly began slapping me, hard, on the side of my head. He hit me with the flat of his hand, very hard, about eight times. Then he went over and began to hit Marc Yager, [another senior Sea Org member] knocking him to the ground.

'Once in 2004, he was giving a group of executives a tour of the RTC [Religious Technology Centre] Building at Gold, and after he had finished showing us one room, he was walking past me out the door when he suddenly punched me in the stomach, hard enough to take my breath away.

'He once hit me repeatedly in the face at a meeting, enough to scratch my face and draw blood. He signalled to his Communicator, Lou Stuckenbrock [the same Lou of the Sci'gy-Leaks messages which the Church deny], who produced a small bottle of disinfectant and dabbed it on my face.

'He hit me another time at a meeting.

'I also saw him physically abuse others. At a meeting in the RTC Building, he knocked one executive off his chair and to the ground. At another meeting he beat Lyman Spurlock about the head. As mentioned above, I saw him beat Marc Yager to the ground. This is not to mention the verbal abuse, profanity, and threats, which were constant. He twice ordered me "overboarded." I was thrown in the swimming pool at the "Star of California" – at Gold Base, in the Californian desert, once, fully clothed. This is about the only use the pool gets any more.

'Another time, just before I was offloaded [quit the Church] in 2005, I was thrown in the freezing lake, at night, in February. My age at the time, 58.

'I was beaten by others as well, numerous times by one of Miscavige's "pets," on his orders. I was once hit by a woman executive, and she demanded of my fellow staff "why didn't one of you hit him?"'

The Church of Scientology and David Miscavige deny all allegations that he is physically violent in any way.

The Church's Freedom Magazine says of Jeff that he is a 'liar to the core' running with an 'honest to goodness terrorist organization' – the usual, in other words.

Some time after we met him, Jeff published an e-book about his experiences in the Church, *Counterfeit Dreams*. In it, he describes the moment he did OT III: 'I sat with trembling hands... an evil galactic overlord named Xenu... they were then dumped into volcanoes, the volcanoes were exploded with H-bombs, and the Thetans then went through days of brainwashing with pictures of angels and devils...'

Back in 2007, Jeff went on to explain that there was a RPF dungeon of the mind hidden inside the Scientology 'Concrete Angel' complex which we had been given a tour of that very day. He drew us a picture of 20 or so Sea Org prisoners, cooped up in a small airless room, paying for their crimes against the Church in a part of the complex he called Lebanon Hall. The prisoners were in bunks. Outside was a guard and a security camera. Jeff also drew us a map showing the location of the dormitory - on the first floor as you enter the building, but accessible through a door from the ground floor if you went round the back. Third, he drew Miscavige beating an executive up, throwing a chair and the man to the ground. The victim? Mike Rinder. That was something to ask Mike, next time I met him.

CHAPTER TWELVE
'You Suck Cock on Hollywood Boulevard'

The Church does not own the skies above their once secret base at Gilman Hot Springs, also known as Gold, on the edge of the Californian desert, at least, not yet. We lifted off, the Hollywood sign somewhere below us, then clattered across the thickly populated chessboard of LA. The cheapest way of experiencing something like the sensation of flying in a helicopter is snorkelling. Floating around on top of the sea, you see the ridges and troughs of the sea bottom rise and fall away from you. It is weirdly like that in a chopper, the land beneath you rising and dipping, the Perspex bubble of the helicopter canopy just a posher version of your snorkel mask.

We were heading east, rising and falling over a fag-end of a dirty brown, dry-as-dust mountain chain till we got to what used to be called Gilman Hot Springs, near Hemet, about 90 miles east of LA. Mr Hubbard arrived here in 1979, pretty much on the run from the FBI. One Scientologist, Anne Rosenblum, who was only familiar with the great man through his approved photographs from the sixties was shocked to discover that he had 'rotting teeth and a really fat gut'. Worse, she had been told the pet dogs of Mrs Mary Sue Hubbard were 'Clear', and would only bark at people who had committed 'overts' – crimes – against the Hubbards. When they started snapping at her, 'I started walking around wondering what deep, dark terrible overts I had committed on LRH or Mary Sue in this life or past lives.' The possibility that the pooches were just reacting to Anne, a stranger, in an ordinary, doggy way eluded her mind-set back then.

The 1977 FBI raids on the Church's offices which had unearthed the documents proving that not journalist Paulette Cooper but the Church had been sending itself bomb threats caught bigger fish in the net. The raids had revealed Operation Snow White, a vast attempt by the Church to seize compromising documents from the US government. More than 130 government agencies were targeted for thefts or infiltration, involving perhaps as many as 5,000 covert agents. At the fag-end of 1979, nine Scientologists, including L Ron's wife, Mary Sue Hubbard, pleaded guilty to specimen charges of subverting the United States government, and she was sentenced to five years. The Church hid Hubbard away at Gilman Hot Springs, an old resort gone to seed, for a while, then moved him on, further into the desert, living a life of total seclusion from the outside world. Paranoid, gibbering, uneasy at the real possibility of arrest, trial and prison, L Ron lived out his last years cocooned from reality by his devoted 'Messengers', hand-picked children of the Sea Org staff, one of them, David Miscavige.

Almost thirty years on, the world has creeped closer to the desert. Instead of miles of nothing, and tumbleweed drifting poignantly in the breeze, a property developer has built a suburban housing estate close by Gold Base. It is as if Barratt Homes has knocked up an estate next to the secret underground lair of Ernst Stavro Blofeld. From up high you can see the effects of irrigation: the green grass of the Scientology golf course where Tom Cruise is supposed to have played, giving way to Gold's cluster of buildings, then the vast brown neck of the mountain to the east.

Our helicopter landed at a small airport near Hemet, we hired a car and tootled off to the secret lair of Scientology.

Sci'gy-Leaks shows how the Church's hierarchy dealt with our going airborne with its customary calm judgment. On Friday morning, Mike reported to Miscavige's Communicator: '*they headed towards STB* [Santa Barbara] *and then turned off and went to Van Nuys airport and goot chopper and just circled Gold. Tommy and i are enroute to gold in case they try to land out there.*'

As ever, Mike and Tommy were keen on telling the Leader's Office how well their campaign was going to stop our Panorama from ever being broadcast: '*This morning we had ltr delivered to bosses at BBC laying out outrageous and bigoted actions of sweeney and attaching dvd clip of his psychotic break at cchr yesterday. UK counsel saw clip and its "extraordinary" and he has never seen anything like it and it alone will embarrass BBC enough that they cld abort the show just on this.*'

So there is a huge contrast between the reaction of the Church's agents the day before – to keep calm and carry on, including a tour of the Concrete Angel and letting me interview Juliette Lewis – and the legal response, which was to big up 'my psychotic break'. Mike was holding one arrow back in his quiver.

' *We havent even told them abt his quote that BBC higher ups are overpaid morons.'*

The overpaid morons remark was made when I sought to entice Anne Archer to make some minor criticism of the Church, in vain.

Mike continued: '*Uk counsel also suggested others write ltrs abt abuses so will get thgese put together. They hv lgl ltr [have legal letter] ready to go but holding onto it until we get response to tommy,s ltr as that will cut off anyone higher up in BBC dealing with us. Ml Mike*'

This suggests that the Church studies the BBC closely. The Church was still waiting for a response from the Panorama team about some previous atrocity by me from earlier in the trip, and they wanted to hold back their big gun of me going tomato until they received that lower-level response. The moment they had that, they could fire the big gun at the top of the BBC. If they didn't wait, then the programme team could reply to the exploding tomato incident, initially, anyway. None of us were in doubt that the Church would make merry with me losing it. We were determined to show it so that they would never be able to claim that we funked showing something embarrassing. Besides, Mole said, it was good telly.

Although Miscavige was too busy to meet us, he – or, rather his Communicator – wasn't too busy to badger his agents: '*Right now you have a record of showing them through CC, Pac, CCHR and the places they refused to go being Flag and Gold (while making demands to interview the pope).*'

The Church's strategy against us seemed to be that they were deliberately seeking to publicly offer us seemingly as much access as possible, report our reluctance to engage with it, and then show that as proof of our lack of fairness and objectivity. But this strategy had two big holes in it: it discounted the detail of their conditions on access, unacceptable to us; and access to beautifully-groomed but empty facilities did not begin to address the credible and grievous complaints made by ex-members of the Church.

'*You two are to solve this.*'

This suggests delusion. Our dogged persistence to make our film on our terms was not a problem the Church's two agents could solve.

Miscavige's office then turned to the making of the Church's parallel documentary, which eventually saw the light of the day as 'Panorama Exposed': '*Solve it as he's expecting your documentary this week - edited and ready for mising [mixing?] and post-prod.*'

On reading this, I cannot but feel sorry for Tommy and Mike. To make any documentary in a week is a real challenge. At Panorama, we call them 'fast-turn-arounds' and they are hell to produce.

Mike replied, filling in his Dear Leader. Quick as a flash, Miscavige's Communicator came back: '*And? Did they show up?*'

I can answer that. We did. Our trip to Gold Base was boring, a crushing disappointment. A public road dissects the base, but thick foliage, walls and high fences blocked our view. Later, we were told that when the media is about, Sea Org members are ordered into lock-down mode, compelled to stay indoors so that they cannot be filmed. There is a tunnel under the road, allowing members to walk across the two bisected halves of the estate without being captured on camera. We didn't go to the booth or security gate immediately, so they found us. A few minutes after our arrival, a Church security goon turned up and started hectoring us that we had parked on private land. Unfortunately, he forgot to use his handbrake and his vehicle slipped back a few feet. But it made for boring telly, and we left and headed back to LA.

The office of the Leader was still babbling: '*As for documentary, it was senseless to explain to you how obnoxious your comm was. Who do you think puts together documentaries in the real world? An Avid Operator (like Dos) or a PR who knows his business.*'

The tone is clear. To be fair to Tommy and Mike, they had just made a Panorama reporter look like a roaring fruitcake and that brilliant PR demolition job on me had been written off, as if it was easy. All Miscavige's Communicator could do was call Mike's message 'obnoxious'.

Mike explained that we had driven back to Van Nuys airport, and that he and Tommy were hurrying back from Gold to LA.

The Leader's Communicator was not happy: '*You blew it. And the phone call was a total waste of time. Just waiting for more orders, like you alwys dO. Tommy (APU) instant Treason all over again. No handling--just... "I couldn't possibly handle it ... "And you have yet to provide any handling.*'

This message is preposterously unfair to the two agents. By this time in the game, we were paranoid and did not discuss our plans with any outsiders unless we had compelling reasons to do so. Tommy and Mike could not predict our movements exactly all the time and to blame them for an occasional failure is well beyond unreasonable.

Very soon after that, a follow-up message from the Communicator, more angry than the first: '*I basically wanted to vomit on that call... The act of treason yesterday of throwing him*' – The Leader - '*up as a target by agreeing hed get contacted all because of tommy having a self important button that he's a big shot... Now answer my comm you CICS!* [Counter-Intentional Cock Sucker]'

Who is the master intelligence behind the messages from the Communicator, David Miscavige or Lou Stuckenbrock? She or He? In 2010 I brought up 'CICS!' with Miscavige's old drinking buddy, Tom DeVocht, and his partner Alison Andrus.

'Counter-Intention...' said Alison.

'Counter-Intention,' echoed Tom.

'...Cock Suckers,' Alison got it first.

'When I spent the time with Dave, Lou was always there,' said Tom, 'Lou is his Communicator, secretary, security, carried a tape recorder around. Records every word out of Dave's mouth, including the "cocksucker this...and that". She records all of it. As the tape is full, she sends it up the hill to Building 50 at Gold and there is two people up there that type full time. When I originally knew her years back she was a sweetheart...'

Alison said she grew up with Lou, or her proper name, Laurisse, at Saint Hill in England: 'When I knew her she was the most wonderful, genuine person incredible person.' Alison had been the Inspector General's Communicator, the same job that Lou has with David Miscavige: 'when you talk, you talk for that person. So when you go to someone and you are told to tell them something, you are telling them, but it is coming from the other person.'

If what you are saying is correct, that is a cut-out. Why have a cut-out? Why can't Miscavige send his own messages?

'Because you would know about it,' said Tom, laughing. 'I sat there and watched him write messages or have Lou write messages like that to Mike [Rinder] or to Marty [Rathbun], to different people... Dave knows that if that came from him somebody could get a hold of it. He is extremely smart and he is extremely afraid, super afraid. He is scared of just about anybody and everybody. So he knows if he can have Lou do that, he could always say, "ah that wasn't me"'.

I asked Alison about Lou. When she was much younger, would she talk about 'Cock Sucking...'?

'Never, ever. Oh, it is definitely not from Lou. It is from David Miscavige, without a doubt.'

The Church of Scientology and David Miscavige deny that he is foul-mouthed and that the messages had anything to do with the Church, its Leader or his Communicator. The Church says I am psychotic, a bigot and a liar.

A third message from the Communicator, angrier yet: '*DID YOU GET MY MESSAGE AND ARE YOU ANSWERING???*'

Tommy replied: '*Yes sir. We got it and mike is answering. I'm driving right now.*'

The Communicator whipped back: '*You are answering and driving? Okay – you just gained a notch on him. He's he passenger and you have more hands to answer. Make sure he knows what the acronym CICS [Counter-Intuitive Cock Sucker] means as that's exactly what he's proving by event REFUSING to answer a comm!*'

Tommy replied: *'Yes sir. He knows what cics means and he is getting this answer to you immediately.'*

Mike joined in the loop: *'Dear Sir. I apoplogize for not answering right away. I have drafted an email to go to him that docuiments his latest criminal act of showing up at gold and aslkin g a securityguard for an interview while we were sitting in la.'*

Mike went on to say that my behaviour was 'beyond the beyond' and that they were not going to waste any more time on providing me with access. Meanwhile, he had got in touch with Bob – Fireman Bob – to film at Westminster Abbey and the BBC.

A Church of Scientology film crew turned up at Lambeth Palace, the historic home of the Archbishop of Canterbury, and knocked on the immense wooden door, demanding an entry. His Grace was not available at that moment, but, to be fair, the Archbishop has given dozens of interviews to the media, the latest of which in September 2012, he admitted to making mistakes with a humility which seems entirely becoming in a religious leader. Then they went to the BBC TV and did the same with the then Director-General, Mark Thompson. He too, was not available at that moment, but he too has been regularly interviewed on television. Had neither Archbishop nor D-G in their various reincarnations not been interviewed since 1992, the Church might have had a point.

The Communicator was still not happy: *'Whatever. These are just tidbits. Of course his [Sweeney's] lies are criminal.'*

That is just nonsense. I had not lied, and nor had I said anything criminal. One gets the impression that no-one in the Leader's circle ever says to him, calm down, mate, you're being silly. The Communicator babbled on: *'No handlings has yet appeared on that and cob [Miscavige] knows he's on his own and can expect nobody in the church to defend him at all... now you are behind the a8 ball.'*

The 8 or black ball in pool is a difficult position to get out of.

'You don't even say where he is right now getting drunk.'

We were now back in LA. I might have been enjoying a beer but I was not getting drunk.

'Maybe you have plans on how to handle but they arebkt [aren't?] listed here.'

Tommy was in dire trouble. He had spoken too frankly when he told Mole: "Well, I report to Mr Miscavige. Is that high enough?"' Now the Communicator was incredibly fearful that Tommy and Mike's 'handling' of the BBC might blow up in their faces and that, he, too might get damaged.

'Sir,' Tommy replied, *'totally got this 100%. He has now sent the answer and also saw the derivation of cics. Tommy'*

The power play from on high continued: *'A) he's gtng the message to me when he wants after 10 MFing* [Mother Fucking] *nudges. B) CICS - the term was originated when the first DNA of a slug was scene by the first sloth.'*

Tommy replied at length, once he and Mike had returned to their office in OSA, the Office of Special Affairs, the Church's intelligence arm, where they were able to speed type on a proper computer. *'Sir, sorry for the crap answer. We are back at osa and making sure this email totally boxes them in and has them utterly smoked and with no choice but to put sweeney out to pasture and shelf this piece.'*

Tommy goes on to prostrate himself before the Leader because of his 'mistake' the previous day: *'So I'm focused on getting the job done and not having it be a flap and fixing my trea-*

sonous caving in and my total betrayal of setting up cob [Chairman of the Board, Miscavige] *yesterday. I caused it so I have to fix it. I have no right to criticize mike or bitch about being where I am with him. Its up to me to be responsible for both of us and not only handle myself but Mike as well. Ml, Tommy'*

That Tommy went out of his way to accept the blame and not place it on Mike's head showed a certain grace, that whatever else was going on inside his head, he retained some sense of dignity.

Back in the office, Mike echoed Tommy in setting out that their representations would sink me with the BBC: *'we are flat out competently hndlng this. This is OK ML Mike'*

Yet again, the Communicator was not content. She (or is it he?) rants at length, concluding: *YS!* [YOU SUCK!] *And have him hat you on the L button as you keep taking hin off as an info. Do you realize everyone of my mssgs are longer than yours. You really are just sp* [Suppressive Person] *aren't you? I wqaited to get this crap? I can't even believe it. You just can't work or do can you? YS* [YOU SUCK!] *YS* [YOU SUCK!] *YS* [YOU SUCK!] *YS* [YOU SUCK!] *YS* [YOU SUCK!]*!!!!!!!!!!!!!!!!!!!!!!'*

The Church denied David Miscavige abused staff with obscene language, saying the allegation was beneath contempt.

One ex-member of the Church later told me that this kind of potty-mouthed, one-way abusive language was standard from David Miscavige. Another of his favourite sign-offs was YSCOHB.

Decoded, it means: 'YOU SUCK COCK ON HOLLYWOOD BOULEVARD.'

257

CHAPTER THIRTEEN
'Is there anybody there?'

On our last day in California we headed directly to the Concrete Angel on L Ron Hubbard Way. Around the back of the left wing of the angel was the door pin-pointed by Jeff Hawkins as the RPF prison. I had called Tommy several times. No answer. But as we approached the door, my phone rang. It was Tommy. I told him we were recording the call and that we had heard that ridiculous numbers of people on the RPF programme were being held in a kind of dungeon in Lebanon Hall.

Tommy: 'John, have you lost your mind?'

'No, Tommy, I have lost my voice.'

That was true. The combination of yelling my head off and doing pieces-to-camera in the chopper had left me hoarse.

Tommy: 'That is the most preposterous ridiculous insane abusatory disgusting thing I have heard you say to date.' I always admired Tommy for his understatement.

'OK, well prove me wrong then Tommy. Let me in to this building.'

Tommy stayed on the phone, as I gave him a running commentary: 'I am knocking on the door.'

Knock, knock, I went, knock, knock, knockety-knock.

It was a 21st century version of *The Listeners*, Walter De La Mare's spooky poem:

Is there anybody there, said the Traveller,
Knocking on the moonlit door?...
For he suddenly smote on the door, even
Louder, and lifted his head:-
'Tell them I came, and no one answered,
That I kept my word...'

As in the poem, no-one answered.

Tommy and I kept batting away at each other over the phone, as was our tradition. Reinforced by Jeff Hawkins, I asked him about Xenu and about David Miscavige – did he go around thumping people?

Tommy was giving no quarter: 'Lies... your behaviour is utterly reprehensible and the level of unprofessionalism is appalling...'

'You won't let me into this building, will you?'

'I will absolutely not. No, considering your behaviour, considering you went so crazy inside of one of my facilities that two of my staff ran off to get help for fear that you were going to become violent because you have what I could only call a psychotic break... you are clearly an unstable individual...'

'Thank you very much, that's very kind of you. But I do not think I had a psychotic break. I reacted under pressure to your attempts to brainwash me.'

You get the drift.

Later, their Scientology attack video, *Panorama Exposed*,

showed an empty meeting room behind the closed door I was knocking on. It wasn't wholly compelling proof that what Jeff Hawkins had told me had never been the case, that it had been a mind-prison and, prompted by our interest, they had moved the people somewhere else. Or Jeff may have been wholly in the wrong, as the Church says.

Tommy and I ripped chunks out of each other, telephonically, for a while and then we were joined by Sylviana, the black clad camerawoman from Sea Org, who started filming me, pounding on the door.

'We are filming for BBC Panorama,' I said. 'What are you filming for…?'

'I love filming,' she said. Sylviana had a cold beauty and an exotic accent – Argentinian, Paraguayan, or something like that.

'Have you ever seen David Miscavige, or anyone…?'

'That is none of your business,' she said.

'It is my business because I am a reporter,' I said, cockily. 'My business is everybody's business. That is what reporters do. So the question is: have you ever seen David Miscavige…?'

'No, I haven't.'

'The Xenu story? Is that true?'

'It is a lie,' stressing the last word with such vehemence that it was quite disturbing. Phonetically, it sounded like: 'Eez a liiiiiie.' Then Bill's tape ran out.

That Saturday, according to Sci'gy-Leaks, was the first day when Tommy and Mike were not fully 'handling' us and were able to engage with their campaign to persuade the BBC to pull our programme before it was broadcast. It was also the first day for the Leader's Office to address their perceived multiple failures at length. Again, the reader should bear in mind that the Church and David Miscavige deny that Sci'gy-Leaks is genuine. Much of the to and fro is boring and repetitive; some of it is meaningless gobbledegook; some of it just plain crazy.

The Communicator waxed long and loud about my failings: '*He missed the JT* [John Travolta] *interview insisting instead of interviewing a nut. And it just continues. We told you COB wasn't doing the interview and that if what you wanted was anything to do with Scn you would have approached him in UK where he was in plain view and greeting people as they entered the Church. COBs role is not to handle public relations and does interviews rarely, if at all.*'

Subject pronouns are words like 'I', 'you' and 'he'. In the above 'He' is Sweeney; 'We' is the Church; 'you' is Sweeney; 'he' is Miscavige. Muddling subject pronouns leads to confusion. This is the linguistic equivalent of a *Dr Who* episode featuring a disgusting scrambled egg style mess called *The Brain of Morbius*.

Miscavige's Communicator, in setting out why an interview was not on, referred to the '*falsehoods BBC preseneted 20 years ago*' – homage to the 1987 Panorama '*The Road to Total Freedom?*' of blessed memory.

The Communicator babbled on for a bit: '-*How come you haven't nade it clear to him that you refuse to forward his request as Sweenys behavior is so bigotted, his conduct so irrational that you sonsider him unstable?*

-Are you actually hiding out and letting him screw around-

outside our properties such as the complex as your handling?'

What is unfair about this message from on high is that neither Tommy nor Mike could stop us from doing our jobs. It wasn't their fault that none of the points the Communicator raised addressed the grave criticisms made by ex-Scientologists to us. This feels like a classic example of the failing of an organisation where top-down control prevents the lower orders from explaining to the bosses what is happening in the real world.

Mike replied by demonizing me – the default position of the Church faced with scrutiny: *'he is a bigot and has psychotic breaks. Tommy said that there is no way he is taking him inside one of our buidlings after he had his psychotic break on wednesday. A break so outrageous two of the female presenmt ran to get help as they were sure john wld get violent.'*

I did shout. I may like a drink. But I am not a violent man.

'*…he then said we had tried to brainwash him!'*

Yes. I believe they did try to brainwash me.

'He also repeated request for interview w COB and Tommy told him he had not forwarded the request and wld nvr ever forward such a request in amillion yrs and wld do everything in his power to make sure sweeney never gets anywhere near cob as he is a bigot and abusive and we hv ansrd every false allegation and will answer to any others. Sweeney ended up hanging up and then geting back into his van and driving off as I am typing this and now heading up Virgil.'

We had not told the Church where we were going. Virgil Avenue was en route between the Concrete Angel and the location of our next appointment, with another ex-Scientologist.

The Communicator replied: '*Your problem on COB is you didn't fill the vacuum but just "da's". That's due to your overts. Specifically hat dump.*'

That sounds like utter mumbo-jumbo but let's try to break it down: '*Your problem on COB is you didn't fill the vacuum* [deal with the BBC] *but just "da's".* [Dead Agents – knocking out critics with a file of black information.] *That's due to your overts.* [Crimes against the Church] *Specifically hat dump* [a failure to carry out your mission – hat means post or job, dump means failure.] Translated, I think it means something like this: 'You failed to do your job properly.'

Lifton's test number six, 'Loading the Language', springs up here and it is worth repeating the psychiatrist's specific point, that 'the effect of ideological totalism can be summed up in one word: constriction. He is, so to speak, linguistically deprived; and since language is so central to all human experience, his capacities for thinking and feeling are immensely narrowed.' The logic of the language from the Communicator is as round and smooth as a billiard ball. It chokes communication and reduces language to a series of Druidic insults to which there is no possible answer. To me, it seems mad.

The Communicator had a lot on her mind: '*As for the stupid allegation of being "afraid" to see Sweeny, anybody who actually knows COB knows what a joke it is… Afraid? He's met individuals from 10 Downing not to mention the home office.*'

No-one in the British government could confirm or deny that Miscavige had met individuals from Number Ten or the Home Office. Who exactly in Number Ten? No-one knows; or no-one is saying.

The Communicator went back to demonizing his staff:

'*You've just gone PTS* [PTS=Potential Trouble Source, one step from Suppressive Person] *and not filled the vacuum as the fact is he barely sleeps AND YOU KNOW IT and doing this BBC thing because he's trying to blackmail with threats of what lies he'll spread is as obscene as it gets and a virtual guarantee it wouldn't happen.*'

The subject pronoun 'he' switches from Hero Miscavige – who barely sleeps – to Demon Sweeney – who blackmails and lies – in the same sentence. We are different. This is primary school English and the Communicator has failed.

The Communicator drones on: '*What the hell happened to the fill the vacuum however? You've got the usual treason...*'

Treason is a heavy word. The Communicator uses it with foolish abandon.

'*...and perfect excuse to do nothing because all of a sudden Tommys on the firing line and is worried he'll choke a question when you idiots already knew if there was something he tommy didn't know it would be the proof of what slime this idiot is...*'

What slime this idiot is? Thank you very much.

The Communicator closes this message with a large dose of self-pity: '*Cob will finish all the materials, all the courses, all the buildings and their contruction, singl hand every event, keep the show on the road, then do TV (which he's tried to get to for a year but god forbid you 2 do anything to ease his lines) and THEN defend himself because you have every excuse not to.*'

Tommy leaps to set out his views on the Leader to the Communicator: '*I have never seen anyone* [Miscavige] *work harder or more hours and is as well the kindest, most genuine caring individual I know.*'

In Lifton's foreword to Singer's book, he writes on cults

264

that 'there is a pattern of manipulation and exploitation from above by leaders and ruling coteries and idealism from below on the part of supplicants and recruits.'

In the normal world, someone might reply to the delusional tone of the Communicator's message by suggesting the real world difficulties the team was confronting. A supplicant in a cult would grovel.

The Communicator swept the applause aside and got on to their version of the story on us: '*Its time our documentary was put together as at this point it will probably be sensational.*'

It was.

The Communicator changed tack, to reply to Mike who was 'handling' my knocking on the door of the Concrete Angel: '*Thanks. You'd better make sure security is in at those buildings. Obviously somebody is spreading more bs [bullshit] about the rpf but you neeed to double ensure secuirty is tight in those buildings as they could try to send somebody in with a hidden camera which is the last thing you need.*'

This appears to suggest that there might be something hidden inside the Concrete Angel the Church would not want the world to see.

'*Yes, his behavior sounds insane. Are you saying he LITERALLY said you guys brainwashed him (SWEENY)? And that this statement is on camera? If so, this guy should practically be under a restraining order... This dungeon bit is desperation and the same crap we've disproven a billion times. He's been exposed as the bigot and dishonest journalist he is.*'

Mike replied: '*Dear Sir. Security is on red alert at PAC and CC. They are now in Griffith Pk... They film every car that goes by as Sweeney accuses us of following and spying on him which at this pt is more of his paranoia.'*

He was dead right about the paranoia.

We had said our goodbyes to the Concrete Angel and drove towards our final interview with a defector. Paranoid, hunted, I thought we were being followed again, one suspect driver a blonde guy, old, moustached, maybe the guy who followed us when we came to LA in the first place in the dark blue Kia, a second, I remember, a tall, dark-haired chap. I pulled our car into a car park and waited. The dark-haired guy followed us, parked, and got out of his car. An ordinary person going about his business? Or a smart private investigator, suspecting that he had been smelt out, pretending to be an ordinary person…

'He's looking back at us,' I said, urgently.

Bill: 'I don't think so. I think he was just sorting out his shit before he got out of the car.'

'It's because we've got a bloody camera in our car, that's why he's looking back at us,' said Mole, boringly.

I drove off, very slowly, the speed of a milk float, so slowly that anyone tailing us would have to crawl along at a suspicious snail's space too. One of the suspect cars overtook us then turned down the far-side of a crescent, perhaps hoping to come back on our tail. I went down the near side of the crescent. We met mid-way, as he rocketed along, almost smashing into us. The guy was jabbering away into a head-set mobile phone, as if demented, but at the last moment he flicked his wheel and we did not crash. Pity. It would have made for a most interesting court case.

Our next defector was ex-Scientologist Tory Christman who we met in Griffith Park. A Scientologist for three decades, she left in 2000, taking my tally of defectors' time inside to 138 years. She, too, had a grim story to tell, of early infatuation turning into years of abuse before she quit. Tory had suffered from epilepsy but medication stopped her fits. However, when she joined the Sea Org, she said, she was told to get off her medication. The fits came back: 'My mom started calling me, saying "Tory, they are going to kill you."'

When Tory started taking medication again, the fits stopped. Once she was utterly loyal. Now she hates the Church, and the Church seems to hate her. She said that she had been defamed by the Church, that its then spokesman Mike Rinder had called her a 'wacko' and her story 'absolute bullshit'.

The 'Religious Freedom Watch' website, keenly antagonistic to any effective critic of the Church of Scientology, says this about Tory: 'a run-away housewife who abandoned her husband when some "new friends" she met over the internet promised her an exciting new life. Christman's new friends are anti-religious extremists... Despite her lies, the media is getting wise to the tall tales of Tory Christman.'

Well, I liked her.

Tory explained the Church's logic in attacking her: 'Hubbard wrote a thing called "Black PR" where he said, "Lie, cheat, steal, destroy someone utterly if they are against Scientology." Because I speak out trying to inform people about scientology they have to slander me, that's what they feel. They have followed me, they have flattened my tyres when I tried to help a family get out. They have not only lied all over the internet about me, they have done all kinds of nasty things.'

Private investigators?

'They sent two private investigators to two of my best friends saying that they were looking for information, was I slandering Tom Cruise? Luckily, my two friends are ex-Scientologists.'

What were you saying about Tom Cruise, I asked?

'I said, I want to thank Tom Cruise for showing the world what an Operating Thetan actually looks like.'

We had to wrap up the interview with Tory quickly and head to the airport.

Back in the twilight zone of Sci-gy Leaks, Mike told the Communicator: *'We are putting togther "greatest hits" clips for BBC execs and compiling everything we have shown, offered and made available and how they hv spent money getting crap and the same disproven crap they had in 87 and it is proven to be so. He is definitely desperate and now we hv to get this put together and have BBC shitcan him as well as our get our own documentary done.*

Thay hv checked out of hotel and hv flight at 945 tonite. ML Mike'

We hadn't shared out flight plans with the Church. Tommy rejoined the conversation: *'we can cut together all the interviews he did and show these beautiful elegant women and dignified men he interviewed and cut to their facial reactions to his off the wal questions and then show photos of the psychotic degraded people he chauffered around CW and SFO (Hines, lonsdale, etc) and show how they are totally DB...'*

DB stands for Degraded Being.

'...and weird and crim and gross. Juxtapositioned against anne archer? Fred shaw? Dr. Root?'

Fred Shaw and Dr Root were the Scientology figures I

had interviewed at the Celebrity Centre whom I had never heard of.

'*Sweeney,*' *Tommy continued,* '*will look like the complete psychopath that he is and I haven't even gotten to the footage of him screaming his head off and then explaingin it away as something to do with a high school play he did or that he was brainwashed. Just gonzo.*'

I'm rather proud of that description.

Tommy sent another message immediately after that, referring to a phone conversation the previous day, seemingly with Miscavige: '*Sir, I want to correct what I said yesterday on the phone with cob. I was and am ready for that interview. I have read every DA* [Dead Agent] *pack I cld get my hands on, went onto the net and saw every disgusting site and read everything I cld about hawkins, hines, donna shannon, lawnsdale and more. I had stacks of the religious expertises ready to literally throw at him and also the DA docs for the OT VII forgery on the net, the san Francisco crap on Narconon and more. I was very entubulated about screwing cob over on wed at cchr* [when he told Mole that he reported to Miscavige directly] *and kicking myself as every other time sweeny brought up cob I said no way and especially not an intervuew with you. I jsut went effect and it was inexcuseable. I have since talked to sweeney today and I went BALLISTIC when he brought up COB and made it very clear that it would be over my dead body that he would ever talk to cob ever. I was being temporarily defeatist when on the phone with cob.*'

The message suggests that they were planning an interview in which Tommy would endeavour to make me go tomato, again, but that his talking about his proximity to the Leader has scuppered it. The logic of that last point seems warped, but never mind: '*I never had any questions about m ability to do that interview and was actually looking forward to it after having drivn sweenmey psychotic on wednesday as I figured I could do it againa d that I would get him to pop off with the most outrageous things. Well this is exactly what happend when I talked to him on the phone today and got him to say that we had brainwashed him!!! And I have this on tape and we are verifying we're got it on video too. He has lost it and I am definitely the person who drives him more psychotic than anyone. He goes nuts around me. And I'm going to keep it up. Ml, Tommy*'

The boast that a member of a Church's Holy Order can drive someone 'more psychotic' than anyone else seems an odd one for a member of a religious order to make. To put it mildly, it wants charity.

The next message is also from Tommy: '*Sir, I'm sorry about not briefing you on Donna. She is a nobody...*'

Donna is not a nobody, but a feisty woman of quality.

'*...Sweeney is nuts and we have it documented and he is such a psycho he's the star of the exposé...*'

The very last message from the Sci'gy-Leaks hoard is also from Tommy: '*Sir, he already told me he is leaving tonight. He and Sarah both told me that. However I was planning on calling him and saying, "hey what's the deal? I spent the last two weeks of my life being available to you for your show and offered you everything. Now from what you told me you are probably leaving soon and you haven't even called to say you are going? I have no doubt you called your good friends Shawn lonsdale, donna shannon and bruce hines. Didn't you? Well good bye John. I can't say it been a pleasure getting to know you but I have no doubt you'll be hearing more from me. Cheers*'

We packed up and drove to LAX. After we had checked in, we went to a bar and drank mojitos. A suspicious-looking man with a briefcase sat extremely close to us and affected not to be interested in us. I stood inches from him and slurped my drink like a baby elephant sucking up water through its trunk, extremely noisily. He didn't run away – proof, if proof were needed, that he must have been an agent. Mole noted: 'We went to the bar and you made awful slurping noises next to some poor passenger.'

CHAPTER FOURTEEN
'Panorama Exposed'

The Church of Scientology's 'Psychiatry: Industry of Death' exhibition turned out to be a moveable feast. A few days after I had lost my temper in its permanent manifestation on Sunset Boulevard, LA, it popped up on Westbourne Grove, just down the road from Notting Hill, West London. We decided it might be a bright idea to ask a shrink to go along and have a peek and then interview him afterwards about the accuracy of the exhibition. Patrick Barrie, our Assistant Producer, arranged to meet the psychiatrist in the Portobello Gold pub beforehand.

Patrick takes up the story: 'I was sitting in the pub – it was deserted – waiting for him when two women, one much older than the other, walked in and marched up to me. The older one, who I later realized as the UK press representative of the Church, Janet Laveau, said something like: "You are Patrick and you have no right to be here. You were told you weren't invited." I was a bit lost for words, but after she droned on a bit more I asked her how she knew who I was and quick as a flash, she said: "From the photos in LA." I told her I thought this was creepy and walked out in a mild state of frenzy.'

I love this story because Patrick is the kind of person who might say that was paranoid, and yet he claims he was frenzied out of a London pub by a Scientologist. No-one will ever believe him.

After the shrink had popped into the Church's unusual House of Horrors travelling show, I asked psychiatrist Dr Trevor Turner what he made of 'The Industry of Death' exhibition? He said: 'A monstrous interpretation of what psychiatry is all about.'

What struck Trevor most was, 'the assault on psychiatrists, on oppressing minorities, causing all the ills of the twentieth century, generating the Holocaust. It's bitter and I don't quite understand why they're so against us.'

Are psychiatrists Nazi?

'Of course not. Clearly any kind of science can be misused in any kind of vicious regime but the idea that we were the cause of the Nazi Holocaust is just part of the logic they mis-use, the association versus causation trick. Because psychiatrists were trying to find out and understand the genetic basis of mental illness, therefore, somehow, they're the cause of Hitler deciding he wanted to round up and kill all the Jews. It's a monstrous form of inappropriate logic.'

Dr Turner had no idea what was Scientology's assault on psychiatry: 'They shout and yell at us in our meetings. They accost us in the streets and film us. They took a photograph of me. I really do not understand. As far as I'm concerned, psychiatrists are doctors doing their best to help seriously unwell people. I suspect it's part of a stigma associated with our patients. As a result of that stigma, desperate remedies have been tried on dreadfully ill people in the past: asylums,

273

lobotomies, ECTs [Electro-Convulsive Therapy]. Looking back retrospectively rather dangerous things have been done in the name of science.'

Some of the images I saw in the exhibition were genuinely horrific.

'Of course. If you or I had been in a psychiatric asylum in the 1930s we would have been terrified. The smells, the sounds, the images, the dreadfully unwell people howling and hallucinations and disturbed thoughts. They were terrifying places because people were horribly unwell. The reason why these remedies were undertaken – ECT, prolonged sleep narcosis, lobotomies – was because in a sense you would do anything to get your relative rescued from that living hell.'

Was there anything in the exhibition that concerned you professionally?

'If I had paranoid schizophrenia and I went to that, I would be very tempted to stop my medication at once. If I was the relative of someone with a severe illness, I'd be very upset by that because it is frightening. It uses lurid images and negative associations and false logic to decry what are effective ways of treatment.'

We went to film the 'Industry of Death' – the London version – from the pavement. A Scientology cameraman filmed us from inside the exhibition but we were also being filmed by a second agent, much more discreetly, in a dark suit carrying a newspaper. 'You could be forgiven for feeling a little paranoid,' I told our cameraman Bill Browne.

I approached the entrance but was swiftly banned from entering by Janet Laveau. That was understandable. Then the Church called the Old Bill. A police van and a police car rocked up and Janet and the Church's Graham Wilson gave the officers the run-down on me. I suspect that they showed the police my impression of an 'exploding tomato' – remember this is weeks before our Panorama setting the context to that explosion was broadcast. All I can be certain of is that the police seemed to be rather wary of me. I walked over to the boss copper: 'Can I put forward the BBC's point of view?'

'Wait over there,' the officer said, not overly friendly.

A third police car pulled up, and two officers got out. I looked around for the drugs bust going down, but it seems they too were on my case: 'They've brought in the Sixth Cavalry,' I said. Some plastic bobbies – Community Service officers – wafted in like dandelions on a breeze, adding to the police presence. Enter a police van, making my running total: four police vehicles and seven law enforcers.

A nice lady who lived on the street brought out an ostentatious cup of tea for me. The natives of Notting Hill seemed friendly.

After around 40 minutes a copper finally set out the score: 'Effectively, there's no allegations of criminal behaviour made about the incident today.'

What incident, I asked, incredulous?

'Effectively you coming here and filming. Whatever we're called to we come to.'

I told the officer that he was dealing with, some people say, a sinister, brainwashing cult that believes that psychiatrists are Nazi pseudo-scientists; that, some say, its leader goes around thumping people and, some say, they have a dungeon of the mind. He took all this in with a dead-pan expression on his face. You've got to feel sorry for the police: they have to

275

put up with some right nutters.

The coppers started to leave. So I'm in the clear? The boss copper almost laughed, and we were left to pursue our lawful business, filming them, filming us. It was beyond surreal, and the day was going to get madder yet.

A few miles further east John Travolta thunk-thunk-thunked along a red carpet on a Harley-Davison. Over the thunk of the Harley, you can clearly hear a man, hoarse but unusually loud, roaring from the back of the crowd: 'Mr Travolta, are you a member of a sinister, mind control cult?' This was the premiere of Travolta's movie, *Wild Hogs*. A couple of police officers came over. They looked bemused, uncertain as what to do. They did nothing.

'The allegation is that the leader, Miscavige, goes around thumping people...'

This lunatic would not shup up: 'Mr Travolta... many of your fans think you're wonderful but some people think your religion is a crazy, mind-control cult?'

I was that lunatic.

'We love you John!' shouted a lady in the crowd – that would be the other John, of course.

A security guard told me to move back. I carried on for a bit. A middle-aged lady with a Cockney accent, clearly a lifelong Travolta fan, had a gentle go at me. I told her that Travolta is, some say, in a brainwashing cult. 'Yeah,' she said, 'but he's in a sexy man cult.' To that, there was no answer. By the time that interchange was over, the film star had disappeared into his premiere.

The *Wild Hogs* premiere was not my finest hour. Behind the scenes, Travolta reportedly phoned the BBC's Director-

General – my boss five levels above my head – to complain about me; the Scientology footage of me yelling at him makes me look unhinged; and there was something clearly uncomfortable about the whole thing.

This is choppy water, where the piety of our celebrity-obsessed culture accords to showbiz deities and the proper scrutiny of the politics of 'religion' clash. On chat shows, in Britain or the United States, presented by people like witty, savvy insiders like Jonathon Ross, you never see celebrities like, say, Madonna, Tom Cruise or John Travolta being questioned, seriously, about the downsides of their beliefs in the Kabbalah Centre or the Church of Scientology. Critics may claim that there is some understanding, written or unwritten, that the chat host will not trespass into certain areas. That means that any 'soft power' celebrities may have, in terms of suggesting to their fans that their off-stage enthusiasms or beliefs are worth taking up, is not critically examined. Power without scrutiny is not good. The alternative is to try and challenge the celebrity when they are out in the open. The danger is that you end up looking foolish, which I did, very much so. Perhaps the greater danger, that the influence celebrities may hold over their fans goes unquestioned, slips by, unseen.

The following Saturday we went along to Tottenham Court Road to film the monthly anti-Church picket outside the Scientology recruiting centre. Even before we got to the picket, I spotted someone filming me surreptitiously, and gave chase. He ran away. As Mole, Bill and I turned the corner, the following scene presented itself: a small crowd of anti-Scientologists, standing on the opposite side of the road from the centre, making amusingly silly noises, a gaggle of police officers, a few police vehicles parked nearby and a Scientology TV crew, a man with a camera and a woman with one of those dead coypu sound boom thingies.

'I presume you're from Scientology because you're dressed in black and you won't tell me your names,' I told them. Sherlock Holmes, eat your heart out.

They held their tongue. It was just like old times. We had missed them; they, seemingly, had missed us; we filmed them; they filmed us; we filmed them filming us; they filmed us filming them filming us...

Shawn Lonsdale would have loved it.

I crossed the road and started chatting to the picket. One woman with long red-hair as if from a pre-Raphaelite painting held a placard, saying: 'Say no to Scientology'. Someone else was handing out leaflets, saying: 'Scientology is evil.' Another chap held a placard on a long stick, proclaiming: 'WARN-ING: You are entering a cult recruitment zone'. From the placard dangled a space alien doll in cosmic grey.

The picket's leaders, if such a chaotic group could have leaders, were John Ritson and Hartley Patterson. Hartley smiled on as John in his tell-tale, sing-song voice advised bewildered shoppers going up and down Tottenham Court Road: 'Never give any money to Scientology. You don't get better, you get worse. They find problems you never knew you had. It's nonsense, it's rubbish. .... People spend more than a million or more to go up the so-called bridge of total freedom. Bridge of total madness more likely.'

He paused, as a red London bus trundled past.

'Just say no to Scientology. They're a barmy cult who just want your money. It's a rip off. It's a scam. Never give any

money to Scientology. They're not growing, they're shrink-
ing.'

In another space-time continuum, I would like to introduce John, Hartley and chums to the denizens of the Celebrity Centre in LA.

Back in the real-world, I turned to our camera and said:
'There's a bloke here who's rather rude about Scientology. He
says...'

That's as far as I got. Mole had spotted Mike Rinder.
Mike and Bob 'Fireman Bob' Keenan crossed the road. Mike
seemed quietly amused. Bob just looked hostile. I shook hands
and battle renewed.

'This is your demonstration that you've set up for today?'
asked Mike in his curious blend of Australian-American.

'It's not my demonstration. It's got nothing to do with
me', I said.

'How did you know they were here?'

'We heard about it.'

'It's a little odd that you suddenly show up. Three people show up for a picket and you're here?' [To be fair, there
seemed to be more than three protesters: say, four. More
turned up later, maybe a dozen.]

'So you didn't know these guys were going to be here?'
asked Bob.

'We did know because we're making a film about Scientology.'

'So you told them to come?'

'No we didn't. That's not right Bob. We knew about the
protest.'

'Because they got in contact with you?'

'Where's Tommy Davis?' I asked, changing the subject, subtly. 'He's dropped off the emails. Where's Tommy?'

They didn't like that. It was just getting going properly when a policeman interrupted: 'You haven't got authority to film here, you are causing a big congestion here.'

He was genial, not officious. The policeman suggested we conduct our interview somewhere else. 'It's not an interview, it's a row,' I said.

The Church's agents beat a retreat back across the road to the centre. We followed them, me calling out: 'Where's Tommy Davis? Is he in the RPF?'

'No,' said Mike.

'Well, where's Tommy? Has he been knocked off?' We assembled by the door of the recruiting centre: Mike and Bob on the threshold, their camera crew close by, me and Mole and Bill on the outside, three police officers swimming around, like goldfish enjoying a trip around their bowl.

'Now we'd really like to interview Mr Miscavige about these allegations that he's been thumping people? So the question is, has David Miscavige thumped anyone? Can we interview David Miscavige?'

Mike turned his back on me, and Bob said: 'You're blocking our door.'

'I take it that's a "no", Sir,' said the police officer, ever the diplomat, and we walked across the road. In the meantime, Janet Laveau and the ginger-haired Graham Wilson arrived to hear John Ritson of the picket loud-hail how one Scientologist who had fallen out with David Miscavige had 'been put in the RPF, their internal prison system. It's a barmy UFO cult – don't give money to Scientology.'

I re-crossed Tottenham Court Road and challenged Mike for old time's sake: 'Just one last question. We've heard from a witness who says that he's personally seen David Miscavige hit you and knock you to the ground.'

Mike launched at me, aggressive, furious, the most animated I had ever seen him: 'John, if you come up with that crap again, I will file a complaint against you. Those allegations are absolute utter rubbish, absolute utter rubbish. Not true, rubbish.'

I pressed him.

'It's a lie.'

That wasn't, as it happened, his last word on the subject.

That day the weird courier asked my neighbour where I lived. That evening Tomiko, my fiancée, my oldest friend, Jonathan Gebbie, his mother, Audrey Gebbie, and I were having dinner in a restaurant in Earlsfield when we noticed that a stranger was sat close to us and paying over-due attention to our conversation. I challenged him to reveal his identity: he refused. I challenged him to deny categorically that he had anything to do with Scientology. He declined, and said that I was invading his privacy. When I asked him who had been talking to my neighbour today, he said nothing but looked embarrassed.

Shortly before our wedding day day, a stranger, a woman, had knocked on the door of Tomiko's mother's flat in Totnes. T's sister, Rhi, answered the door and the stranger who said she was from Dawlish – a coastal town in Devon – implied that she knew us well and knew that we were getting married but wasn't quite sure where. Rhi told her about the fort.

Tomiko and I got married in the Cornish fort in late

April. It was a stunning day: blue clear skies, an absurdly happy party, with a pig on a stick and buckets of alcohol, preceded by an open air ceremony conducted by Jonathan, who just happens to be not only a rocket scientist who worked on Beagle II's trip to the Red Planet – a top secret success that initiated first contact with the Martians, covered up as a great British disaster – but also a lay Anglican to boot. The Church of Scientology – or maybe someone connected with them – came too. The iconic picture of our wedding day is of the bride and groom looking grave after my son, Sam, and his mate Tom Reeves spotted somebody hiding in the shrubbery and taking pictures. Sam, Tom and my BBC colleague Patrick Barrie gave chase but whoever it was got away. I have to say it helped being inside a massive Napoleonic era fort surrounded by enough food and wine to feed an army. We kept calm and carried on.

Back at the BBC's Current Affairs department, in White City, Team Panorama struggled to cope with a torrent of letters from the Church's lawyers, American and British. The Church seemed to be making most use of those awfully nice people at Carter-Ruck.

By this time, our group paranoia was comical. When we held meetings, we would take the batteries and SIM cards out of mobile phones and leave them and walk to a meeting room 50 feet away from where we had left our little silicone puddles of micro-electronic wizardry. We were determined that they would not find out who we were going to talk to. We wanted to tell one story of how the Church impacted on the life of a British family. Our research team, Patrick Barrie and Uli Hesse, found a mother who lived three hours train ride from

London. We hopped on the train and crossed England to see her.

You know what happens next. 'Betty' gave us a very moving interview about how her daughter, 'Sam', had disconnected from her. Before we got back to the office, 'Sam' walked through her door for the first time in two years and the next day asked her mum to kill the interview with Panorama.

The Church being the Church, it wasn't difficult to find another family that had been split by them. We interviewed Sharon in North London, bereft that her daughter had joined the Church and later disconnected from her.

On May 3rd, a couple of weeks before transmission, Mike Rinder arrived in the BBC lobby to talk face-to-face to BBC executives. This was viewed as a deliberate attempt to put pressure on our journalism, and Mike and the Church of Scientology was left unseen. But not, thanks to Carter-Ruck, etc, unheard or unrepresented.

Behind the scenes we were editing and re-editing. After a lot of argy-bargy, we pulled the allegations that Miscavige went around thumping people. In 2007 we had only one on-screen interview from Bruce Hines in which an ex-Scientologist alleged that he had been hit by the Leader. British libel law is, some say, a rich man's game which places the burden of proof on the publisher. Many newspapers were critical of the then leading judge on the libel bench, Mr Justice Eady, who had, fairly or unfairly, developed a reputation for favouring rich plaintiffs over cash-strapped newspapers and broadcasters.

A tsunami of letters from smart, expensive lawyers like Carter-Ruck in London and others in LA were coming in, attacking this and that aspect of the programme. Celebrities who I had interviewed in LA now claimed that I had invaded their privacy and refused consent for the interviews to be shown, even though they had sat down in a room in the Celebrity Centre in front of me and the BBC's cameras. In the programme we addressed that concern by showing the celebrities but paraphrasing their views and, when I asked about Xenu, hearing Tommy voice his incredulity. The cumulative effect of the attacks from the Church's lawyers was to bring most of us to a state close to mental and moral exhaustion. The hardest thing for me was that any internal argument I made in favour of x or y was enfeebled by my 'exploding tomato' impression. The team swung behind me, carrying me across the finishing line.

On the Saturday before our Panorama, 'Scientology & Me', was due to air, the Church's John Alex Wood put up a 41-second clip of me losing it in 'The Industry of Death' on YouTube. The calls from the Sunday newspapers piled in, and Panorama editor Sandy Smith and I fielded them. We told all of them I had been in the wrong to lose control and I used the phrase 'exploding tomato' to describe my hapless interviewing technique. If the newspapers thought that we were going to cover up my loss of temper, they were wrong. But we also said there were things in the programme about the Church that would give the viewer context and grounds for concern. We released an equally short clip of Tommy Davis going nose-to-nose with me at Plant City, when he lectured me about America's freedom of religion and then trotted off when I started talking about freedom of speech. But, by and large, the story in everybody's minds was me losing it, and that's what the papers ran with.

It was an interesting experience being rubbished 24/7 around the world for three days. My son Sam was at the gym, on a double treadmill machine, with a pal, both of them watching the BBC News Channel when the exploding tomato popped up. 'Look at that nutter losing it,' said Sam's pal.

'That's my Dad,' said Sam.

On the Monday of transmission, Panorama's editor, Sandy Smith, got a letter from Mike Rinder. Then it was marked 'PRIVATE AND CONFIDENTIAL NOT FOR BROAD-CAST OR PUBLICATION' but the Church have since published it on their website.

Mike was reacting to an interview Sandy had given to the BBC's *Heaven and Earth* religious affairs programme in which he had apologized for my loss of temper but defended our investigation in robust terms. Mike ripped off Sandy's face, as it were: 'Your blatant disregard for the truth with respect to the *Panorama* episode being produced on the Church of Scientology is appalling...

You have repeated Mr. Sweeney's avowed reason for losing his temper in the US: "he fell into a trap ... he'd been watching a 90minute exhibition of supposedly proving that psychiatry is a Nazi science ...I feel he was baited, he lost it." This is false.'

Mike hit all the Church's G-spots: 'psychotic break', Carter-Ruck, 'discredited sources', and concluded: 'Please retract your false and inflammatory statements that have been quoted in the media, with utter disregard for the documented facts.'

It was drizzling that afternoon, wet, soggy, miserable

weather. The fire bells starting ringing and 2,500 BBC employees trooped out into the rain as the building was cleared, and every single one of those 2,500 seemed to be looking at me, as if it was all my fault.

Panorama's '*Scientology & Me*' peaked at 4.9million viewers, the highest figures for Panorama that year. This was almost certainly because of the Church's attack video which seemed to have alerted every single news organisation on the planet to our journalism about them. After a fair bit of stuff for the lawyers – the 1984 verdicts of Judges Latey and Breckenridge – the Panorama settled down to the Tommy and John show, with him chasing, harassing and yelling at me across the United States. The show climaxed, as it were, with Mr Tomato.

The best line of commentary in the show was the pay-off, written by Sandy: 'So: Scientology? Those of its disciples who find it useful? Good luck to them. We don't doubt their sincerity. But its leaders have their work cut out if they want to be hosting *Songs of Praise* anytime soon.'

After the programme went out, there was that awful wait until the comments came in. I was saved by the sheer bloody-mindedness of the Great British Public who pay my wages. On the internet, on YouTube and via email, thousands commented that I was wrong to lose it, but I had been goaded into it. Two comments stand out. Over time I've polished these comments so they gleam like shiny conkers, but this is how I remember them. The first was from the Green Watch of the Lambeth River Fire Brigade who said, words to the effect: 'we were with you the whole way, and we all shouted with you, and, in our view, you should have punched the xxxx.' The very next email read: 'Mr Sweeney, you're my hero but then I am the Vice-President of the Royal College of Psychiatry.'

A few days later bleary-eyed BBC staff arrived at work to be handed copies of a CD called *'Panorama Exposed'*, illustrated with a screaming fruitcake on the cover. I am that screaming fruitcake. This was the Church's film about our film on them. They printed around 10,000 CDs and posted them at random to people in Britain – fancy goods salesmen, vicars, lollypop ladies – many of whom kindly got in touch with me, letting me know that they had received this oddity through their letterbox.

'Panorama Exposed' starts strongly with a typewriter effect tap-tapping out grave concerns about standards at the BBC; shows me denouncing BBC bosses as a bunch of morons; segues into the 'Exploding Tomato'; cites Mike Rinder having a go at me at the hotel at midnight; shows us interviewing Shawn Lonsdale, sex pervert; and does a brilliantly edited cut-down of the celebrities being asked my 'some say' questions.

They show me asking Kirstie Alley is it a sinister brain-washing cult?

Kirstie Alley: 'Would you ever sit with a Jew and tell them that their religion is a cult?'

JS: No.

JS: [fast inter-cut] Some people... some say... some people say... some people say... that it's a sinister brain-washing cult.

Juliette Lewis: I know and some people say women are really stupid and shouldn't have the vote.

JS: Some people would say you're a member of a brain-washing cult, in some way brain-washed, brain-washed, brain-washed...

Anne Archer: Do I look brain-washed to you?

JS: (Silence)

Anne Archer: How dare you!

What is odd is that Scientology's celebrities had been objecting that I had invaded their privacy; then the Church broadcast their encounters with me. Intercut with the interviews were contributions from pundits warning about the BBC and tabloid journalism.

One pundit stands out. The Right Reverend Graham James, Bishop of Norwich, who was once a serious contender to become the next Archbishop of Canterbury, told the Scientology crew: 'The thing that worries me the most is the way in which unexamined assumptions get taken as read – so Church of England congregations are in free fall, the Roman Catholic Church doesn't do much about sex abuse, Opus Dei, Scientology, the Moonies are all mind-numbing and brainwashing cults – those are the sort of things that are taken for granted, as if these are proven.'

The bishop may question whether the Church of Scientology and the Moonies are brainwashing cults. But in my experience few people choose to call them that lightly. That view of the Church of Scientology is not 'unexamined' but expensively protected by, for example, Carter-Ruck.

As I've said before, I'm sorry I lost my temper with the Church. But it did have one wholly unintended and very welcome consequence.

Cut to two years later...

...nine rockets crashed in, just after sunrise. They killed one soldier and badly wounded the Havildar, or Sergeant-Major. The Taliban would have wired up their solar-powered detonators, triggered by the sun's rays, the night before so they were long gone by the time the Pakistani Army found the firing site high on a bluff of land overlooking the army base, set up in an abandoned girl's school – no education for girls in the Swat Valley these days, and not much in the whole of the North West Frontier Province. The Taliban had seen me, the only European in this part of the Valley, the previous evening filming the ruin of a mosque one of their suicide bombers had blown up. The bomber had wanted to blow up an army post but a sentry started shooting at the bomber's Land Cruiser and he swerved towards the mosque and hit his trigger, wrecking it, bringing down the minaret and killing six children queuing for water at the mosque's tap. The rockets were the Taliban's response.

What went through the mind of the suicide bomber in the last moments of his life? Did he really believe that he was part of a force for good? Or did he see that he was about to crash into the holy building? Did he see the kids lined up with their plastic water containers by the water pipe? On the internet you can find dozens of Taliban snuff movies, showing 'brave, idealistic' Pakistani or Afghan young men garlanded with explosives before they drive their truck bomb into the pre-selected target and BOOM! The Taliban is, some say, a nationalistic resistance movement against foreign invaders. Others feel that it is a death cult and those 'brave, idealistic' men have been brainwashed into killing themselves and others.

The chopper came to take me out of the Taliban's way, sharpish. The rush of wind through the open doors burnt my eyes but the view from two, three, four thousand feet was spectacular, the ridges of the North West Frontier Province rising and dipping as our ancient Pakistani Army Huey chugged over the terrain. In the back seat, just behind me, the half-dead Havildar lay on a stretcher with a medic hard at work, pumping his heart. Beneath him, the coffin containing the corpse of the dead soldier.

Back in Islamabad, I did my best to grow my beard. We got stuck in a traffic jam and were crawling around a roundabout when my Pakistani fixer said the police had caught a suicide bomber at this very place, waiting for a European. When, I asked? 'Yesterday,' he said.

I wanted to get some GVs – General Views – TV twaddle for the wallpaper shots of a country you can stick anywhere in a film over which you can make some boring blah-blah point. We found a mosque, climbed up the minaret and the cameraman shot bucket-loads of GVs. Down below, five, six, seven SUVs had rolled up. We were being stared at by men in dark glasses and sharp suits. We climbed down, icicles in our bowels. We were descending towards the ISI, the Pakistani secret police. Not the Taliban, but not nice either. The ISI torture and kill. We must have filmed something they did not want us to film from the minaret.

The main dude spoke exquisite Oxford English, wore a rather fine suit and had pitted skin.

'Who are you?'

'My name is John Sweeney and I work for BBC Panorama.'

'Can you prove it?'

'Yes. Here is my passport and here is my press card.'

He inspected them, and handed them to a goon who got in a big SUV and drove off, kicking up a storm of dust. As soon as the dust died down Pitted Skin turned back to me and said: 'Who are you and can you prove it?'

'My name is John Sweeney and I work for Panorama and I have seven million hits on YouTube. Look me up.'

He came back and handed over my passport and press card and we were allowed to go on our way. So, for making me instantly identifiable in this and all other galaxies, I would like to thank the Church of Scientology.

CHAPTER FIFTEEN
The Defector

I n the summer of 2007 Allan Henderson – the father of
Mike who, with his wife Donna, had told me about the
reality of life inside the Sea Org back in Clearwater – lay mor-
tally ill in hospital in California. Allan had six children and
24 grandchildren but only Mike and his daughter were at his
bedside. The rest had disconnected from him because he had
left the Church. The dying man had a simple message for his
family: 'I'd say stay together; family is family and if somebody
is trying to talk you out of being a member of the family...you
better question that group.'

Not one of the disconnected attended his funeral.

After Allan died, Mike Henderson told me about his
father's death and I sent him a note of condolence. Not long
after, Mike got in touch. He had heard a rumour about a defector who had very quietly left the Church. When we heard the
name of this supposed defector we were astonished.

I did some digging, and a mole – not, obviously, the Mole
– told me that the defector was selling second hand cars in
Virginia. As his final verdict on me had been that I was an
'asshole', it was decided that Mole should fly across the pond

and see whether she could smoke him out. Mole was sceptical that he would be where my mole said he was, and thought the trip a complete waste of time. I sent her a photo of some flying geese, adding to her fears that this was the wild goose chase to end all wild geese chases. She was, satisfyingly, wrong.

And so in late 2009 I stood in a room on top of the Tate Modern with a superb view of the Thames – liquid history – flowing through London and St Paul's beyond, waiting, waiting, waiting. It was like the scene in John Le Carré's *The Spy Who Came In From The Cold*. But in this version, the defector defected, safe and sound. He walked across the Wibbly-Wobbly footbridge, the one that wobbled so much they had to rebuild it, bang on time.

Zombie Mike Rinder was a thing of the past. The spooky, hollow-eyed corpse-in-the-making sidekick had become a different human being: fitter, browner, heavier, happier, funnier. He'd spent 46 years inside the Church, taking my tally of ex-members' service up to 184 years.

After '*Scientology & Me*' had been broadcast in 2007, he had toured the TV studios, rubbishing me, boasting of how the Church had done 'a John Sweeney to John Sweeney'. But he also felt that Miscavige had hated the programme and was angry that the Church had not been able to stop the Panorama. Mike feared that he would be the fall guy – banished to The Hole or given a ghastly foreign assignment in some faraway country, where he would rot, far away from his family. He knew all about disconnection, about what happened when a Scientologist left the Church. For some years he had run the machine, the Office of Special Affairs, that had made disconnections happen. He knew that if he left the Church he would be saying goodbye to his wife, his son and daughter, to his brother and mother, to all his friends, to everything he believed in. But he couldn't bear it anymore.

So one day in the late spring of 2007, he left the Church's office in Fitzroy Street in central London and set off towards Saint Hill near East Grinstead. But he never got there. Instead he turned off his phone, rented a room in a poky B&B near Victoria and walked out of the Church, the only life he'd known for damn near half a century.

He was amused when Mole found him in Virginia and although he played impassive and uninterested there was something on his conscience, a lie he wanted, he said, to deal with. So when he gave his first TV interview he gave it to Panorama, to get it off his chest.

Is it true that David Miscavige hit you, I asked the former head of the Office of Special Affairs?

'Yes.'

And you denied it?

'Yes. That was a lie.'

How many times did he hit you?

'Fifty.'

It was an extraordinary moment. The Church of Scientology is weird, weird, weird, a real thing that defies the wildest imaginings, so far beyond fiction as to stun the mind. Once upon a time its spokesman Mike Rinder vowed to me that Miscavige was some kind of living angel. Once upon a time Mike Rinder had been at our hotel at midnight, supporting Tommy and demonising us. Now white was black, black white, the Leader of the Church the thumping Pope – a charge the Church and the Leader deny.

I questioned fifty. Mike explained he could not be exactly certain of how many times he had been beaten up by Scientology's pope but described it as routine. Miscavige hit, punched, slapped, kicked and otherwise physically abused many members of the Church's Holy Order, he said. The culture of violence spread outwards from the top of the Church, he said. The Church and Miscavige deny this.

Mike reflected on Tommy, the man who, according to Sci'gy-Leaks, could make me psychotic. He said he felt sorry for him, a decent guy, but perhaps his personal integrity is a little lacking if he were able to sit down in front of me and say that Miscavige never hit anybody.

'You can't lie like that and live with it,' said Mike. 'It's one of the reasons why I eventually walked out. You were the straw that broke my back. Because you stood there and said to me, "did David Miscavige ever strike you?" and I said, "no".'

Over the years, Mike told me, he had faced a lot of questions from the media about Scientology. Many of them were ignorant or silly or uniformed, and easy for him as a believing Scientologist to knock down or dismiss. But my question floored him: it was direct and, he said, true, and what he told me in 2007 was a lie. Mike added that even though our Panorama did not air the violence allegations against Miscavige, he was still on the wrong end of the Leader's anger, and he thought that was crazy, a kind of insanity. I asked him whether he thought Miscavige was sane. Mike replied that he was very intelligent, a very fast learner but no, not sane.

The Church and Miscavige deny that he is insane.

We discussed Miscavige's idiosyncratic way with words. Back in 2007, Miscavige, Mike said, called him and Tommy:

'Cock sucking ass hole. Cock sucking mother fucker. Useless piece of shit. He has the most vulgar vocabulary of anybody I have ever heard in my life. There used to be Blackberry messages, he would have his assistant Lou send them and they had little acronyms and you had to figure out what the acronyms meant. "YSCOHB". And then the next one would be, "well did you figure it out yet?" Like five seconds after the one before. "Did you figure it out yet? Come on. Answer, answer, answer!" And what that stood for was: 'You Suck Cock On Hollywood Boulevard.'

Mike thought this slightly unusual for a religious leader.

The reason why he had looked as though he had been in prison when we first met in 2007 was because he really had been in a prison – 'The Hole', two big trailers at Gold Base in the Californian desert where 100 of the Church's most senior people who had angered Miscavige were locked up and tortured by each other. Immediately before we came on the Church's radar, Mike had spent the previous nine months in 'The Hole'. The conditions he described were barbaric. He is not alone: Debbie Cook in her evidence in open court in Texas in 2012 spoke of unbearable heat, of physical torture and mass humiliation.

'It is totalitarian,' said Mike. 'It's insane. It's psychosis, probably not seen in the entire history of the religion. It degenerated into people hitting one another, putting people in garbage cans, having people crawl around on their hands and knees until their knees were bleeding, torturing people with water.'

Did that happen to you?

'Absolutely. I crawled around on my hands and knees

on this indoor, outdoor carpet until my knees were bleeding maybe a dozen times.'

Why did he put up with it for so long? Mike set out explaining the greatest puzzle of all. Although he had left the Church of Scientology, he still believes in the faith of Scientology, is still a disciple of L Ron Hubbard.

'There is a principle in Scientology,' explained Mike, 'called the greatest good for the greatest number: dynamics. One judges whether something is good or bad based on whether it enhances survival across those dynamics. For a Scientologist probably the single most important thing is expansion of the church, the expansion of the religion. Here, the person that is responsible or is the driving force behind that expansion has hit someone or slapped them.'

So the heart of the problem was a conflict of loyalties: as a Scientologist he felt he had to endure abuse because otherwise the expansion of his religion would be imperilled, and that would imperil humankind.

Mike described the first time David Miscavige hit him. It was sometime in the late 1990s when he was working at Gold Base in the Californian desert: 'He called me up, he had an office that was up the hill. I ran up the hill because you had to get there in a hurry because you don't want to keep the dear leader waiting. I ran around the corner and he literally, "Wham!" cold cocked me and then tackled me and pushed me into a tree and then had me in a headlock and was shoving me in the bushes and kind of pushing me around. You can't really fight back because that would be the end of your career. That went on for, maybe, probably two minutes or something. He then calmed down and I had a cut on my mouth and [he] said: "OK, come inside" and I walked inside the little lounge and he handed me a glass of scotch and said, "drink that," and pretended that nothing had happened.'

Why?

'For whatever his whim was at the moment. Looked at him the wrong way, answered the question the wrong way, said something that was in his mind inappropriate, had something that he thought was incorrect, had happened to be standing next to someone else that he was hitting so just kind of hit that guy and then, oh well I'll give you one too just for good measure.'

It sounds as though he was out of control?

'He is. It's insanity, and that's why this is so bad. Look, someone getting hit, slapped across the face or whatever is not going to scar them for life. But the fact that the person who is the pinnacle of the Scientology religion is unable to control himself and has such what would be called in Scientology evil purposes towards others…it would be, like, the pope was a devil worshipper. It's so diametrically opposed to what Scientology should be and what the example of a good Scientologist is. That's what's so troubling about it, not the fact of hitting someone but the fact that the person who is supposedly at the pinnacle of the religion is that nutty. That's bad. David Miscavige is an anti-Scientologist.'

The Church of Scientology and David Miscavige deny allegations of violence.

I put it to Mike: they deny this.

'Of course. Just like I did. It would be destructive in the minds of Scientologists because it would not be the greatest good for the greatest number of dynamics because David

Miscavige is driving forward the massive expansion of Scientology. So, therefore, anything that would undermine him or undermine his position or undermine his public persona would be destructive to this greater good, the greater good being – he is driving the expansion of Scientology. But that's a lie.'

Why did you put up with it? I asked again, unsure that I had properly understood what he was telling me.

'Because I believed, like I said to you, I believe that the greater good and the expansion of Scientology was more important than my personal wellbeing.'

And that included being beaten up by the Leader?

'Yes.'

The Church of Scientology...

'I mean,' Mike interrupted, 'if he came and punched me now, we'd have a little difficulty...'

I laughed out loud.

I put it to Mike that if he was telling the truth, then Tommy was lying. He said he was, and that Tommy would continue lying until he was no longer in post, and that goes for all the senior Scientologists. They had, for example, sent statements to us and other journalists setting out that the allegations against David Miscavige were baseless, and that people alleging abuse were, in fact, the abusers. Mike had read these statements. His view was they were 'frankly absurd. They look like and read like they were written by someone who just came out of a North Korean concentration camp.'

In the light of Lifton's work, that is a fascinating observation from a man who spent half a century inside the Church of Scientology.

'They talk,' Mike continued, 'about the wonderful virtuous David Miscavige and that here is a man who walks on water and never does anything wrong, he saves sparrows who have fallen out of trees... He can do nothing wrong. I mean his breath doesn't smell, nothing, everything about him is perfect, now that is obviously ridiculous. There is nobody walking on planet earth today that is quite as virtuous as he is made out to be.'

Did Mike beat anyone up?

'I did. On a couple of occasions. It was really something that I am not proud of and don't feel good about. I don't really have any excuse for it because something that I will never do again and if I ever see those people I will certainly apologise.'

Mike described one attack: 'I grabbed his shirt collar and held him up against the wall, making a point rather forcefully, maybe an inch away from his face.'

He attacked the man because, he said, Miscavige had told Mike to give him an SRA, a Severe Reality Adjustment.

Violence flowed from the top: 'You see what happens at the very pinnacle and then that becomes the code of conduct of those immediately beneath and then that eventually makes it way down the organisation, especially when you have an organisation that is so hierarchically structured as the Church of Scientology.'

Bruce Hines had told me the same thing, that he had hit another Scientologist because he had been told to. They both may have been lying, of course, but they both showed remorse which I found convincing.

What seems to anger Mike more than the physical or emotional abuse was the lack of honesty about the growth of the

Church. He described how Miscavige had been making up the numbers, claiming millions of Scientologists as members when the real figures were pitifully lower: not ten million but something like 40,000.

I have only once seen a packed Church of Scientology and that was the one Mike and Tommy took me into in LA. He told me that had been staged for Panorama, that they called people up to make the place look packed.

Stepping away from the interview with Mike for a moment and to the only ever newspaper interview Miscavige has given, in 1998 to Tom Tobin of the St Petersburg Times, a reporter who has vigorously covered the Church against a howling wind of legal threats. Miscavige recalled meeting the founder in 1977. The newspaper's story read:

'Hubbard, then 66, wore a straw cowboy hat, slacks, a short-sleeved shirt and boots. He was leaving a dining room when the teenager from Clearwater introduced himself. "Oh I know who you are," he remembers Hubbard saying. "Welcome aboard." As most Scientologists do, Miscavige often refers to Hubbard by his initials, LRH. He says Hubbard called him by the nickname "Misc" (pronounced Misk).' [No other ex-member of the Church has used the Misc nickname to me.] "I never thought LRH was looking at me as: Oh, Dave is 17 years old or 18 years old," Miscavige said. "It was just Dave, person to person. Spiritual being to spiritual being, so to speak."'

So to speak. Miscavige used his proximity well. By the age of 21, he succeeded in persuading Hubbard's wife, Mary Sue, to step out of the way and when Hubbard died it was Miscavige

301

who emerged as the new pope. There were no elections, or anything like that. 'People keep saying,' Miscavige told Tobin, '"How'd you get power?" Nobody gives you power. I'll tell you what power is. Power in my estimation is if people will listen to you. That's it.'

I put it to Mike that Miscavige was close to Hubbard. Is that right?

'Partly true. He controlled the communications to and from him. So therefore he was able to manipulate what information went to L Ron Hubbard and then what went back and he always manipulated it to make himself look very good, and others look not so good.'

Stalin did that with Lenin, though I am not directly comparing Stalin with…

'Yes, you are.'

I pleaded that it was not a useful analogy. What was the difference between Miscavige then and now?

'He has the same energy and intelligence. There is no question that he has always been very intelligent, smart, but that doesn't make him good. The difference between now and then is that now he firmly believes that everybody else is dirt and he is God.'

On reflection – and I hadn't studied Lifton's work at this stage – Mike's analysis fits exactly with Lifton's cult criteria of a charismatic leader who becomes the dispenser of immortality, a god.

Why hasn't Miscavige given a TV interview since 1992?

'In part because he thinks it's beneath him. In part, because he will only do it under extremely controlled circumstances. He doesn't think it's going to get any better than the interview that he did with Ted Koppel.'

The 1992 ABC interview by Koppel with Miscavige is fascinating because in it the Leader – forceful, fluent, intense blue staring eyes, speaking in a gravelly New Jersey/Philadelphia twang – sets out arguments that Tommy, Mike and the Scientology celebrities had made to me in 2007, fifteen years later, sometimes almost word for word.

For example, the film package prior to the interview showed ex-Scientologists complaining that they had been ripped off inside the Church and then spied on, threatened and followed once they had left. Miscavige replied, talking about the Church's betterment programmes, defending auditing and demonising its critics: 'every single detractor on there is part of a religious hate group called Cult Awareness Network... [This was an allegation Koppel denied on their behalf.] Now, I don't know if you've heard of these people, but it's the same as the KKK would be with the blacks. I think if you interviewed a neo-Nazi and asked them to talk about the Jews, you would get a similar result to what you have here.'

That is the same trope Kirstie Alley hit me over the head with – not literally – in the Celebrity Centre, as if she was an actor and Miscavige had written her script some 15 years before.

Later on, Miscavige riffs on psychiatry: 'The Fascists, the Communists have used psychiatry to further their ends. That's just a fact. You want to look at the studies that brought about the Holocaust of the Jews, that the Nazis justified killing the Jews, they were done at the Max Planck Institute of Psychiatry in Leipzig, Germany, and that justified the killing of six million people... But let me tell you what our real problem is. Number one, understand this. Psychiatry, psychology, that comes from the word psyche. Psyche means soul. These people have preempted the field of religion, not just Scientology, every other religion. They right now practice and preach the fact that man is an animal, and I guess that is where philosophically we're at odds with them. But to understand what this war is, this is not something that we started. In fact, 22 days after *Dianetics: The Modern Science of Mental Health* came out, the attacks from the American Psychiatric Association started.'

How did Miscavige respond to critics? Time reporter Richard Behar 'is a hater', who set out to kidnap a Scientologist – a charge that Richard Behar denies. Former high-ranking Scientologist Vicki Aznaran told ABC: 'They hire private detectives to harass people. They run covert operations. You name it, they have never quit doing it. It would like, they would have to quit being Scientology if they quit doing that.' On Miscavige, Vicki alleged: 'He said that we will use public people, we'll send them out to the dissidents' homes, have them, their homes broken into, have them beaten, have things stolen from them, slash their tyres, break their car windows, whatever. And this was being carried out at the time I left.'

Miscavige said of Aznaran: 'This is a girl who was kicked out for trying to bring criminals into the Church, something she didn't mention… She violated the mores and codes of the group. She was removed for it. I was a trustee of that corporation. She knows it. The words she said to me is, "I have no future in Scientology. " She wanted to bring bad boys into Scientology, her words.'

Mike went on to suggest to me another reason why the

Leader hasn't given a newspaper or TV interview for years: fear.

'If something were to go wrong and he was made to look like a fool or couldn't answer the allegations that were being put to him, then that would crumble some of his image in the mind of Scientologists.'

We went through the details of our weird encounters back in 2007. Mike explained that Miscavige had been aggressively contemptuous of Tommy's 'handling' of us, that he was 'pussy', that he had failed to stop us from talking to the heretics, Mike Henderson and Donna, so Tommy decided to ambush us at our hotel, late, the expectation being that we would not have had our camera with us. It was pressure from Miscavige that drove the midnight ambush. We showed Mike a clip of the two cars following us when we were arrived at Los Angeles airport and me challenging the driver of the Blue Sidona: 'are you from the Church of Scientology?'

Was I being paranoid?

'No, you were being followed.'

Who gave the orders to follow us, I asked.

'I did.'

There is no doubt in your mind that we were followed by the Church of Scientology?

'No doubt whatsoever.'

Simple test. There is a gap, we were in Florida and then we went to LA. Where did we go in between?

'You went to see Bruce Hines in San Francisco.'

How did you know that?

'I was there.'

What do you mean you were there?

'See… I was better at following you than the other people.' They would have been the private detectives.

I never saw you.

'I know. I followed you from San Francisco airport to the hotel that you stayed at, that one sitting on the corner. I was there.'

So you spied on us, the Church of Scientology spied on us?

'Yes, absolutely.'

The Church of Scientology has always denied following and spying on the BBC.

'And they probably would do so again.'

Will they be telling the truth?

'No, that will be an absolute lie.'

Why spy on people?

Mike explained from the perspective of the Church, that they knew that the Panorama we were making was not going to be friendly, so that they wanted to know exactly who we were seeing and what we were finding out, so they could reply immediately that the things we were being told were not true. The only solution is to spy. The person driving this approach is David Miscavige, he said, and he admitted that as far as the media goes it is counter-effective. He touched on the colossal expense of private eyes. One in London costs around £300 a day or $50 an hour; lawyers, of course, cost far, far more, around $750 an hour.

The Church, for its part, said we weren't spied on. David Miscavige said the suggestion that he and his office monitored any such operation communicating with Rinder and Davis is absolute and total nonsense. The Church categorically denied it too, but admitted private eyes were tasked to track and document us. An overt operation, they said, not spying.

Making the Scientology film was the strangest thing I have ever experienced in my entire life, I told Mike. And towards the end of the days we spent with you in the States in 2007 I felt as though I was beginning to lose my mind. And I can remember saying to Mole, on the day, that I lost my temper, 'I don't think I can do this any more.' Tommy Davis in particular was attacking me, again and again and again. Is that deliberate?

'Absolutely. Tommy Davis believed that he could score brownie points with Miscavige by driving you psychotic. If you had some of the fundamental technology and Scientology that you could apply, it wouldn't have created that effect on you. He was doing something that's called in slang Scientology "bull-baiting". He was attempting to goad you into a reaction, do that routine and then have it appear in the press all over the world. It made you look bad and it was from our perspective something that made you lose credibility.'

I was as good as gold for five, six days before I went tomato.

'You held up pretty good. It was a deliberate effort to get you to lose your cool.'

And when I lost it, how did you feel?

'Pretty cool.'

But the new, un-Zombie Mike was ashamed of what they had done in 2007 and felt that it was an abuse of their powers as Scientologists, a betrayal of what Scientology stood for. Mike explained that the greater problem for the Church was that Tommy had boasted of his immediate access to the Leader, because in Miscavige's mind that countered his ability to plausibly deny his agents – a disastrous mistake. Faced with the Leader's anger, Tommy vanished to Las Vegas, leading Mike to run the show. That was the explanation for his absence in London: Tommy had gone AWOL. Mike was too modest to say so, but he was, in the end, the more professional PR man.

The allegations of being beaten by Miscavige, the spying, the lying, The Hole - all of this, I asked Mike, I've got to ask you: were you lying to me then in 2007 or are you lying to me now: 'I was lying to you then.'

I know this word cult is a very difficult word for you and you don't accept it as far as Scientology as a principle is concerned.

'Correct.'

But is the Church of Scientology under David Miscavige a cult?

'It's degenerated into the cult of David Miscavige. He has become someone who is infallible, who is all-knowing, all-seeing, expects absolute obeisance and people now look to him like he is beyond any criticism or beyond any reproach and will blindly follow the things that he says to do.'

The Church, of course, was not best pleased with Mike Rinder giving an interview to Scientology's devil, which we broadcast in the autumn of 2010. Its on-line Freedom Magazine has even created a special graphic, a cartoon of Mike looking at himself in a mirror and suddenly morphing into a fanged, green-skinned cobra, complete with chilling sound effects. The Mike-into-cobra cartoon is compelling evidence that the organising intelligence behind the Church of Scientology is very troubled. It strikes one as being nasty, pathological and pathetic. If this man really is so incompetent and lacklustre as the Church suggests, then why bother attack him so viciously? And how does the Church square blackening its enemies in this way while advancing its claim to be respected as a religion? It's schizoid.

Weirdly, the Church's Freedom Magazine and I ask the same question: 'Was Mike Rinder lying then, or is he lying now?' It then adds its own gloss: 'Regarding the anti-Scientology drivel he now funnels to the tabloid media? You be the judge after reading the following verbatim quotes from Rinder when he served the Church as spokesperson... "Look, there is a string of these people...that goes back 25 years. Most of them you will never see again. They have their moment of glory where they make their wild allegations. They get coverage in the media. And then, they disappear. Their claims are proven to be untrue, and they're gone."

Mike Rinder to BBC Panorama in 2007...

'In a 2007 letter to the BBC, Rinder again set the record straight: "[W]e repeatedly requested the name of any source alleging 'bullying' and 'beating.' The only individual you name is (B.H.) [Bruce Hines]. You must find it at least a little strange that [he] has appeared in various media in the United States, France and the UK over the last two years and has never made this allegation before. In each case he has told stories that the media at the time wanted to hear. You are just the latest, and obviously this is what you wanted to hear from him, so he manufactured a tale."'

This is weird on weird to the power of ten. The Church's Freedom Magazine is seeking to disgrace its former spokesman and make his word appear unreliable by quoting his remarks to me and a letter to the BBC. The obvious retort is, having defected from what he now says is a cult, Mike has changed his mind. Painting Mike as a cobra or reminding the world of what he told me in 2007 does not address the substance of the grave complaints made by Mike and other senior ex-members of the Church, that they were beaten, abused and humiliated by David Miscavige when they were inside the Church. These are allegations which the Church and Miscagive deny.

The next day Mike introduced me to Marty Rathbun, the former Inspector-General of the Church and once David Miscavige's right hand man. After 27 years inside, he left in 2004. Marty used to be Scientology's confessor to, amongst others, Tom Cruise, Kirstie Alley, and John Travolta, and he had offered to give me an opportunity on the E-meter. I sat opposite him and picked up the cans while he twiddled with a dial on the E-meter.

'What I am going to do is I am going to pinch you. And I want you to just check and see what the needle does when I pinch you, just note it ok.'

He pinched me.

'Ow!'

'Now what I want you to do, keep watching the needle, is recall the moment of that pinch. Now right....John.'

I recalled the moment of pain from the pinch, and the needle jagged to attention. I laughed nervously as my scepticism queued up for the bus home.

'That's a bit creepy,' I said, 'because my mind remembered the pinch and then that registered.'

The E-meter, Scientologists both within and without the Church believe, helps you uncover repressed thoughts. It didn't take Marty long to find a naughty thought of mine.

'Are you nervous or concerned about something?' asked Marty.

'I am fighting this. Also I am thinking of something that I am not going to tell anyone about...'

'I can tell that....' said Marty, laughing. 'You don't have to. OK.'

'Yes. I am not going to.'

'And I am not going to try to make you so, although I know when you're thinking it.'

'Right. This is a naughty thought. Does it tell you it is a naughty thought?'

'It tells me that you don't want to share it, that's all.'

'You can tell whether I am agitated about a line of thinking, a line of questioning.'

'You got it, you got it.'

The E-meter scared me. My lesson in what lay behind Mr Hubbard's tech was not over. We watched a clip of Tommy having a go at me back in 2007, relentlessly piling on the pressure: 'Bigot... bigot... bigot,' said Tommy, 'I, Tommy Davis, say you, John Sweeney, is a bigot.'

Marty explained what was happening, if you had been trained in Scientology: 'People have emotional buttons, things that set them off and they study you for that.'

'Bigot,' snapped Mike.

I'm not a bigot, I said. To call me a bigot annoys me because I am not a bigot.

'I understand that but that's...' said Mike.

But hold on a second, I struggled to interrupt.

'If I keep cutting you off like this,' said Mike, 'I will actually drive you nuts if every time you start to say something I cut you off...'

I tried to cut in, in vain.

'That's another...' said Mike.

I babbled...

'... if every time you start to say something I cut you off...' said Mike.

Eerumpfg, I said.

'...It's another way of getting you so that you become emotionally upset...'

'Yeah, it builds up like a dam,' said Marty. 'All these things you want to originate, keep getting cut off and it builds up like a dam and then finally explodes.'

'And its one of these things...' said Mike.

It's very annoying, I said, I want to say something interesting.

'No,' said Mike, 'you're not allowed to say anything right now...'

'Bigots are not allowed to talk,' said Marty.

I collapsed in half-annoyed giggles, pleading that they stop. But again, this made me just a little bit afraid. The two Scientologists could tie me up on knots verbally and I get paid for talking the hind leg off a donkey.

Mike and Marty told me about black or reverse Scientology, about how its power to do good had been corrupted and turned to the dark side. 'In Miscavige's Church,' said Marty, 'you see Scientology and dynamics, good principles, being twisted around, used in a negative fashion. The whole thing is to help the guy communicate, to help the person freely communicate, to help the person you know examine his own life and to communicate about it. Reverse the process, you're going to feel worse.'

Having met Russell Miller and read his heretical biography of L Ron Hubbard, and the books of other ex-Scientologists who felt they were victims of the Church under its founder, I am not convinced that there was a 'White Scientology' to be corrupted. But there is a clear difference in the openness with which Mike and Marty explain their faith, and their belief in L Ron Hubbard, and the flat refusal to do the same by David Miscavige.

And that extends to Xenu. When I asked Marty about the space alien stuff, he talked about Buddha reaching enlightenment underneath a tree and Jesus exorcising demons: 'If you look at early Christianity, they fully believed in the existence of spirits amongst us. So this whole thing about the stuff you're talking about, I call it a creation myth.'

Is Xenu true, I asked Mike?

'That's not what Scientology is about. It is a creation myth, no different than the creation myth of God creating the world in one day...'

It was six days, I interrupted, and then the seventh...

'Six days, you know, whatever...'

These were not perfect answers, but both men answered my question about Xenu civilly, without incredulity or scorn. The problem is when you claim respect and tax relief for secret belief, for something holy or unholy you keep dark from the world.

Later, Mike and Marty and I went on a tour of the

313

Church's London properties. They were disgusted that they all looked empty, that the footfall was so sparse. For Mike and Marty, who truly believe in Scientology, this was the worst thing of all – worse than the abuse, The Hole, the obscene language – that the man in charge of the Church they used to love was driving people away from it.

We were spied on, filmed overtly and covertly: the usual.

CHAPTER SIXTEEN
Broken Lives

The man in the dark suit walks into the centre of the screen and welcomes you to the Church of Scientology. His presence is Magus-like, just this side of sinister, hinting at knowledge of dark matters, beyond ordinary human ken, the voice urgent, probing, concerned, the hair – and everybody's hair was like this in the eighties – absurd: 'Right this instant you are on the threshold of the next trillion years.' Behind him, a steady stream of young, attractive people walk through two large doors, into some place the camera cannot go. 'You will live it in shivering, agonized darkness. Or you will live it triumphantly in the light. The choice is yours, not ours.'

If you are a committed Trekkie you might recognise the actor from the movie *Star Trek: Insurrection* in which he plays a Tarlac officer – that's a space alien with an enormous head with reptilian ridges to go – proclaiming: 'Activating injector assembly... Injector assembly has separated.'

Larry Anderson, the man on the screen, is now out. He's left after 33 years inside the Church. He's an Out-Out, no longer a member of the Church or a Scientologist.

We met in Hollywood, probably the most over-rated place

in the world, a fantasy factory parked in a smog-rich, overly-expensive industrial estate of dreams gone rancid. Not too far away on the street where the stars have their names in cement sad wannabes dress up as Batman and Robin, Cat-Woman, Spiderman and Freddie from the horror movie. They strut to and fro, barking at tourists who take their picture but don't hand over five dollars. Behold our cheap celluloid gods… five bucks, please.

There was a time when the Church of the Stars love-bombed Hollywood, and Hollywood returned that affection. But the times, they are a-changing.

Larry has become an avenging angel, turning his voice against the Church. Back in 2007 he started to question the faith he once promoted: 'I began to speculate that those early gains and wins as they say in Scientology were, in fact, the bait, the hook to bring you in. As a Scientologist you're not only encouraged – you really had your arms twisted never to look at media. If you see a story on the Church, turn it off because it will only destroy the gains you've achieved up to now. Well, I said, I'm not doing that anymore. I'm going on-line.' He trumpeted the word 'on-line' as if it was a statement of personal freedom, a super-hero breaking his chains, not an ordinary thing to do in the twenty-first century.

As a 'public' Scientologist, Larry did not get much of an insight into the innards of the Church. But when he became a presenter, advertising Scientology, he went to Gold in the desert to work on films to promote the Church. There, he saw things ordinary Scientologists never got to see: 'The edict came down this film needs to be done tonight, it's got to be done, so we were working through the night, one, three, five in the morning, and of course I might have gotten a very nice night's sleep the night before and just had to work a long shift to get the film done but the Sea Org members who were the crew didn't get a good night's sleep the night before. They're working seven days a week, often times 20 hours a day getting literally three, four hours of sleep. Here and there falling asleep like I saw on the set and then of course they'd get punished for that.'

Once, at Clearwater, at Christmas, Larry saw Sea Org members on the RPF, dressed in black, not talking to anyone, moving 'like robots': 'They were scrubbing the stage floor with toothbrushes.'

As well as the treatment of the Sea Org members, Larry came to resent the constant high-pressure salesmanship: 'Back in summer 2008 they released the basic Hubbard books again. Over the course of the 33 years I bought those books, I think, on four different occasions. Each new release we were given the story that they had now found corrections that weren't integrated into the previous release and a chapter wasn't there or some story about how we would now be getting fully official fully documented L Ron Hubbard basic books, the definitive works are now here.'

On inspection, the books turned out to be essentially the same: 'It's just another slick packaging thing and what drove me nuts was that the primary reason they were being re-released – and I was expecting some really clever story that they were now on their fourth release, you know, boy, they'd better come up with a great story – was that they discovered that the people who transcribed L Ron Hubbard's audio tapes goofed. It was the most ludicrous explanation and yet every-

one was standing up and doing standing ovations, "I can't wait to shell out another 3000 dollars on my basic books again.'"
David Miscavige was doing the pitch.

After filming we went to a café to take a bite to eat with Larry. As we were relaxing, we noticed someone filming us: the usual.

A few miles up the coast lives Jason Beghe, star of *GI Jane* and a good number of American TV shows. I thought we were being tailed by a white Audi, but whoever was behind the wheel drove too fast. Beghe's house has a fantastic view of the Pacific. I found myself spouting Keats, never a good sign: when stout Cortez, tumpety-tum, stood silent upon a peak in Darien...

'Oh, Truth is beauty, beauty truth, and all of that nonsense,' deflected Jason, nicely. He spent 13 years inside and around a million dollars. Now Jason thinks he was in a cult. He said it was hard to describe why he spent so long inside because 'you lose your own ability to make a rational decision'. The starkest evidence of it being a cult was disconnection: 'I can't think of many religions where such a large percentage of people are willing to dump their own son, daughter, best friend, wife, husband because they won't have Scientology anymore. That's going too far. It's insanity to me.'

I told him that Tommy Davis said that disconnection is a lie.

Jason talked about the day when he finally left, the cut-off was sheer: 'Nobody ever talked to me again. All my old friends were gone. My son, Bix, four years old in a Scientology pre-school, kicked out, no friends, boom!, cause he was connected to me. It was like boom! I went to call some people and say, "Hey," and they wouldn't take my call. And if I left a message, never returned, and these are people that would come to me, hug me, kiss me and tell me how much they love me and blah blah blah. So that's disconnection. My wife was made to disconnect from her mother. That's my personal experience. I know many, many, many, many people that were forced to disconnect.'

What Tommy was saying about disconnection not happening was 'just a lie.'

The mind-holes inside the Church went deep: 'We're these wonderful, powerful, superhuman OTs [Operating Thetans] and Clears and we're well beyond anyone else. Then why is it that you can't even see a differing opinion on the internet? That to me is a show of just incredible weakness. These people are not stupid but they go well, OK, and then not read the newspapers. If you can't handle a newspaper, how OT are you?'

Jason, who plays a psychiatrist on the television but freely admits he's no expert, said: 'Even the most degraded criminal will protect his mother. These people drop mothers like a hot potato because they have decided that this philosophy or the superstructure of the Church itself is more important. So they say: "Well, you're dead to me." How do you make that leap? It's something like mind control. It's totally unnatural, it's hypnotism, I don't know what the hell it is but it's something. The bottom line is handle or disconnect. In other words get them to behave in a way that they're not a danger to me or the group or else dump them.'

Our mutual acquaintance cropped up: 'Tommy was one of the most beautiful, sweet and enthusiastic guys. He liked

319

to have fun, and was I think a person worthy of admiration. He was born with a silver spoon in his mouth and he could have been out partying with Paris Hilton and he decided he was going to dedicate his life to helping others for no money. That's a personality trait that's rare. So his intention is spectacular, very admirable person.'

Tommy was weird with me, I said, off camera, very nice, cameras around, aggressive.

'I've done a lot of acting scenes with people and you get to know when someone's really there and when they're acting. He's not good at doing that. I don't buy it. Looks manufactured to me. It smacks of "methinks he doth protest too much". It looks like an admission of guilt to me.'

He was faking it?

'It's much worse. For Tommy's sake I wish he knew he was lying but he's convinced "I'm telling the truth" which is further along the line of brainwashing. Instead of having a tool to use, you are used by the tool.'

Jason explained that in 1999 he had a terrible car accident, broke bones, broke his neck and fell into a coma for three and a half weeks. Tommy Davis and another Scientologist from the Celebrity Centre came to the hospital: '24 hours one of them was always by my bedside'.

Later, Jason discovered that Tommy was encouraging his family and doctors not to use 'certain drugs – Psyche drugs – that may disqualify me from being eligible to continue in Scientology. Don't construe that as evil. Construe that as love: Jason needs Scientology.'

There is compelling evidence that L Ron Hubbard when he died was full of psychiatric drugs, I said. Why on earth should the Church continue to challenge the use of psychiatric drugs in the way that they do?

'If you're looking for logic you came to the wrong place,' said Jason. 'This is not logic.'

When Jason tried to leave, they made it difficult for him to do so amicably. Frustrated by the delay, he took a step from which there was no return. Following 'months and months and months of this I finally knew the deal breaker. I just said, that's it, give me my money back and then the fucking guillotine went down and the party was over.'

I brought up the space alien Satan.

'If you want to believe in Xenu and this whole routine, that's fine. The justification for keeping it secret is that this is such powerful information that somebody who hasn't done the previous steps would go into something called Freewheeling, they wouldn't be able to sleep, they would go insane and they would die.'

That's the official reason. But Jason suspects the real reason is different: 'Keeping something rare keeps it more valuable and it's a way to keep people interested and to pay a premium to gain the information.'

In that sense, question: is it a religion or is it a racket?

'They are not necessarily mutually exclusive, are they?'

The Church of Scientology says of Jason that he is an 'apostate poster boy', 'a D-list actor' and 'Hollywood Psycho'. He seemed like a good bloke to me.

Private investigators tracked us around California: the usual, from LA to Gold base, which we visited with Marty and Amy Scobee, pointing out The Hole from the safety of the public road. Marty and Amy told me about what they saw as the madness at the heart of Scientology under the rule of David Miscavige, telling me the stories I've set out in Chapter Five. The private eyes in 2010 were robots. They said very little. Two stood out: a thin one and a fat one. The difference between 2007 and 2010 for us was no Tommy popping up here and there like a jack-in-the-box. Hiring private investigators to follow us around must have cost the Church thousands of dollars – and provides a simple definition for a religion: a belief system, open and honest about itself, which enjoys the respect of society and does not employ private investigators.

The Hollywood stars who have now got out lost money and peace-of-mind. But members of the Sea Org? They lost years of their lives. Ask an ex-follower of the Church of Scientology how do they get along with their family members still inside and the answer seems to be universally depressing.

Claire and Marc Headley were practically born into the Church. Earlier, we've heard how Claire said she had to relay obscene messages for the Leader and how Marc said he was once beaten up by him – claims the Church and Miscavige deny. They both signed the billion-year contract of loyalty to the Sea Org, becoming adepts when they were both just 16. Claire said: 'My mother joined the Sea Org when I was four years old.' Claire had no choice. The hardest thing for Claire was that she had no knowledge whatsoever of the outside world, and feared it, us, out of total ignorance.

Trapped inside the Sea Org, Claire knew something was wrong: 'There was 24/ 7 security cameras, people everywhere, it was definitely a very strict operating environment. Fear and intimidation was the dominant controlling emotions of my life for 20 years.' As a woman in the Church, Claire had to put up with a lot.

The most bizarre behaviour, she said, came from the Leader. Once, he told Claire, she said: 'I was "a f***ing c**t" because I greeted one of his staff members in an enthusiastic manner.'

Marc chipped in: 'One time when we were in a meeting with David Miscavige. He said that the only expansion that two senior executives in Scientology had ever caused was by sticking their cocks in each other's assholes. That's David Miscavige in a nutshell.'

Now they are both out. In the Sea Org, there is no sex before marriage. When Claire, just 19, and married to Marc, realised that she was pregnant, she had a horrible decision to make. You can't have a child and stay in the Sea Org.

Marc explained: 'The Sea Organisation is not in the business of raising children or raising babies. It's not in their business model.'

For Claire to have her baby she would have to leave the Sea Org. Fearing it meant leaving her only home and breaking from her family she felt an abortion was her only option. Two years later, the couple were posted 2,000 miles apart.

'I was in Clearwater, Florida,' Claire told me, 'when I found out I was pregnant again. I requested authorisation to be able to call Marc. That was disapproved, not allowed. So I literally could not even tell him about it until eight months after the fact when I next saw him in person.'

If she chose to have the baby, she faced never seeing him again. Unable to talk things through with her husband, she had another abortion: 'It was absolutely the most horrifying, upsetting, deeply disturbing situation I've ever been in.'

For its part, the Church said Claire made a statement at the time that she did not want the child and never wanted children. It confirmed pregnant women cannot remain in the Sea Org but they are free to leave with their husbands.

Marc left the Church on his motorbike on a rainy day. Chased off the road by Church security, he said, he crashed, picked himself off the floor and was rescued by a cop. He got back on the damaged bike and drove into the town of Hemet at its new maximum speed: five mph. Claire got out a short while afterwards. But since that say, both sets of parents, still in the Church, have shunned them. The couple have two sons, both seriously into Thomas The Tank Engine. The little boys have never seen their grandmothers.

'My mother,' said Marc, 'has never met her only grand-children and Claire's parents have never met their only grandchildren.'

The day after Claire fled, she said, 'my mother, my stepfather, my half-brother, my two half sisters were all pulled into Scientology and told I was a Suppressive Person. They could have no further contact with me.'

The Church said it is a fundamental human right to cease communication with someone. It added disconnection is used against expelled members and those who attack the Church. It said Marc and Claire Headley were declared suppressive persons and expelled. The family's decision not to have contact was theirs alone.

'Speaking to me,' said Marc 'would risk their and all of mankind's future eternity.'

Claire said: 'The last phone call I had with my sister was

her bawling her eyes out, telling me that she could never talk to me again and she could not talk she had to hang up. That was the last conversation I had with my sister in Jan 2005 – I haven't talked to her since.'

The couple tried to sue the Church, saying they had been abused at work, used as slaves, working illegal hours and paid a pittance. Because the Church is classed as a religion in the United States, they lost the case. Members of the Sea Org – in America, a religious body – are legally exempt from labour law. As a result, they ended up owing the multi-billion dollar Church $40,000 – and had to hand over their savings, sell many of their possessions, including their children's swing, to try and make up the money. Word got around the ex-Church community – both ex-Scientologists, Out-Outs, and people who have left the Church but still believe in L Ron, Outs, – and tens of thousands of dollars was donated to the Headleys. In Britain, where the Church is not officially recognised as a religion for the purposes of English charity law, they might have stood a chance. So the difference between religious recognition and non-recognition is not academic. For the Headleys, it almost drove them bankrupt. It did cost them their boys' swing.

Like the Headleys, Tommy Davis was practically born into the Church. He was three years old when his mother, Anne Archer, became a Scientologist. There you are: sympathy for the devil. Thing is: he's not a devil.

We flew to Florida, to catch up with Mike Rinder. I interviewed Mike on top of the car park in downtown Clearwater, just as I had Shawn Lonsdale three years before. Not long into the interview an enormous black SUV approached. It boasted a squaloid radiator grille and tinted windows, making it look the most passive-aggressive motor vehicle I have ever seen. I walked towards the SUV, my hand upraised. Coincidentally, I am sure, the driver elected to park somewhere further back and he started to reverse slowly. From the perspective of Bill's camera, it looked as though I was forcing the SUV backwards by the telekinetic power of my hand, like Magneto in the film *X-Men*. This image of my superhuman powers was so disturbing, so challenging to the rational mind, that the BBC elected not to broadcast it. Shame.

When it finally stopped the SUV disgorged two men. One of them was the fat robot who had filmed us at Gold, two thousand miles away and less than 24 hours before. They were silent. The cameraman was working but the other man was not. I offered him my hand. He refused it.

'Have you been told by the Church not to talk to us?'

Silence. Good answer.

We got back into Mike's car and drove down the multiple tiers of the car park to the ground level. In the side mirror the black SUV loomed monstrously large, as if we were living inside a Hollywood thriller. Immediately outside the car park was a disused drive-in bank, essentially lots of car lanes, open and empty. Mike drove down one lane; the SUV followed. Mike reached the end of the lane and turned hard around and drove back along one of the lanes; the SUV followed. It was a stately gavotte in metal, chrome and rubber. Following them, following us, was the BBC back-up car driven by assistant producer Jon Coffey with producer Kate Stead riding shotgun. Mole was lurking in Essex, having a baby. After a prolonged to-and-fro-ing inside the empty drive-in bank facility, all of us in the car were in danger of being car sick. Mike headed home. The black SUV followed. Jon and Katy followed them, until a car containing two chaps in white-ish uniforms stopped them. Jon wound down his window, assumed that they were Scientology security, patronised them and drove off. Too late, it dawned on Jon that they were, in fact, officers from the Clearwater Police Department.

The black SUV followed us all the way back to Mike's home, where it parked outside. I rapped on the window, and accused the private investigators of harassing Mike in the name of religion. No reply.

The level of harassment was extraordinary and unbecoming.

Mike's mum and dad joined the Church when he was six years old. He has known nothing else since primary school. He married and became a father to son Ben and daughter Taryn while inside. After he got out, Mike's family became part of the battleground. Mike has tried to see his son, Ben, who is still in the Church and has disconnected from Mike. Like the rest of Mike's family, Ben has refused to have anything to do with him.

In late April 2010 Mike drove his girlfriend Christie to a medical appointment. He sat in the car, while Christie was in the clinic. Seven people started walking towards him, including Cathy Rinder, his ex-wife, Taryn, his daughter, Andrew, his brother and four other Scientologists, one of whom is a massive chap. It was seven members of the Church against one ex-member. Mike had not seen his ex-wife and daughter for three years.

What happened next is disputed. But Mike was on the

phone to a reporter who was taping the call – and that reporter was me.

First, you can hear several people screaming at the same time: 'Fuck you, Mike, Fuck you.'

Jenny Linson, the ex-wife of Tom DeVocht screeches: 'You look at your daughter. You piece of shit.'

Mike: 'Oh, Fuck off Jenny.'

Jenny: 'Fuck you. You deserted your family, you piece of shit!'

Cathy Rinder: 'You walked out on me, you fucker.'

Taryn Rinder: 'And you tried to fuck with Benjamin, you tried to fuck with Benjamin.'

Mike: 'Taryn…'

Taryn: 'You're trying to fuck with me. You're trying to fuck with my home.'

Mike: 'Taryn…'

Taryn: 'Your church, and my church, you're fucking with everything I believe in.'

Cathy: 'You leave Benjamin alone, you knock it off.'

Mike: 'That's fine, Cathy.'

Cathy: 'No, it's not fine, you fuck off, you fucking stop.'

Jenny: (nonsensically) 'Your family came here to talk to you, and you refuse to talk to your family.'

Andrew Rinder: 'Talk to me Michael, talk to me.'

Sweeney (from London, down the phone to Mike): 'Mike, are you OK?'

Andrew: 'Don't be a dick, don't be a fucking dick.'

Cathy: 'I'm telling you, you better stop, you better stop… You have no fucking idea, Ok. I don't give a fuck. All I know, is that what you've been doing and what you're doing now is committing SP acts every minute, of every fucking day...'

At one point Mike says his brother and ex-wife tried to take the car keys off him. In the scuffle Cathy's arm got grazed. The police arrived. The police report stated the injury was incidental contact – not intentional assault. No charges were filed.

Mike was stoical when he reflected on it: 'The intention was intimidation. It was to make me worried. It was very unpleasant.'

The evidence from the audio is clear: seven members of the Church approached Mike and began screaming at him. The effect on him of seeing his ex-wife, daughter and brother after three years of no contact must have been extraordinarily painful.

CHAPTER SEVENTEEN
A Space Alien Cathedral

New Mexico, USA.
November 2012.

I f you don't have a flying saucer, Trementina Base is not an easy place to get to. If you're a visitor from Outer Space, it's a doddle because the Church of Scientology's Church of Spiritual Technology has etched on to the top of a mountain side in the desert scrub of New Mexico, west of Los Alamos and due north of Roswell, two vast connecting circles, 1000 yards in radius, containing two diamonds. Just follow – not the Yellow Brick Road – but the Space Alien Signs.

I'm not joking. Dial up Mesa Huerfanita on any satellite map such as Google Earth. Go west from that mountain – New Mexico state road 104 trundles along the bottom of the picture – and you will find a second nameless mountain scarred by a long concrete strip with a short leg at the northern end pointing to the east. That's the Church's private airport. A ziggy-zaggy white line from the strip heads north. That's the Church's private road. It leads to two enormous intersecting circles with diamonds in them. You can't see them from the road because they are on top of a mountain. But if you have that spaceship you can see them fine.

Down on the planet, it's not so good. The mobile phone signal dies as soon as you turn off the freeway, the old Sante Fe trail. The road tapers through the buttes of high New Mexico, great cliffs of rock on which you half expect to see a Red Indian in full plumage on a horse being pursued by John Wayne, or vice versa. You cannot drive through this landscape without marvelling at the raw courage of the pioneers in their wagon trains and feel great sympathy for the Native Americans. The sheer immensity of America is stunning, that and the absence of people.

Trementina itself turns out to be a ghost town, abandoned after the end of the Second World War. The only signs of life are the steel windmills, still turning in the cold early winter breeze, but they are misleading. At the foot of each and every windmill is an old homestead with broken walls and 1940s tractors, rusting gently on the humidity-free mile-high plateau.

To get directions we drive to Trementina Post Office. It is round the back of someone's house. Out front is a car with the keys in the ignition. No dogs bark. Only the autumn leaves scurry and tumble through the scrub, snagging on the occasional cactus. The Post Office is shut. I shout, 'Is there anybody there?' The silence is oppressive.

Not far away is another house, but this one has a dog outside. I hail the owner and eventually an old chap emerges tentatively from his house and gives me directions to Trementina Base: go two miles past the fire station, take the dirt track, and drive for 30 miles. Then you'll find a gate...

Driving me to the base is Marc Headley, the ex-Scientol-

331

ogist who says he was audited by Tom Cruise and beaten up by David Miscavige. The Church denies both and says that Marc is a cyber-terrorist.

As we drive down the bumpy dirt track in a gulch between two walls of rock a certain nervousness creeps over us. Here, even the windmills have no life. They have not turned for decades. A great black bird circles in a thermal high above. We come to a gate marked NO TRESPASSING. Gingerly, we go through the gate and drive on. If a crazy hillbilly shot us – there is, of course, no suggestion that the Church would do any such thing – then you get the feeling that no-one would find the bodies for six months.

Two more gates, marked NO TRESPASSING. Trementina Gulch is the creepiest place I've ever been to because the faint memory of life here makes you wonder why everyone left. Our courage dries up and we turn back, all the way to Trementina, and park at the Fire Station. It's closed. There is dust on the door. We drive on and find somewhere. It, too, looks empty of life. I shout. There is no answer. I knock on the door. No answer. I open the door and walk into an empty room. I shout again, and another door opens. It is the first proof of humanity we've seen for about two and a half hours. This chap gives us firmer directions and we head back down the dirt track.

Ex-Scientologists say that the Church spent millions of dollars building a space alien cathedral deep underground in the 1980s. In the vault are housed L Ron Hubbard's lectures on gold discs locked in titanium caskets sealed with argon. The cathedral is H-bomb proof, behind three separate 5,000 pound stainless steel airlocks. The signs on top of the mountain are for Clears, returning from outer space, to find Mr Hubbard's works after nuclear Armageddon has wiped out humanity. Ex-Scientologist Chuck Beatty of Pittsburgh has said: 'The whole purpose of putting these teachings in the underground vaults was expressly so that in the event that everything gets wiped out somehow, someone would be willing to locate them and they would still be there.'

It is an odd thought that if all of humanity dies out then at least there will be some Scientologists left or at least some evidence of Scientology.

Anyone who drives along this dirt road for 30 miles knows that burrowing a great hole into the mountain in this part of the world would have been astonishingly expensive. They would have needed to import labour, immense earth-moving machines, tunnel drills, steam rollers – or whatever the modern equivalent is – for the airstrip, and a small city of concrete and steel.

It feels terrifyingly remote. The word is that one security man was driven so melancholic by the solitude of the base that he killed himself. I would fear to be a believing Scientologist and end up in this place. Contact with the rest of humanity would be close to zero.

The light is beginning to die, the shadows creeping up the side of the gulch. I have come 4,500 miles to see this thing, and it is looking like the worst wild goose chase ever. We turn one last corner and suddenly Marc and I are staring at something out of *Lost*. We have become attuned to the primitive landscape, pretty much untouched by man, and suddenly we are staring at 21st century technology: a massive steel gate, secured by an alphabet lock and guarded by two security cameras which watch our every move like Hal the psycho computer in *2001: A Space Odyssey*. I press an intercom button. A lonely voice – German, Scandinavian accent? – says: 'Hello?' I tell the disembodied voice that I'm John Sweeney and I ask nicely for a tour. The intercom spouts white noise. As we drive back to civilization we wonder what kind of religion is it that builds a space alien cathedral underground in the middle of nowhere?

Only later does it strike me that a Church is not the right word for an organization that places gold in a vault under the ground. In English, we call that a bank. Had it been 'The Bank of Scientology' I could have stayed in bed all these years.

We stop the night at a Best Western in Las Vegas, New Mexico. That night at one o'clock in the morning Marc gets four mystery phone calls to his room. Each time the caller hangs up as soon as Marc answers. Both rooms were registered in my name. They got the wrong room. But still impressive, in a way, because I hadn't booked in advance and I paid cash.

The next morning we drive back to Marc's new home in Colorado. On the road, we talk about the Church he spent his whole life from the age of six in. His book, *'Blown For Good: Inside the Dark Curtain of Scientology'* has become the bible for Scientologists thinking of leaving the Church. They often call him up and he chats through his arguments for getting out.

As we drove across the endless wastes of New Mexico, Marc explained what he tells them: 'I don't criticise Hubbard, I don't say it's all bad. I start with money and math. The E-meter costs $40 to make. I know that number because I used to make them. There is a picture of me making an

E-meter. The Church sells an E-meter at $4,000. That's a profit of $3,960 on each one, and everyone needs two in case one breaks down. In 2004, we in Sea Org started making the new generation of E-meters, the Mark 8 Ultra. They still haven't been rolled out yet. Since that time, the iPhone has come out. You can put all of Hubbard's work on the iPhone or similar. You can make an app which would do the same thing as the E-meter. If you really care about spreading the word of Scientology to the whole planet, why not go digital? You could have it all for free on an iPhone which costs you $400?'

At 11:30am we stop off for a bite to eat. We sit on our own in a barn of a restaurant. As we get up to leave we notice a man sitting in the next booth, oddly close given the emptiness of the restaurant. He asks which team do we root for? I reply: 'Tranmere Rovers', my dad's team, those bonny boys from Birkenhead. He looks nonplussed. I ask him who does he support? He says: 'Manchester.' Which one? I ask, puzzled that anyone would presume that there is only one team in Manchester. With a visible effort of memory he says: 'Manchester United.'

The miles roll by. The Man U fan follows us is his car. We drive off the freeway and stop. We are close to the state line and if you are a New Mexico PI you cannot follow someone in Colorado without risking being nicked for stalking unless you have a separate PI license for that state too. We don't see him again. As usual, he could just have been a friendly American fascinated by British soccer who just happened to have never heard of the current Premier League Champions Manchester City.

Marc continues: 'The goal, Miscavige says, is getting the

whole planet clear. OK. I figured out that if you take zip code 90027 around L Ron Hubbard Way in Los Angeles,' – centred on the building I call the Concrete Angel – 'you have 50,000 people. After Clearwater, it has probably the highest concentration of Scientologists per square mile in the world. The organisation within Scientology that makes people clear is called the American Saint Hill Organisation or ASHO. ASHO has a newsletter and it printed that it had two Clears in one month. That got me thinking.'

Clears, to repeat, are on the first big step on the road to total freedom – a journey that costs around $50,000. Beyond that and much more expensive are the Operating Thetan Levels I, II, III – the Wall of Fire where you learn about Xenu – on to OT VIII when you become a kind of God.

'So let's be generous,' Marc says. 'They make two Clears in one month. In one year, that's say 24 Clears. In ten years, that's 240 Clears. In one hundred years, that 24,000 Clears. So in a century, the Church will only get to make half the zip code of one of the greatest concentrations of Scientologists on the planet Clear. Under Hubbard, if you made Clear in a previous existence that stayed with you, so "Last Life-Time Clears" could carry on at that level into a new life. Miscavige killed that policy, so once you get to 100 years and everyone is dead, you have to reset the whole thing to zero. All those 24,000 are no longer Clears in the next life. So the stated goal of the Church of Scientology, to Clear the planet? It is not going to happen – on their own numbers.'

Marc and Jason Beghe, the Hollywood actor, travelled together to Germany to attend a conference on Scientology organised by Ursula Caberta, yet another woman the Church greatly dislikes. Caberta is in the vein of shotgun-toting cult-buster Margaret Singer. Caberta opened the conference, Marc said, by noting that Church officials had not been allowed to attend and they had protested about this denial of their rights. Caberta said: 'If you hold a conference about drug addiction, you don't invite the drug dealers.'

The Church says that Caberta is the 'Wicked Witch of the West', 'Hamburg's modern-day Grand Inquisitor' and has printed a picture of her against the backdrop of a bleak building it identifies as the Gestapo HQ from the 1930s.

Marc told me: 'Ursula says that the best way of working against Scientology is using Scientology.' He said that she has more of L Ron Hubbard's works than he ever saw in the Church and that when people asked for her help with refunds she would state Hubbard's policy advice at Church officials, reading out chapter and verse.

Marc took Ursula's advice and applied it to the Church's Holy Scriptures. Several times ordinary 'public' Scientologists have been asked to re-purchase Hubbard's works because technical errors had led, the Church said, to his wisdom not being correctly put down. 'If that is so,' said Marc, 'then all the writings locked inside the earth in Trementina Base back in the 1980s are wrong. What a waste of money.'

It is arguments like this, Marc says, that make ordinary Scientologists wonder what they have been paying for.

While her two young sons played making a fort out of a blanket, Marc's wife Claire reflected with me on the absolute worst moment for her since she got out. Until this moment she had let Marc do the fighting. Having suffered two abortions because of the Sea Org's then policy against its adepts having children, she was determined to be a good mother and leave talking to reporters about stuff to Marc. That changed when a social worker from Child Services knocked on the door of their home. He had received an anonymous complaint alleging child abuse. It didn't take long for the social worker to work out what I saw: that their boys are greatly loved and smashing kids. She was and is incredibly angry that someone sought to make trouble for her as a mother.

Claire and Marc were both brought up inside Scientology. They didn't see much of their parents, didn't have many toys or holidays, left school very young and learnt L Ron's works rather than the 'false data' of what you learn at university. They strive to give their little boys the very best. But neither boy has a grandmother worthy of the name: both women are in the Church and have disconnected from the Headleys and that means disconnecting from their grandchildren too. To make up for that, they have Cindy, an ex-Scientologist who lives close by, whose own daughter is in the Church and disconnected from her. Cindy spoils the lads rotten, just like a real grandmother would.

This book opened with the story of Betty being disconnected from her daughter. The good news is that her daughter has left the Church, and they are back together on good terms. But how did the Church find out that Betty had given us an interview in the first place?

One of the funny things about the Church is that it has a lot of secrets but it is not good at keeping them. One source has told me that I was followed in Britain by a London firm of private eyes. I phoned the firm. No reply. I sent an email asking to talk them. No reply. Next I visited their offices which turned out to be a fancy accommodation address. This gives the company the allure and status of an expensive address and a smart receptionist but in reality its staff do not work there full-time, if at all. It is not a shell company because it does exist, just not in the bit of space the business address suggests. And so it being an accommodation address, they were not in. I wrote them a series of follow-up emails, saying that I had heard on good authority that they had been working, effectively, for the Church. Did they spy on me for the Church? Thus far, I have received no reply which is odd because in my experience, if you contact anyone or anything suggesting they are close to the Church of Scientology you get a reply.

For example, I was told by a source that the credit rating firm Experian had sold six sets of its people-tracking software kit, 'Name Tracer Pro', to the Church of Scientology for £60,000 in 2008. This software would enable the Church to track down anybody they fancy – me, you, someone on the run from Sea Org – with the very latest commercially available information kit. Experian spokesman Bruno Rost admitted that this was true, saying: 'We can confirm that The Church of Scientology is no longer a client and in 2009 ceased using this product. The product uses publicly available information and its use is governed by the Data Protection Act.'

So that's all right then.

The silence, thus far, from the firm of private eyes who I'm told spied on me is intriguing and leads to more questions, such as: has the Church used private eyes to spy on people who have embarrassed its celebrities?

Take *South Park*. In the episode called *Trapped In the Closet* the cartoon team present their take on L Ron's Second Coming. The Church's seer returns to earth as Stan. Immediately Tom Cruise turns up and asks the reincarnation of Mr Hubbard what he thinks of his acting. When Stan pooh-poohs his talent, Tom Cruise is upset and hides in Stan's closet, leading to the immortal line: 'Dad, Tom Cruise won't come out of the closet.' John Travolta pops in and he follows Tom into Stan's closet and won't come out. Xenu is portrayed as an evil space alien frog. The show concludes with Stan saying, 'to really be a church, they can't charge money to help,' and then coming clean: he's not L Ron Hubbard but, Stan says, 'Scientology is just a big fat global scam.'

It's hilarious satire: bitingly funny. Marc Headley and I watched it together and howled with laughter. Perhaps unsurprisingly, all of the credits are either John or Jane Smith.

After Comedy Central aired *Trapped In The Closet* in 2005 it was booked for a rebroadcast the following spring, but the show mysteriously fell off the air amidst gossip that Cruise had used his power in Hollywood to stop the repeat. *South Parks's* creators, Trey Parker and Matt Stone, issued a statement to Variety on March 17th, 2006: 'So, Scientology, you may have won THIS battle, but the million-year war for earth has just begun! Temporarily anozinizing our episode will NOT stop us from keeping Thetans forever trapped in your pitiful man-bodies. Curses and drat! You have obstructed us for now, but your feeble bid to save humanity will fail! Hail Xenu!!!'

The statement was signed 'Trey Parker and Matt Stone, servants of the dark lord Xenu.'

Did the Church take that comic defiance lying down? A document from the Office of Special Affairs, the Church's version of the CIA, for the very next month suggests otherwise. It reads as follows:

'CONFIDENTIAL WDC OSA
24-4-06
CC: CO OSA INT
D/CO EXTERNAL OSA INT
RE: INVEST REPORTS
Dear Sir…

SOUTH PARK

The PI was out today at the South Park Studio near Marina del Rey. The inside of their offices has different work cubicles in an open space. The staff mainly appear to be in their 20s and 30s. They do not go out for lunch, it is brought in by a catering company called Prestige Services Inc, which does catering for the entertainment industry. There are two parking spots marked "SP" in one section which is covered. The two vehicles there are most likely owned by [Trey] Parker and [Matt] Stone. One is a gray [model and plate details I have deleted] and a blue [model and plate details I have deleted].

The LA office of Comedy Central where Doug Herzog works is in one of the towers in Century City. The special collection there is not possible.

Research is being done on writers and others who have been or who are currently connected with the show to find lines that can be used.'

The OSA document goes on to list people connected with South Park to be targeted for further investigation and concludes: 'The next action will be for the investigator to work out a resource to get the above people interviewed.'

Clearly, *Trapped In The Closet* as far as the Church of Scientology is concerned was no laughing matter. There is no suggestion that either Tom Cruise or John Travolta knew of or condoned this spying operation on the satire show.

One of the very weirdest things among the host of weird things I have learned during the past few years is that ex-Scientologists have created among themselves quite the best intelligence network I have ever come across – and that includes MI6, the Russian FSB, the CIA, the Chinese State Security Bureau, the Belarus KGB, Saddam's Mukhabarat, Mugabe's C10, Ceausescu's Securitate, Albania's Segurimi and the Czech StB back in 1988 whom I dodged to see Vaclav Havel. They know so much about Hollywood, power, Clinton and Blair, sex, money. Their network stretches around the planet. But their speciality is, of course, the Church of Scientology.

In the autumn of 2012 I just happened to be in a pub in Soho downing a swift pint when I phoned a member of the ex-Sci network. The pub was noisy. A few feet away a gang of drunks were singing Abba's *Knowing Me, Knowing You*. Bloody drunks. Through the din of the Scandinavian threnody to a defunct love affair I distinctly heard the words: 'Tommy Davis has left…'

I was so astonished I left my pint in the pub and raced out to the street to hear the ex-Sci properly: 'Tommy Davis has left the Sea Org. He's quit California and started a new life selling real estate in Texas.'

You could have knocked me down with a copy of L Ron Hubbard's *Battlefield Earth*. I zoned out and thought back to the first uber-weird moment – the midnight ambush – when both Tommy Davis and Mike Rinder were waiting for us at the hotel in Clearwater. Now both of them were out of the Church's Holy Order. Astonishing.

The ex-Sci network might be good but it didn't tell me everything because I still don't know why Tommy left the Sea Org. I do know he's told people that his allegiance has not changed, so he is still with the Church but no longer in the Sea Org, its high command. New people are talking officially on behalf of the Church and Tommy has gone off the radar. Whatever the cause of this, starting over in Texas is a long way from Gold.

Soon after that the ex-Sci network provided me with Tommy's precise address. He once told me that he knew where I lived. Well, now I can return that favour.

Having heard and seen so much from so many different people since I first poked my nose into Scientology I think I now have some understanding of what it must have been like to be virtually born into the Church, as Tommy was. And as a human being, I can only feel sympathy for him.

Another thing: getting old is not good but one compensation is that if you live long enough you can watch what happens to your enemies. Sometimes they even become your friends. With that in mind, I flew from Colorado to Texas.

Tommy now lives 1,500 miles from Gold Base in a smart apartment block – Americans call it a condo – somewhere lovely in the Lone Star State. As I arrived at the front door a man in a Maserati convertible pulled up and an attention of valets fought to park it. I strode through the valets and marched towards the lift. The bad news is that I'd grown a beard and my clothes were still covered in dust from Trementina. The concierge thought I was a hobo and wouldn't let me through the lobby so I left Tommy a note asking him to get in touch with me, if he ever wants to, along with a copy of my novel, *Elephant Moon*. It's about elephants rescuing orphans on the run from the Japanese in Burma in 1942 and one of the heroes is an Indian officer who sides with the enemy – proof that I'm not a bigot.

At the time of writing, late November 2012, I have not heard from Tommy. I hope to meet him again. I imagine it would be like one of those reunions the chaps from the RAF and the Luftwaffe have, when they laugh and joke about that time during the Battle of Britain when they tried to kill each other. I wish Tommy well.

The Church is under attack these days in a way that it was not back in 2007. But it still is extraordinarily rich and aggressive. Do not doubt its power. While we were making our second Panorama on the Church in 2010 we heard that the FBI was investigating the Church, too. They seemed to be asking the right people the right questions, and we kept our mouths shut about the FBI investigation. Nothing has happened. One ex-Scientologist who assisted the FBI told me: 'They were good. They got it. The investigators we were talking to knew what they were doing. Then someone upstairs seemed to raise the stakes. They had to have video evidence of wrong-doing, an admission of guilt, or else nothing would happen.'

All I know for certain is that an FBI investigation was running and nothing has happened. It turned out, my source said, that the Church had more money and more resolve than the FBI. The thing that may have killed the investigation was the FBI was afraid of taking on an official religion. If true, that does not sound good. Of course, all of the above may well be untrue and the FBI investigation may have failed for the simple truth that there was nothing to investigate.

In my time as a reporter money and power always seem to get on sweetly; power and the poor, the wretched, even, perhaps, the 'disconnected' less so. So will the authorities, those in government, crack down on the Church of Fear? I doubt it.

This is a personal account of my time inside the Church's embrace and I have deliberately concentrated on my first-hand experiences of the Church, events I can report directly and confidently because they happened to me with our cameras running and even that seemingly simple task has not been easy. But outside that narrow focus the Church seems to have been very successful at emerging intact from what appear to be great scandals, in particular in the United States. The Church has reportedly got a billion dollar war chest. Its teams of lawyers are ready to fight tooth and nail.

Take the tragedy of Scientologist Lisa McPherson. She was declared 'Clear' then dead in an embarrassingly short time frame in 1995 on David Miscavige's watch as Leader. Florida's medical examiner reported that Lisa had been the victim of negligent homicide and the Church was indicted on two charges, abuse and/or neglect of a disabled adult and practising medicine without a license. The case collapsed after the state's medical examiner changed the cause of death to accidental in 2000. Ex-Scientologists say that there was a cover-up operation aimed at hiding Miscavige's role. The Church and Miscavige deny that emphatically. Law suits related to the McPherson tragedy are still trundling through the courts but the Church has survived Lisa's death – evidence, the critics say, of the power of the Church to block scrutiny. The Church denies that.

Narconon – Scientology's anti-drug therapy praised in the House of Commons by Charles Hendry MP and by the Church's celebrities to me – is now in trouble after a series of young addicts have collapsed and died in the Church's treatment centres in worrying circumstances. But again the Church's legal teams are working hard to prove the Church has done nothing wrong. The Church, of course, says exactly that: these personal tragedies do not reflect on the good work that Narconon does in treating thousands of addicts. The ex-Scientologists say Narconon kills people. It is fair to say that addicts die in non-Scientology centres all the time.

The evidence suggests that the authorities will not do very much to encumber the Church of Scientology. But that does not mean that ordinary people are powerless. Richard Behar, the *Time* magazine journalist who wrote 'The Thriving Cult of Greed and Power', once told me that in the long law suit between *Time* and the Church – which *Time* won – the thing the Church most seemed to be afraid of was the prospect of their celebrities being embarrassed.

Katie Holmes' divorce from Tom Cruise is a seismic event in the glitzy media world, but ordinary Scientologists may have noticed that while they have to disconnect from their family members declared 'Suppressive Persons', Tom Cruise has not disconnected from his daughter Suri after his divorce. 'If you meet Tom Cruise,' says Claire Headley, 'ask him about disconnection.' Here in this book, I repeat my request to interview Tom Cruise. He is an action hero and an Operating Thetan. He will have nothing to fear from me.

In the mean time, the Church's culture of celebrity endorsement could, the ex-Scientologists say, be reversed against itself. If Tom Cruise and John Travolta face public shame about some of the Church's extraordinary conduct, then things might change, they say. Marc Headley, for example, does not choose to watch the latest Tom Cruise thriller. He would rather see his mother see his sons. The same goes for all the former members of the Church who have left: Mike Rinder is disconnected from his family, Amy Scobee from hers... The list is long and cruel.

The critics say the next time Tom Cruise or John Travolta or Kirstie Alley pop up on the sofas of Jonathan Ross or Jeremy Clarkson or Oprah Winfrey they should ask three questions:

'Why can disconnecting grannies from grandsons be good?'
'Who is Lord Xenu?'
'What kind of Church hires private eyes?'

The answer is, of course, a Church of Fear.
John Sweeney, December, 2012.
THE END

NOTES

Introduction

'John Sweeney is genuinely evil' see: http://gettothechoppa.word-press.com/2010/09/28/john-sweeney-is-genuinely-evil/

'Exploding tomato' see http://www.youtube.com/watch?v=hxqR5NPhtLI and many other sites. Scientology & Me, the 2007 BBC Panorama documentary is here: http://www.youtube.com/watch?v=rFRSt_viosc The Dalek impersonation is worth a watch, too: http://www.youtube.com/watch?v=cLI1Al3S_pE

'Hysterical rant' from the *News of the World, May 13, 2007. Five years later Rupert Murdoch changed his tune, tweeting:* 'Very weird cult, but big, big money involved with Tom Cruise either number two or three in hierarchy.'

'Secret police interrogator': Charles Moore was writing in The Spectator, May 25, 2007.

'Whose bunny was boiled': watch here: http://www.youtube.com/watch?v=ecWhXP2jM28

'Create the new reality': watch Tom Cruise espouse Scientology here: http://www.youtube.com/watch?v=UFBZ_uAbxS0

Chapter One: First Contact

'Psychotic, a bigot and a liar': for the Church of Scientology's considered view on the author:

http://www.freedommag.org/special-reports/bbc/panorama-exposed.html

http://www.freedommag.org/special-reports/bbc/panorama-desperate-lies.html

The first draft of this book was written before the Savile scandal engulfed the BBC in the autumn of 2012. What happened was wrong, and the failure of BBC Newsnight to broadcast the stories of Savile abuse in 2011 compounded that wrong. But the BBC did air programmes strongly critical of BBC management, including a Panorama made by my colleagues and a BBC News Channel interview in which I openly criticized the then Director-General George Entwistle:

http://www.bbc.co.uk/news/world-20024904

Entwistle faced difficult questions about his conduct from the BBC on air. Commentators have noted the contrast between the BBC's openness to effective scrutiny and Entwistle's subsequent resignation and the reactions of many newspaper groups to accusations of phone-hacking.

'How warm space is': http://www.xenu-directory.net/practices/ot.html

'Con man': *Bare Faced Messiah,* Russell Miller, London, 1987.

'Mark of the Beast 666': *L Ron Hubbard: Messiah or Madman* by Bent Corydon and L Ron Hubbard Junior, Lyle Stuart, New Jersey, 1987, p48.

'Star shape behind': *L Ron Hubbard: Messiah or Madman* – illustration opposite p195.

'Wog': Saint Hill Briefing Course-82 6611C29.

'The production of plant mutations': *Bare-Faced Messiah*, p305.

'Mental therapy': http://www.cs.cmu.edu/~dst/Library/Shelf/anderson/index.html

'The other cheek': *Believe What You Like, CH Rolph, Andre Deutsch, London, 1973.* http://www.cs.cmu.edu/~dst/Library/Shelf/rolph/chr06.htm. Rolph, a former police officer, wrote about the Church and gave the warning about fatuous credulity at the start of this book.

'Or destroyed': HCO Policy letter of 18th October 1967, LRH directed: 'Enemy- SP Order. Fair Game. May be deprived of property or injured by any means by any Scientologist without any discipline of the Scientologist. May be tricked, sued or lied to or destroyed.'

'In 1984...' http://www.gerryarmstrong.org/50grand/legal/a1/breckenridge-decision.html

'His autopsy...' http://www.xenu.net/archive/hubbardcoroner/hubbard_toxicology_report.jpg

'Discarded the body...' http://www.xenu.net/archive/hubbardcoroner/hubbard_toxicology_report.jpg

'Disgrace to the German nation': http://www.xenu.net/archive/hubbardcoroner/hubbard_toxicology_report.jpg

'We'll get them to them last': http://www.sptimes.com/Tampa-Bay/102598/scientologypart4.html

'Scientology is not a religion':
http://www.charitycommission.gov.uk/Library/start/cosfulldoc.pdf

'Smart thing to do': "Celebrities are very Special people and have a very distinct line of dissemination. They have comm [unication] lines that others do not have and many medias[sic] to get their dissemination through" L. Ron Hubbard, from Flag Order 3323, 9 May 1973 http://www.xenu.net/archive/celebrities/

'Brief fling': http://www.youtube.com/watch?v=PKYn5xAfHKQ

'I don't think Scientologists get a fair deal': *Why do I say these things?* Jonathan Ross, Bantam Press, London, 2008, pp269-271.

'What is brainwashing?': *Thought Reform and the Psychology of Totalism,* first published in the USA, 1961. The page numbers I will refer to for this book are from the Lifton edition published by Pelican, London, 1967.

'Supplicants and recruits': *Cults In Our Midst,* Margaret Thaler Singer, Jossey-Bass, San Francisco, 2003, p*xii.*

'Eliminated': Lifton, p482.

'Posse of vindictive liars': http://www.freedommag.org/special-reports/bbc/panorama-desperate-lies.html

'Total villain': http://gettothechoppa.wordpress.com/2010/09/28/john-sweeney-is-genuinely-evil/

'Is not a cult': Hansard, July 11, debate on the Racial and Religious Hatred Bill;
http://www.publications.parliament.uk/pa/cm200506/cmhansrd/vo050711/debtext/50711-29.htm#50711-29_spnew4

'Hotly deny': Vanity Fair: What Katie Didn't Know by Maureen Orth, October, 2012.

'I am the baddie.' Panorama Exposed: http://www.freedommag.org/special-reports/bbc/panorama-exposed.html

Chapter Two: What do my socks have to do with spiritual freedom?

Panorama, 1987: 'The Road to Total Freedom?' http://video.google.

com/videoplay?docid=-3608301463793011770

Chapter Three: Ill-met at midnight
'The man in black is the Scientology cameraman': http://www.you-tube.com/watch?v=5R5KqNG9HLo
'Now you listen to me': http://www.youtube.com/watch?v=0HGM8DSnYh0

Chapter Four: One man against the crowd
'Cult Watch': http://www.youtube.com/watch?v=K4uwcB2uZBs
'He is crazy': A piece on Shawn in the St Petersburg Times by Robert Farley brilliantly captures his lonely courage – http://www.sptimes.com/2006/09/17/Floridian/Scientology_s_scourge.shtml
'A singular American': http://www.youtube.com/watch?v=YDHXu1PjoRA

Chapter Five: Your needle's floating, Tom
'An astonishingly successful drug therapy': http://www.cs.cmu.edu/~dst/Stop-Narconon/sfusd-articles.html
While checking a few details with Nanette Asimov over the phone in my study in 2012, Bertie, our dog, ate my dinner, a dish of microwaved lasagne. I report this to give readers a true flavour of the glamorous nature of investigative journalism.
Charles Hendry MP on Narconon: http://www.publications.parliament.uk/pa/cm200506/cmhansrd/vo050711/debtext/50711-29.htm#50711-29_spnew4
Scientology confession: *Abuse at the Top, Amy Scobee, Washington, 2010, p32.*
Hemet on Google Earth: dial in Golden Era Golf Course – and to the left Gold Base straddles Gilman Hot Springs road.
The Church on Bruce Hines:
http://www.religiousfreedomwatch.org/anti-religious-extremists/bruce-hines/
Panorama in 1987 on David Miscavige: http://www.youtube.com/watch?v=65nU9YIizPM

The Church on Tom DeVocht:
http://www.freedommag.org/special-reports/cnn/tom-devocht-the-consummate-con-man.html

Marc Headley's book: *Blown for Good: Behind The Iron Curtain of Scientology*, BFG Books, LA, 2009.

'Most disgusting experience': *Blown for Good: p231*.

The Church on Marc and Claire Headley: http://www.freedommag.org/special-reports/sources/mr-and-mrs-headley-anonymous.html

The Church on Steve Hall: http://www.freedommag.org/special-reports/sources/steve-hall-the-man-who-tells-it-straight-from-the-straitjacket.html

Amy Scobee's book: *Abuse At The Top*
http://www.amazon.com/Scientology-Abuse-Top-Amy-Scobee/dp/0692008012

'Mind-glue': *Combating Cult Mind Control,* by Steve Hassan, Park Street Press, Vermont, USA, 1988.

The Church on Amy Scobee: http://www.freedommag.org/special-reports/cnn/amy-scobee-sex-lies-and-the-blogosphere.html

Debbie Cook's testimony: District Court, Bexar County, Texas, 9th February, 2012, CAUSE NO. 2012-CI-01272

CHURCH OF SCIENTOLOGY FLAG SERVICE ORGANIZATION, INC. v DEBRA J. BAUMGARTEN, AKA DEBBIE COOK BAUMGARTEN, AKA DEBBIE COOK, AND WAYNE BAUMGARTEN.

http://markrathbun.files.wordpress.com/2012/04/baumgartendayone.pdf

Lifton's eight tests for brainwashing: *Thought Reform, pages 477-497.*

Marty Rathbun's blog: http://markrathbun.wordpress.com/

The Church on Marty Rathbun:
http://www.freedommag.org/special-reports/cnn/the-rathbun-family-madness-mayhem-and-mysterious-death.html

Richard Behar's report in Time Magazine, 1991: http://www.cs.cmu.edu/~dst/Fishman/time-behar.html

Amy Scobee's book on abuse of confession: *Abuse at the Top, p80, p121*

Chapter Six: This is the word of the Church of Scientology

On Eugene Ingram: http://www.holysmoke.org/cos/ingram.htm

Brent Sampson: http://www.webpronews.com/navigating-the-amazon-sales-ranking-2006-06

Scientology speak: easily the best glossary of Scientology terms is available here: http://www.xenu-directory.net/glossary/glossary_a.htm#A

Hubbard on Dead agenting: L. Ron Hubbard, *Board Policy Letter, PR Series 24: Handling Hostile Contacts/Dead Agenting,* May 30, 1974.

Cults In Our Midst, Margaret Thaler Singer, Jossey-Bass, San Francisco, 2003

For more on Singer, she was a former board member of the Rick Ross Institute: http://www.rickross.com/groups/singer.html

Press archive on Singer: http://www.csj.org/infoserv_profile/singer_margaret.htm

Chapter Seven: Do I look brainwashed to you?

For the Church's take on my interviews with the celebrities, watch: http://www.youtube.com/watch?v=M3ecx_6xOaU

Chapter Eight: They want you to be afraid

Rick Ross: http://www.rickross.com/

The Church on Rick Ross:

http://www.religiousfreedomwatch.org/religious-experts/false-experts/rick-ross/mental-instability/

Chapter Nine: The Industry of Death

'They lie so truly': Lifton, p169.

'Extortion, mayhem and murder': http://freedom.lronhubbard.org/page080.htm

Harold Wilson and the psychs: http://solitarytrees.net.silver.alpha-megahosting.com/cowen/misc/psywar.htm

William Battie: 'Treatise on Madness': http://books.google.co.uk/books?id=F6JbAAAAQAAJ&printsec=frontcover&redir_

esc=y#v=onepage&q&f=false
George III and the Mad-Business by Ida Macalpine and Richard
Hunter, London, Allen Lane, 1969. The authors were mother and son,
and psychiatrists, and the grandmother and father of the publisher of
this book, Humfrey Hunter, an accident of history I only learned this
summer. Their book was turned into a play and then a film by Alan
Bennett.
On Benjamin Rush, see Brodsky, Alyn. *Benjamin Rush: Patriot and
Physician*. New York: Truman Talley Books/St. Martin's Press, 2004.
The Church is also a dark critic of the pharmaceutical industry.
But you can be that, and not be a Scientologist. See Ben Goldacre's
excellent *Bad Pharma: How drugs companies mislead doctors and harm
patients*, Fourth Estate, London, 2012.
For more on Rivers, read Arthur Anderson, 25 March 2006: Anxiety
and Panic History, 1900-1930 and Judith Herman, MD, "Trauma and
Recovery; The aftermath of violence – from domestic abuse to political
terror," BasicBooks, New York, NY, 1997
On the Church's operation against Paulette Cooper, see:
http://www.holysmoke.org/pc/pcof1.htm

Chapter Ten: The Tethered Goat
http://www.cs.cmu.edu/~dst/Fishman/time-behar.html
The Church v Channel Four: see
http://www.independent.co.uk/life-style/focus-why-channel-4-is-haunted-by-scientology-1293089.html
http://www.lermanet.com/persecution/tv4harrass.html
Gumbel on the Industry of Death:
http://web.archive.org/web/20060427102908/http://www.lacityb-eat.com/article.php?id=3137&IssueNum=136

Chapter Eleven: The Concrete Angel

The Church on Jeff Hawkins:
http://www.freedommag.org/special-reports/cnn/jeff-hawkins-sympathy-for-the-devil.html

See *Counterfeit Dreams by Jeff Hawkins, 2010.* http://
www.amazon.co.uk/Counterfeit-Dreams-ebook/dp/
B008228CX0

Chapter Twelve: You Suck Cock On Hollywood Boulevard
The pooch that can detect an overt: Miller, p456.

Chapter Thirteen: Is There Anybody There?
Lifton's preface to Singer's book: Singer, p*xii*
The Church on Tory Christman:
http://www.religiousfreedomwatch.org/anti-religious-extremists/
tory-christman/

Chapter Fourteen: Panorama Exposed
The Church's filming of the Wild Hogs premiere:
http://www.youtube.com/watch?v=80sxnBfja9M
The Church's clip of me going tomato:
http://www.youtube.com/watch?v=hxqR5NPhtLI
Mike Rinder's letter to the BBC complaining about me:
http://www.freedommag.org/sites/default/files/Mike-Rinder-Let-
ter-to-BBC-2007.pdf
Panorama Exposed:
http://www.freedommag.org/special-reports/bbc/panorama-expo-
sed.html

Chapter Fifteen: The Defector
Allan Henderson's story:
http://www.heraldscotland.com/news/home-news/i-know-the-
dark-side-of-scientology-i-almost-lost-my-friend-when-she-became-
obsessed-with-it-1.930802
Miscavige meets Hubbard:
http://www.sptimes.com/TampaBay/102598/scientologypart1.html
Lifton's definers for a cult: Singer, p*xii*
Miscavige's one TV interview:

http://www.youtube.com/watch?v=fP6yXOEgHjs

The Church on Mike Rinder:

http://www.freedommag.org/special-reports/sources/mike-rinder-a-walking-hate-crime.html

Chapter Sixteen: Broken Lives

Larry Anderson greets you into the Church:

http://www.youtube.com/watch?v=FmnU28gYmBk

The Church on Jason Beghe:

http://www.freedommag.org/special-reports/sources/jason-beghe-apostate-poster-boy.html

Private eyes harassing Mike Rinder:

http://www.youtube.com/watch?v=6n0Y9WXIZvI&feature=relmfu

Chapter Seventeen: The Space Alien Cathedral

For precise details of how to get to the gate of Trementina Base, go to my website at http://www.johnsweeney.co.uk/

The Washington Post on Trementina:

http://www.washingtonpost.com/wp-dyn/content/article/2005/11/26/AR2005112601065.html

Marc Headley's Blown For Good is available at http://blownforgood.com/

Tom Cruise not opening the door of his Bugatti Veyron:

http://www.youtube.com/watch?v=riR-yw0S5xs

For Elephant Moon, see my site http://www.johnsweeney.co.uk/ or go to Amazon or Silvertail Books, www.silvertailbooks.com

To watch South Park's hilarious 'Trapped In The Closet', sites come and go so trawl the internet.

BIBLIOGRAPHY

Corydon, Bent and Hubbard Junior, L Ron: *L Ron Hubbard: Messiah or Madman* Lyle Stuart, New Jersey, 1987.

Hawkins, Jeff: *Counterfeit Dreams,* 2010.

Headley, Marc: *Blown For Good, Behind the Iron Curtain of Scientology,* BFG Books, Burbank, 2009.

Robert Jay Lifton: *Thought Reform and the Psychology of Totalism,* Pelican, London, 1967.

Miller, Russell: *Bare Faced Messiah,* Sphere Books, London, 1987.

Morton, Andrew: *Tom Cruise: An Unauthorised Biography,* St Martin's Press, New York, 2008.

Rathbun, Marty: *The Scientology Reformation,* Corpus Christi, 2012.

Rolph, CH, *Believe What You Like,* Andre Deutsch, London, 1973.

Scobee, Amy: *Abuse at the Top,* Scobee Publishing, Washington State, 2010

Singer, Margaret: *Cults In Our Midst,* Jossey-Bass, San Francisco, 2003.

ACKNOWLEDGEMENTS

Rinder, Mike; Rathbun, Marty; Headleys, Marc and Claire; Hines, Bruce; Scobee, Amy; Hawkins, Jeff; Beghe, Jason; Hall, Steve; Henderson, Mike; Shannon, Donna; DeVocht, Tom; Andrus, Alison; the late Singer, Margaret; Ross, Rick; Lifton, Prof; Behar, Richard; Miller, Russell; Morton, Andrew; Childs, Joe and Tobin, Thomas C; Ortega, Tony; Christman, Tory; Lonsdale, the late Shawn.

Moles, various; Mole, Sarah; Browne, Traitor Bill; Barrie, Patrick; Hesse, Uli; Smith, Sandy; Giles, Tom; Kemp, Darren; Edwards, Clive; Law, Roger; Leask, Damian; Richardson, Adam; Stead, Katy; Coffey, Jon; Harte, Alys; Stott, Chris; Hunters, Humfrey, Charlotte and Ringo.

Newson, Tomiko; Sweeneys, Sam, Molly, Barbara, Bertie.

The great British public who via the BBC pay my wages and who forgave my exploding tomato outburst.

And to everyone who is still in. If you've read this far, you might consider getting out. Humanity, for all its faults and foolishness, is not as bad as you've been told.

40802186R00221

Made in the USA
Lexington, KY
18 April 2015